Bye-Bye Blackbird

Bye-Bye Blackbird

◆

An Anglo-Indian Memoir

Peter Moss

iUniverse, Inc.
New York Lincoln Shanghai

Bye-Bye Blackbird
An Anglo-Indian Memoir

iUniverse, Inc.

For information address:
iUniverse, Inc.
2021 Pine Lake Road, Suite 100
Lincoln, NE 68512
www.iuniverse.com

ISBN: 0-595-31373-6

Printed in the United States of America

For my parents, Frank and Holly
and my brothers, Paul and Robert

Contents

Introduction

In her treatise *Identity in Motion: Bhowani Junction Reconsidered*, Kathleen J. Cassity, of the University of Hawaii at Manoa, points out that "Today there is certainly no shortage of novels concerning British colonialism in India, India's independence and partition, and the aftermath of the Raj". The late twentieth century, she goes on to remark, has seen a literal explosion of novels on the subject, penned by both British and Indian writers, invoking a variety of perspectives ranging from staunch anti-imperialism to colonial nostalgia. "Yet few of the novels concerning the Raj invoke, or even acknowledge, the unique role and perspective of the Anglo-Indian community, an ethnically and culturally hybrid people of mixed European and Indian ancestry known also, at various times, as 'Eurasians', 'half-castes', 'half-breeds', 'blacky-whites', 'eight-annas' and 'chee-chees'."

Half a century has elapsed since John Masters' *Bhowani Junction* made its appearance in 1952. Cassity calls it the "one notable exception to the relative invisibility of the Anglo-Indian community in narratives of empire". Unlike *Bhowani Junction, Bye-Bye Blackbird* is not a novel. It is an autobiographical account of my childhood in the Anglo-Indian community that populated the railway colonies scattered all over the sub-continent, a community that has largely vanished from the Indian scene.

The song *Bye-Bye Blackbird*, with words and music by Henderson-Dixon, was popular during World War Two. Sung in chorus by Allied soldiers and airmen, homeward-bound aboard their troopships, and directed at Anglo-Indian girlfriends bidding them farewell at the dockside, the lyrics took on a different but unmistakable meaning.

Peter Moss
Hong Kong
March 2004

With the Gift of Hindsight

It was apparent to my Indian hosts that my stop-over at Dum Dum airport, en route from London to Hong Kong, must have been prompted by some curiously compelling reason to see inside. Therefore a caretaker was summoned to unlock the huge Institute doors for my benefit.

I gazed up at dusty rafters, hung with shreds of cobwebbed tinsel and streamer from long-past festivities. In the darkness of the vaulted roof beyond I detected a faint, brief rustle of membranous wings. Stretched far around me in the gloom, the empty dance floor ached with its burden of memories. The windows were shuttered, the skylights screened, the atmosphere was of a cave, an immense, sealed sarcophagus in which to bury a forgotten legacy.

The caretaker looked at me, a quizzical, speculative smile on his lips. Was I here for the ghosts? Why else would I visit this mausoleum? Why else indeed? It was borne home to me, as I stood in that abandoned temple of our scattered tribes, that I myself was a resurrected wraith from a world beyond the new India that lay outside these walls.

My India, my Anglo-India, was an Atlantis vanished beneath the waves of history, dispersing its survivors to their separate and distant landfalls. The lingering few of us who had been part of it held on to the remnants of a collective memory that would die with us, inadequately recorded, imperfectly lodged in the greater saga of mankind.

Thirty-four years had passed since I had last seen the Bell Institute, social centre and spiritual hub of our little railway colony, one of many scattered all over India. I had been nine years old when I left. At that time, across the Assam hills, the tide of war was turning, the Japanese were in retreat and we were spared further nocturnal raids by their long-range bombers. And now, in 1978, I was back, after so prolonged an absence, to rediscover this tiny corner of Bengal that had burned its image deep into my retina.

Why had we, who were once so many, who had formed the cartilage in the anatomy of India, buffering the bare bones of the Raj from the multitudinous flesh of those they governed, been so poorly chronicled? Why was it so hard to trace our descent or track down our history? Why was so much of who we were, what we had done, vanished beyond recall? Because we had been taught to live with shame. Because to admit that we were who we were was to accept the disparagement, perhaps even the scorn, of those we desperately strove to emulate; those who would see us as "touched by the tar brush".

I had dismayed many of my relations by daring to show my colours, asserting my pride in my Anglo-Indian origins. Yet I could understand and sympathize with their sensitivity to that label, for they were of that earlier generation who had risked suffering the consequences of confessing their miscegenation; the arched eyebrow, the upturned lip, the suddenly averted gaze of those who had suspected as much and who now had their suspicions confirmed.

It seems grotesque today, in an increasingly intermingled and miscegenated world, to conceive how such a situation could ever have arisen. It seemed absurd even in 1978, when imperialism and the colonial ethos were long nailed into their coffins, with stakes driven through their hearts to prevent any possibility of resurrection. But in the Kanchrapara of my childhood, back in 1944, the barriers raised by the embattled Raj were still in place. Struggling through the death throes of their presence in India, the British were as punctilious as ever in preserving distinctions between themselves, their "also-rans" and the hordes of natives with their tides and counter-tides of nationalism led by such as Mahatma Gandhi, Pandit Nehru and Mohammed Ali Jinnah.

Hence it befell us, of the in-between, to maintain the pretence, to practice the subterfuge, with deceits so carefully contrived and zealously pursued that we fooled even ourselves. And in doing so we paid the penalty of losing our true identity, and our ability to draw from it the spiritual solace and pride that all people need to be fundamentally whole and psychologically secure. Those of my parents' generation, broadcast to all compass points by the massive diaspora resulting from India's independence in 1947, were still living in the shadows of the great counterfeit they had erected to conceal their true provenance. But if I was among the few to defy that subterfuge, I was—at least in this one degree—whole and content to be so; Anglo-Indian and proud of it.

Yet my eagerness to declare my motley lineage was in itself a camouflage. I employed one unorthodoxy to divert any suspicion of another; the possibility that I might also be "queer"—as we used to call it then. For back in 1978 the world (and especially Hong Kong where I had made my home) was taking longer to accept that particular aberration. So I too was living a lie; locked away in the bastion of my inner self. Outside that perimeter, my Anglo-Indian colours could bravely fly as much in defence as in defiance.

Farewell to All That

I am the product of an empire ingrained into my bones. Its echoes have resonated throughout my life. If there was ever a moment when my childhood ended, it was when I stood in the noonday heat of 1946, on the deck of the Cunard liner *Brittanic*, anchored off Port Said, wearing for the last time my obligatory solar topi. As a child, I had never cared for this form of headgear. I saw in its pith helmet the cranial equivalent of braces for teeth, cramping and confining my mind. While it might shield me from the sun, its hard, unyielding lining allowed little room for ideas to grow. And what was so wrong with the sun anyway, that I must be perpetually protected from it?

That late September day In the harbour of Port Said—the symbolic dividing line between East and West—I abandoned my last solar topi with a sigh of relief and a pang of regret. For even as I knew I would never wear one again, I also saw that I would never again be given a reason to do so. I was vaguely conscious of the fact that the world for which I had been nurtured and prepared was heading for the scrap heap. The unthinkable had but recently—and rapidly—translated itself into the inevitable. What would continue to elude me, until many years later, was the realisation that this was no accident of history but the outcome of a deliberately planned obsolescence, embarked upon before I was born.

My family left India because we knew that our allotted place in an epic progression of events, more than three centuries old, was coming to an end. The pageant was in the closing scene of its last act, the termination notices already prepared, closure stickers waiting to be pasted across the billboards. It was simply a matter of time.

The initiative must be perceived to emanate, not from the management, but from the pressures for change foisted upon them by those waiting to take possession of the stage. So that when surrender appeared the only remaining option, those who offered it could be seen to submit with good grace, accompanied by a shrug of resignation and a twinge of sadness.

India was the blueprint for a more general retreat, demonstrating that age-old responsibilities could be shed within a few frantic months of abandonment. The curtain descending here was merely the prelude to a succession of diminutions that would eventually and permanently close all the global chain of His Majesty's Imperial Theatres.

In the jaundiced introspection of my immature years, when I was prone to bitterness at being dislodged from everything I had grown to love, I would muse on the fact that Britain should not have walked away from an empire that embraced half the world, shrugging her shoulders as if it never existed. Why behave as if the whole imperial enterprise could now be regarded as a colossal miscalculation? It irked me that when a production line ended, or a factory closed, the workers laid off could seek re-employment elsewhere, yet when an empire foundered, whole communities disintegrated and died, just as did the Anglo-Indian community to which I had belonged, extinguished with scant regard for what might become of the survivors.

Lesser powers had their dominions wrested from them. Britain surrendered hers on tarnished silver salvers, with little to take their place other than the Commonwealth Club, an *alma mater* for old boys that once a year assembled for the obligatory group photograph in the Queen's drawing room.

Time, if not wisdom, has long cured me of such over-simplifications, making me see that there were reasons for this withdrawal that went beyond the more obvious historical trends. Not least of these was the dawning apprehension, in Whitehall, that the *Big Bang* of imperial acquisition must inevitably produce its counteraction. Once the limits were reached, the waning energies of that explosive force that had projected British colonisation across the face of the planet would collapse, giving way to a gigantic implosion that would bring its wreckage hurtling back towards the epicentre.

We have all witnessed the consequences, which have changed the very nature of Britain and altered the definition of what it means to be British. For me, one encapsulating image is a newspaper photograph of an Indian woman in Trafalgar Square, holding up a placard in a demonstration against ever-tightening immigration laws. The placard reads "We Are Here Because You Were There".

I was "there", and in a sense I have never really returned. I have lived much of my life floundering in the wake of that doomed vessel of state emblazoned with the word *Empire*, scrambling aboard the flotsam and jetsam it left behind. Just so potent and life-conditioning was the leviathan in its passing that I have been unable to break entirely free of the backwash. Its eddies have inundated all the pages of my experience.

Others in my family could not understand my preoccupation with the past. We were British. We had always been British. The British had left India. Ergo *we* had left India, long before the lowering boom posed by passport addenda and codicils could restrict our ability to do so. Why was I stuck in this time warp?

I had no clear-cut answer to that question. I only know there was a particular quality to the Indian sun. Its ferocity had seared its images on my retina, so that the afterburn lingered on. I still suffer, without warning and at frequently inappropriate moments, the recurrence of unbidden evocations, overlaying present realities like double exposures. For who can account for what the mind gathers or chooses to discard? At best, memory is a wilful archivist. Which is why, instead of beginning at the beginning, my careening mind goes back to that September afternoon in 1946, when I discarded my last solar topi; if only because that moment marked the first distinct watershed of my life.

We had just traversed the Suez Canal. We were on the line of demarcation where Asia ended and Europe—or at least the proximity, the sense and the smell of Europe—began. Asia was all I had known. It was important for me to extract from that moment the utmost in significance.

Not that I detected any immediately perceptible change. The shabby but still dignified harbour frontage of Port Said, half asleep in the afternoon heat, was as imperious and impervious as the one we had left in Bombay, in neither case giving a hint of the titillating curiosities rumoured to be available in the back streets. We would not be going ashore. We were heading west in the *Brittanic*, freshly restored from wartime camouflage to civilian colours, but with her lower decks still serving as troop quarters. Before us lay the Mediterranean, where the threat of stray mines surviving the recently ended Second World War obliged us to wear life jackets at all times.

I had been told it was customary for soldiers, returning from their tours of duty in India, to toss their solar topis overboard at Port Said in a collective "goodbye to all that". It had dawned on me that this time the goodbye would be a leave-taking not just of a brief sojourn in India, but of the very idea of India itself. I waited on the boat deck with my younger brother Paul, assuring him it was simply a matter of time before we witnessed a spectacle to remember.

Reluctantly I resigned myself to the fact that it wasn't going to happen. Importuning vendors had provided a brief diversion, clambering up the sides from their bumboats, with carpets and brassware, until repelled with fire hoses to appreciative caterwauls from the lower decks. And now the ship had lapsed again into boredom and ennui. The moment was passing, and the opportunity would soon be lost. Somebody had to give the signal!

I doffed my pith helmet and sent it sailing in a wide arc, an inverted khaki saucer briefly hovering above retreating bumboats. A great cheer went up from the lower decks, but nothing—not a single item of headgear—followed in its wake. One of the bumboats changed course so its sodden occupant could retrieve the topi. My brother, susceptible to what he saw as the unwarranted embarrassments I frequently inflicted upon him, withdrew indoors. He wasn't going to lose *his* solar topi, and certainly not in an act so recklessly exhibitionist as mine. He left me hatless in the sun we had been taught would fry our brains if we lingered uncovered in its thrall.

Through the perspective afforded by advancing age, I now see the irony of my gesture. Of all aboard the *Brittanic* that day, I should have been the last to sacrifice my solar topi. For I wasn't going "back to Blighty". Though my father had been born there, England was no home to me. I was being torn away from everything that topi signified. In the years to come, I would stand witness to the loss of three imperial possessions; India in 1947, Malaya in 1957 and Hong Kong in 1997. But for me the first strand of that protracted severance was sundered on that day I lost my distinctively imperial hat.

A Cockney in Love with Kipling

Though I was unaware of it at the time, my father, William Frank Moss, suffered an even keener pang of regret for what we were leaving behind. Before the year was out, his inability to re-acclimatize to the country he had last seen in his early teens would be the cause of a nervous breakdown.

Born within the sound of London's Bow Bells, and proud to call himself a Cockney, he had accompanied his parents and two sisters to India when my grandfather was sent there on his first overseas posting since the Western Front of the First World War. The year would have been about 1924. A Regimental Sergeant Major in the Royal Horse Artillery, William George Moss was a small, wiry martinet with a sarcastic tongue and parade ground manner that extended into his domestic life. I believe lack of paternal affection was the principal reason why my father elected to leave home at the earliest opportunity.

Not that my grandfather would have stood in his way, for he was always advocating the virtues of an early start in one's career. He thoroughly approved of my becoming an apprenticed journalist at the age of fifteen—even before I had properly completed my grammar school education.

My father embraced India with enthusiasm, never hesitating in *his* choice of career. Fascinated with railway locomotives since childhood, he had himself apprenticed as a draughtsman on the Indian railways—also at the age of fifteen—and embarked on the happiest years of his life. I still envy him his youthful discoveries. Weaned on the imperial literature of Kipling, he wanted to devour India, and set out to do so by motorcycle. An inveterate tinkerer with objects mechanical, he acquired a machine of such slimness and grace that it looked little more than a bicycle with a thin petrol tank slung between seat and handlebars. Illumination was provided by a stuttering naphtha lamp. With it he went racing up and down the Grand Trunk Road, following in the tracks of Kipling's hero Kim.

Kim was possibly the first Anglo-Indian ever featured in a novel. He would become my hero too when I was old enough to discover him. I felt we had much in common, just as I would see that his father, "poor O'Hara that was gang-foreman on the Ferozepore line", had much in common with mine.

> "Though he was burned black as any native; though he spoke the vernacular by preference, and his mother-tongue in a clipped uncertain sing-song; though he consorted on terms of perfect equality with the small boys of the bazaar; Kim was white—a poor white of the very poorest. The half-caste woman who looked after him (she smoked opium, and pretended to keep a second-hand furniture shop by the square where the cheap cabs wait) told the missionaries that she was Kim's mother's sister; but his mother had been nursemaid in a Colonel's family and had married Kimball O'Hara, a young colour-sergeant of the Mavericks, an Irish regiment. He afterwards took a post on the Sind, Punjab, and Delhi Railway, and his regiment went home without him."

Ever to remain in envious competition with his son, my grandfather, William George Moss, was not to be outdone by my father's escapades. He too acquired a motorcycle, together with a sidecar shaped like an aircraft nacelle in reverse, its sharp end dauntingly to the fore. This contraption was described to me years later, in one of many stories my grandfather endlessly recycled and embroidered until they acquired mythic dimension.

While his embarrassed wife Rose busied herself with her knitting, not daring to contradict, he would relate how he rode the combination through a crowded Indian marketplace, refusing to slow down for sluggardly pedestrians. One who failed to step aside in time was speared by the sidecar, through the cotton *dhoti* between his thighs, and deposited in my grandmother's lap from whence, according to her husband, she ejected him with a few deft blows of her handbag. I doubted my grandmother's role in this, and looked to her for contradiction, but she continued clacking away with her knitting needles.

I learned to steel myself against my grandfather's seldom amusing recollections of India. They invariably had to do with unfortunate Indians being in the wrong place at the wrong time, or rendered hapless victims of some arbitrary event over which they could have no control. An instance of the latter was his description of range practice, when the guns were sighted on a target located on a hill at the far side of town. One of the practice shells, for whatever reason, had fallen short, in the middle of the intervening market place. I did not wish to ascertain the extent of damage caused.

Among his few stories I remember with affection was one set on the platform of a typical cantonment station, where the stationmaster would turn the clock hands forward five minutes to tally with the noonday gun fired from the nearby military camp. Ten minutes later, when the stationmaster had gone about his duties, the camp commandant would ride up on his charger, set his wristwatch by the station clock, and go galloping back to his office.

I have a photograph of the Moss family, posed before their bungalow in Jhansi some time around 1925. Jhansi is now the headquarters of a district in Uttar Pradesh. There were two conditions in the original treaty between the British and the Raja of Jhansi. The first stipulated that, whenever the British needed help, Jhansi should help them. The second required the consent of the British to any decision as to who should rule Jhansi.

In the final stages of the Indian Mutiny, when British forces were regaining control of a country torn by rebellion against their arrogant authority, an army under the command of Sir Hugh Rose reached Jhansi. Rose sent word to the widowed Maharani, whose adopted son had been denied British recognition as her late husband's heir, commanding her to come unarmed to meet him. The Rani replied that she would attend only if escorted by her own army, whom she had been training for months. She had given her guns names such as "Mighty Road", "Bhavani Shankar" and "Lightning Streak", and they were fired, in turns, by both men and women.

Sir Hugh Rose launched his attack on Jhansi on 23rd March 1858, and for twelve days the tiny state was besieged and imperiled. When Rose's army entered the city, the Rani, attired as a man, fought in hand to hand combat until her shrinking band of warriors persuaded her to escape with them through the enemy lines. She fought on through subsequent encounters, far away from her beloved Jhansi, until she died of a dagger thrust from one British soldier and the sword of another, whose arm she succeeded in severing even though she had lost an eye in the encounter.

I only learned the story of Rani Lakshmi Bai many years later. As a child I was brought up on the British view of history, whose heroes were such as Clive of India and the tarnished but vindicated Warren Hastings. Even Tippoo Sultan, revered in India for his stand against British usurpation of his kingdom of Mysore, was reviled and demonized by the British as a man who enjoyed torturing their captured soldiery by throwing them to his tigers.

My only link with Jhansi is through that family portrait. A carefully arranged tableau of cantonment life, this was probably the work of a local photographer adept at producing such vignettes as keepsakes for those about to complete their tours of duty in the tropics. My uniformed grandfather stands to the left, striking an appropriately military attitude, his face in semi-profile.

My father, young and dapper in white flannels, is also looking off camera, but at least he is smiling, I like to think at the prospect of his imminent freedom from parental restraint. My grandmother and the eldest of what would eventually be three daughters, Alice and Susan, make up the rest of the group, with servants paraded in the background. There must have been, in family albums or framed on mantelpieces all over the British Isles, thousands of such photographs in the heyday of the Raj. To me this one represents a set-piece of England-in-exile, dutifully suffering durance vile on foreign soil in the cause of empire. Those servants, hovering in the rear like stage props, provide a closer link with the India I knew.

Improving the Blood

His family had long returned to "Blighty" when my father met, assiduously courted and eventually married my mother. Learning of this at long range through the mails, his parents may have had their suspicions regarding their daughter-in-law's provenance, but to give them credit they did not voice disapproval or attempt to interfere. And in time they would come to accept her as one of their own.

My mother had spent most of her childhood—when she wasn't away at boarding school—in the small railway community of Tundla, in the Firozabad district, not far from Agra. And Tundla was a minor outpost of the extensive Anglo-Indian domain. Colonies we called them—railway colonies—as if the railways, spreading remorselessly across the Indian plains, had taken on an independent life under the very noses of the overweening British who had unleashed them.

There was a time, in the early days of Britain's empire in India, when the term Anglo-Indian described British families so long connected with the sub-continent that they adopted the Indian suffix with pride. But that definition fell into disuse long before my parents met. My father would have been well aware that by then Anglo-Indian had come to mean Eurasian; a person of mixed ancestry. And the caste-ridden Raj, whose hierarchical intricacies—largely at the bidding of its machinating memsahibs—were the equal of anything India could concoct, looked upon Anglo-Indians as the muddied middle ground between itself and the masses it governed. The railways were allotted us as our particular reserve.

To be Anglo-Indian was by then something one no longer claimed with pride. My mother's family was one of many that clung to the original definition, with varying degrees of success. We traced our forebears back to a Doctor Watson who had arrived here from Scotland in the early nineteenth century. Other families maintained they had only recently emigrated from England, exaggerating slender associations with towns or cities in the British Isles to support their claims, or inventing spurious bloodlines that did not bear close examination. The general rule was that the darker you were, the more British you pretended to be. When my maternal grandmother, Kathleen Maude Staerck Watson, learned my mother was hesitant about accepting Frank Moss's proposal, she urged, "Marry him, Holly. He'll improve the blood."

How that proposal came about is as tenuous a circumstance as anything that had ever preceded—and dictated—my existence. My mother was a reluctant participant in social events, and especially loath to attend railway institute dances, where she was invariably overshadowed by her elder sister Zena. The beautiful, blonde and surprisingly Nordic looking Zena was a stand-out in Tundla society, and her reputation had spread so far afield that young men would travel miles from neighbouring colonies for the opportunity to dance with her.

In order to do so they would have to brave the wrath of her ever vigilant father, Arnold Watson, the local stationmaster and a champion boxer whose fists would clench at the mere sight of a lecherous glance in her direction. Zena's dance card was nevertheless filled within minutes of her stepping into the institute ballroom, whereas her sister Holly—if she could be prevailed upon to attend at all—would shrink into the shadows, content to remain a wallflower.

One of my mother's earliest memories of *her* childhood was of Arnold Watson returning home, from his long hauls on night mails as a railway guard, to lavish love and affection on Zena. He would pick up the adorably cute little girl with the golden ringlets, whom I envisage as a prototype Shirley Temple, while his younger, raven haired daughter, still in nappies, tugged at his trousers. "I pretty too, Dada," Holly would squeak. "I pretty too."

By the time the two sisters were "coming out" in Tundla society, Frank Moss had fully immersed himself in Anglo-Indian life. To have become so young an apprentice in a railway locomotive workshop in India he could hardly have done otherwise. It was unusual for a young Briton, straight out from England, to end up in the lower rungs of the railway ladder. British officials still formed a thin veneer in the upper echelons of railway administration, and might return "home", to write their memoirs, at the close of their careers on Indian soil. But for most there remained an invisible barrier between "them" and "us".

My father chose to spend more time among those of "us" who comprised the majority in any railway colony. In these circles he met and made lifelong friends, from whom he acquired most of his knowledge of India and in whose company he gained most of his Indian experience. Firmly lodged among this group were my mother's family, who were just about as predominant in their environment as it was possible to get.

It was a chance suggestion from one of his friends, Alec Lees, that brought Frank Moss to the Tundla railway institute on one of the rare nights when Holly Watson happened to be there. Alec had assured him that Tundla girls, and Zena in particular, were worth the fairly considerable journey by motorbike in order to verify the claims made concerning their beauty.

Arrived at the institute, Frank acknowledged that Alec had not exaggerated. Zena's commanding presence on the dance floor was certainly the focus of attention. But Frank's eyes went beyond her, to the doe-eyed, raven haired girl seated among the spectators. He strolled across and asked this shy and uncertain young woman for a dance.

Months later, returning by train from one of his frequent visits to the Watson family in Tundla, Frank overheard the conversation of two fellow passengers, who were discussing the astonishing rumour that one of the two Watson girls was engaged to be married, and it *wasn't* Zena. My father declared himself the Paris responsible for that judgment. Zena was no less surprised. Quiet, taciturn Frank Moss wasn't exactly her idea of a hell of a good time, but for him to choose Holly in preference to her—well, that was something else. Yet with that sororal intensity so often displayed between siblings of entirely opposite temperament, she loved Holly as much as Holly loved her, so that no one would dare supplant Zena as maid of honour at her sister's wedding.

The Blackest Sheep

I cannot claim that my blood, as firstborn of this union, was improved in the way that my grandmother had hoped. If anything I was the darkest progeny the family had seen, though any dismay at that consequence was quickly smothered in the affection lavished upon me by my mothers' parents, her brothers, Trevor, Roland and Denzil and of course Zena. As a child, I experienced the very reverse of the paternal asperities my father had suffered. My mother was the first of her generation to marry and I was the foremost issue of the next. If I had materialised in a manger on Christmas morn I could hardly have commanded more attention.

Small, dumpy and indomitable, my grandmother, Nana Watson as I knew her, included in her maiden name that of the German family that had expelled her own mother for daring to marry into the Eurasian community. What, if any, contact Kathleen Maude may have had with the Staercks I will never know. She spoke only of the Thomsons, the family into which her mother had married. And Kathleen Maude, in turn, married Arnold Watson, tall, built like a boxer, white-haired at twenty and so indubitably Scottish in appearance that nobody dared dispute *his* origins.

Nana was barely fifteen when he swept her off her feet, into the kind of marriage I could well believe was ordained by God, so unassailable seemed its perfection. I was closer to them than I was to my parents, and spent more time in their company, yet I never heard a cross word exchanged between them. Nevertheless crosswords were something Kathleen Maude excelled in, to the extent that the *Statesman* newspaper in Calcutta eventually informed her they would accept no more of her entries because she won so consistently as to deny others the chance.

I remain mystified as to where Nana acquired her wide-ranging knowledge, her literary and artistic attributes and her intense appetite for life. Doomed to spend all her formative and most of her adult years in tiny railway colonies like Tundla, she seldom had the opportunity even to visit one of the major cities like Delhi or Calcutta. But she read everything she could lay her hands on. And she painted in oils; never scenes from life or from the vast vistas of India, but always of imaginary European landscapes she had never set eyes on, complete with snow capped peaks and stags in groves of oak. She wrote a novel whose hero and heroine were brother and sister, separated in childhood and unsuspectingly reunited, as adults, in a haplessly incestuous romance. She ordered by catalogue the latest musical scores from London and New York and produced and directed, at the Tundla railway institute, some of the first performances on Indian soil of such stage hits as *No, No, Nanette* and *Anything Goes*.

She was a tremendous organizer, and hostess of lavish and ambitious parties, involving party games that occupied entire evenings. These generally climaxed in a grand treasure hunt, leading participants on an exhausting cross-country tour to destinations that must be deciphered from anagrams buried in the verses one had discovered at the last port of call. In the course of one such hunt, two contestants had collected, from the troubled caretaker of a *dak* bungalow, a pair of tiger cubs the man had been foolish enough to remove from their lair. Should their mother track the scent of her offspring, the caretaker would have done better to leave the cubs and make his own escape from the *dak* bungalow. What became of him I never learned, but the cubs were eventually handed over to the Calcutta zoo.

Party Tricks and Guessing Games

An invitation to one of my grandmother's parties would be accompanied by instructions to come dressed as—or at least wearing some clue to—a song or film title. For this reason I first took the word "guest" to mean someone who guessed, and was guessed in return. My father, quick to enter into the spirit of these occasions, achieved an early sensation, looking as if he had been caught in some violent fracas, both his eyes apparently badly bruised. Denying he had finally been thrashed by over-protective Arnold Watson, known to relish knocking out young men who made advances towards his daughters, Frank eventually explained his appearance was but a clue to the song *Two Lovely Black Eyes*.

Granddad's temper was a constant worry to Nana. She was gratefully bemused as to why he never vented it on my father. Perhaps because my father defied his expectations by courting Holly rather than Zena. Where Zena was beautiful in a grand operatic manner, so Aryan as to seem a slim, athletic Brunnehilde with a voice to match, Holly was timid, retiring and convinced Frank Moss must have some motive in mind other than his alleged attraction to her. She resisted his advances until, by sheer perseverance, he wore down her defences.

They went to Calcutta for their honeymoon and had a miserable time because nobody had told my mother what to expect and he was too gentle to force himself on her. Zena tracked them down to their hotel, accompanied by her latest boyfriend, Leonard Sharp, and saved the situation with some much needed advice.

And it was Zena who antagonized my father when, some eighteen months later, I was born at Allahabad hospital, shortly after nine in the morning of 27th June 1935. Determined to be first at the bedside, following the arrival of her sister's child, she hurriedly pedalled her bicycle home to inform the family, still seated at breakfast in preparation for their hospital visit, that she had beaten them to it and that Holly was delivered of a son.

This was but the first of what would become a growing list of instances my father would quote as evidence of his in-laws' interference in his parental rights and obligations. He had never met anyone like them. He had married not just a wife but her entire entourage, constantly visiting, constantly expecting to be visited, treating him as but the latest addition to the matriarchal empire at whose unquestioned head was the diminutive but omnipresent Kathleen Maude Staerck Watson.

They in turn, having encountered no one more in need of familial affection—even if he would never admit it—smothered him in their embrace and pretended not even to notice his efforts to resist. Gradually he relented, as he had done on nearly every point until then. Nearly but not all. In order to marry my mother, he had agreed to abandon the Anglican faith and become a Catholic. Only when the priest, a dogmatic French rustic of the type one too frequently encountered in provincial India, dictated that as a convert he could not be married within the altar rails, did my father back down and stubbornly resist apostasy. He agreed to marry outside the altar rails of a Catholic church but not as a Catholic. He further agreed he would permit his children to be raised as Catholics—which I certainly was until, much later in life, I became a collapsed Catholic under the weight of all that dogma.

Bursting the Balloons

Much as he might grumble about the suffocatingly unfamiliar experience of total immersion in a family as close as the one in whose coils he was now firmly entwined, my father's capitulation developed into a grudging fondness for his ever-imminent in-laws. His only defence was his major failing. For if he acquired no other trait from his sardonic father, he inherited a streak of sarcasm guaranteed to provoke my mother's bitter retaliations. Intensely loyal to those she loved, she would brook no criticism of them, and would be equally ready to spring to Frank's defence if the tables were turned.

At times the rows between my parents would climax in pillow and cushion fights, enough to make me cower in my cot from all the sound and the fury. But they never reached the point where anything more substantial was thrown, or where rage degenerated into physical violence.

No matter how provoked, Dad would seldom criticise his diminutive mother-in-law, whose wit and intelligence commanded his respect, and whose love of music, painting and writing he happened to share. He was no mean talent on the banjo, taught himself to play the piano, was a skilled artist, especially in the medium of Indian ink drawings, and so loved to commit family adventures to prose essays that he became unofficial chronicler of its more significant landmarks.

He especially enjoyed performing in Nana's plays, musicals and other theatrical presentations. For years after he left India, he kept mementos of those productions, including the wig and collar he had worn to portray the puritanical Quaker uncle in Lionel Monckton's *The Quaker Girl* which, although it had seen its first performance at the Adelphi Theatre, London, way back in 1910, remained one of their mutual favourites, especially for the song "Come to the Ball".

Nana understood my father better than anyone else in the family. She saw him as the product of an upbringing that held any excess of affection to be a weakness, and detrimental to character building. This, she realised, had made him slow to accept the unrestrained abundance of affection he found among the Watsons.

I of course was raised on the very milk of human kindness. Yet despite the love showered on me, I remained perpetually dissatisfied. Never an intrinsically attractive or endearing infant, I pushed to the limits the tolerance of those around me by spending most of my long waking hours screaming my entirely bald, over-large, saucer-eyed and egg-shaped head off. Most of this voluble distress had to be borne by a succession of *ayahs* employed to nurse me. Generally they quit after a few weeks if not days. The hardiest of these survived tenaciously, and far too long. She had mastered the art of bringing me to heel, by threatening the disapproval of a whole pantheon of Hindu gods and of the entire animal kingdom at their command.

By this time my paternal grandparents had returned to India for a second tour of duty. They took immediately to the daughter-in-law they were meeting for the first time, and even, unexpectedly, to their grandson, encouraging my eager parents to surrender me to their care and seek brief respite from my caterwauling presence with a holiday in the hill station of Nainital.

My mother was by now horrified to discover she was pregnant again, and had become so within a mere six months of my delivery; a sure indication, she thought, that she was a morally loose woman. Since abortion was out of the question, she took it upon herself, during the Nainital vacation, to ride hired ponies at full gallop every day in the hopes that this would induce a miscarriage. Unable to explain this sudden and uncharacteristic interest in riding, she assured Frank it must be the mountain air. Her efforts were thwarted with the birth of Paul on Friday 13th November 1936.

Paul's arrival put a damper on my disposition to scream. He was a remarkably appealing baby, and I recognised when I was beaten. Having exhausted my lung power, I now settled into the phase of wide-eyed wonder at all around me which was to last through most of my childhood. Nana and Granddad Moss were sufficiently encouraged by this development to spend their last Christmas in India with their grandchildren, and this inspired another of Granddad's interminably recycled stories.

He described the labours my father had expended on decorating the drawing room for our descent on Christmas morning. In the centre of the room stood the Christmas tree, for which a casuarina was substituted, and around this, supported on trestle tables, was a model railway layout, complete with landscape moulded in papier-mâché; mountains, tunnels, bridges, the lot. Piled under the tables were presents from family and friends and the whole effect was decorated with balloons, hanging listlessly under the overhead fan.

When Paul and I made our appearance, the electric train was set in motion and various mechanical toys embarked on expeditions across the tiled floor. But it seems the only things that engaged our attention were the balloons, with which we became totally preoccupied until they had all burst, whereupon we withdrew in tears. By this time, explained my grandfather, the room was filled with the stale halitosis of whichever street vendors had inflated the balloons.

I have only one recollection of Nana and Granddad Moss from my Indian years, and that was on the morning of their departure, when we saw them off on a regimental troop train destined for their embarkation aboard ship at Bombay. Granddad was in uniform, with puttees and pith helmet making him look, if possible, even more daunting and inaccessible. Adding to this effect was the lack of a platform on which to stand, so we grandchildren had to be elevated at arms length to kiss him goodbye as he towered above us in the open carriage door. I had a vivid impression of somebody about to ascend to a remoteness quite outside my limited terrestrial experience.

Life on the Rolling Rails

My childhood was a more wandering existence than even my mother's family had known. I remember a succession of railway colonies, some large, some small, with names like Alighar, in Uttar Pradesh, Jamalpur and Tatanagar, in Bihar, Kanchrapara and Asansol, in West Bengal, and Lilloah, near Calcutta. Most were attached to fair-sized cities, but when I knew them these colonies themselves were barely large enough to qualify as townships. And what I saw of them, even then, was limited to the territorial ambit of the resident railway community, generally rotating around that bastion of Anglo-Indian social life, the railway institute.

Such outposts were connected by a network of rails that ran like quicksilver in the sun, stretched tight as wire to their vanishing points on the horizon. Those rails were our lifeline; our one reminder that we were linked to a greater world, a world I sometimes feared I would never get to see. The platforms of our railway stations—our embarkation points for that network—were effectively the brake linings that clamped the tracks on either side, briefly detaining them in their passing. But the rails were too quick for them, too slippery and shining, impatient to be off on their volatile errands, singing in the noonday glare with the faint sounds of that distant world humming in the steel.

Our sojourns in these various colonies were interrupted by seasonal trips to the mountains, specifically to Darjeeling, to escape the pre-monsoon temperatures of the plains. The elevation from one state of existence to another—from the heat, aridity and drudgery of endless flatlands to the coolly sublime heights of the Himalayas—was equivalent to transition from the mundane to the celestial in some mediaeval altarpiece of religious exaltation.

Although I could know nothing then of drifting continents, or the infinitely patient reworkings to which our planet had been subjected through countless millennia, something in that craggy panorama triggered recognition. I was curious to see a resemblance to an effect I could create myself, simply by ramming the toe of my shoe into the crust of a mud pile; the same brittle striations where ripples of impact had rebounded on each other, fold upon fold.

It seemed absurd to suppose I was gazing at a supreme magnification of that effect, on a scale which threw up the icy ramparts of such peaks as Kanchenjunga. I was too young to comprehend that before me were the remains of an immense cataclysm, produced when island India, breaking off from the original single continent of Pangea, had hurtled across what is now the Indian Ocean to collide with Asia.

Fly away Peter, Fly away Paul

But such serene mountain prospects left a less durable impression than the wavering curtains of heat haze hovering over unobstructed horizons of the plains. The very fluidity and intangibility of those unmeasurable distances reinforced the sense that we were adrift on an endless ocean of land.

One particularly potent image lingers from a visit to my grandparents in Alighar, where Granddad Watson was stationmaster. Why this should be I have no idea, for I could then have been no more than three years old. Even my parents, years later, could not recall the topography of our Alighar environment as clearly as I. Perhaps it was imprinted on my mind because of its desiccated nature, for Alighar that year was locked in a formidable drought.

The Watson bungalow was set in a "compound", the name given to the extensive square or sometimes rectangular space that bounded such dwellings on all sides. Typical of neighbouring compounds, ours contained a garden so parched that a team of water carriers, known as *bhistis,* spent their evenings with the aid of inflatable buffalo hides, watering its flower beds from our well. Adjoining this compound, and accessed through a wicket gate, were concrete tennis courts on which my grandmother once organized thoroughly mixed doubles, for which men and women exchanged tennis attire—all very "forward" for those days, and suspiciously regarded by some of our less unconventional neighbours.

On a large expanse of farmland, stretching away from the opposite side of our compound, a blinkered ox plodded patiently in circles, hour after hour, turning a wheel that raised leather buckets of water to irrigate the barren fields beyond. I agonized over the predicament of this blinded creature without knowing why. I doubt I consciously saw it as I would much later; serving as a metaphor for life itself.

Granddad Watson was given to recounting his own hair-raising tales to his grandsons. But unlike those of Granddad Moss, his anecdotes were calculated to instill a deep respect for—if not actual fear of—native customs and traditions. We brothers, "Fly-away Peter" and "Fly-away Paul", would perch uncomfortably on his knees, braced for his spine-tingling worst. He would be sprawled in his cane lounger on the *chibuthra*, a circular concrete platform that served as a sitting out area for whatever sensation of coolness could be wrung from the brief Indian twilight. Invariably his tales would be bizarrely contrasted with little party tricks performed with his fingers, his favourite involving the disappearance of digits to accompany the nursery rhyme that accounted for our nicknames:

> Two little Dickey Birds sat on a wall,
> One named Peter, one named Paul.
> Fly away Peter, fly away Paul,
> Come back Peter, come back Paul.

The story that sticks most clearly in my mind concerned a *sadhu*, an itinerant Hindu holy man, discovered travelling without a ticket in a third class railway compartment. My grandfather claimed he witnessed this *sadhu* hauled unceremoniously off the train by its German guard, who allowed no latitude for impoverished mendicants stowing away in his carriages. Denied permission to continue his journey, the *sadhu* uttered a bloodcurdling curse, promising that the guard would not board his train alive. Dismissing the absurdity of this claim with a contemptuous grin, the guard flagged the train into motion and waited for his van to catch up with him. Leaping for the running board, he missed his footing and was crushed between carriage and platform edge.

We slept outdoors through desperately hot nights, on canvas cots under mosquito nets. A habitual insomniac—which might account for my unceasing distress as an infant—I would lie awake, wondering at the phases of the moon and the slow revolutions of stars, listening to crickets and distant hunting cries of jackal packs and, one night, the hullabaloo that broke out in the servants' quarters when a matrimonial dispute led to the departure of a miscreant husband.

In the afternoons the dark green garden shrubbery wilted under fierce onslaughts of unclouded sunlight, forcing our retreat into shaded torpor behind verandah blinds kept watered by the *malis* in an effort to lower the temperature. The streets of Alighar were even more dry and dusty than our compound. There slow-plodding camels hauled carts at a pace that would cover barely a dozen sand dunes of desert in a day.

Hothouse Heat

Jamalpur is the colony I associate with the greater store of my earliest memories. Paul was born there, and caused me panic attacks as I watched him wilfully expose himself to endless varieties of danger. Asia's first and largest railway workshops were located at Jamalpur, which owed its existence to the railways, as did virtually every one of its inhabitants. Locomotives were designed and built there from scratch. Nothing was imported. This otherwise unexceptional township was strategically located on the country's first railway line, linking the winter capital of Calcutta to the summer capital of Simla.

Kipling had much to say of Jamalpur in his *From Sea to Sea and Other Sketches*:

> "Jamalpur is the headquarters of the East India Railway. This in itself is not a startling statement. The wonder begins with the exploration of Jamalpur, which is a station entirely made by, and devoted to, the use of those untiring servants of the public, the railway folk. They have towns of their own at Toondla and Assensole; a sun-dried sanitarium at Bandikui; and Howrah, Ajmir, Allahabad, Lahore, and Pindi know their colonies. But Jamalpur is unadulteratedly "Railway", and he who has nothing to do with the E.I. Railway in some shape or another feels a stranger and an interloper. Running always east and southerly, the train carries him from the torments of the North-west into the wet, woolly warmth of Bengal, where may be found the hothouse heat that has ruined the temper of the good people of Calcutta. The land is fat and greasy with good living, and the wealth of the bodies of innumerable dead things; and here—just above Mokameh—may be seen fields

stretching, without stick, stone, or bush to break the view, from the railway line to the horizon."

For my father, the locomotive sheds of Jamalpur were Santa's toy factory. His training as a locomotive draughtsman had fulfilled a boyhood passion and now he was reaping the harvest. He brought his work home with him, setting up a drawing board over which he would spread blueprints that would occupy him for hours and reinforce his anti-social attitude. He hated to be disturbed, least of all by his children, who were, in any case, increasingly becoming the property of his in-laws.

As in Kipling's day, an invisible but unmistakable barrier divided the railway colony from the plebeian remainder of Jamalpur. I am told little has changed in the sixty and more years since I was there. Thoroughfares still bear names such as Albert, Warwickshire and Club Roads. In front of the imposing Jamalpur Gymkhana, built six years before I was born, stood—and still stands—a little Shantipur locomotive, polished and shining as if newly commissioned. But the handsome red façade of the Gymkhana itself was less accessible, to be viewed only from a distance across its trimly circular lawn.

A more familiar haunt was the inevitable railway institute, where Paul and I, accompanied by other extremely well behaved children, all of us escorted by our *ayahs*, attended formal birthday parties. The central feature of these parties, or the main event as it were, was the ceremonial bursting of the *khoia* bag, a ritual resembling what Mexicans call the *piñata*. *Piñatas* may have originated in China. Marco Polo claimed to have discovered the Chinese fashioning figures of cows, oxen or buffaloes, covered with colored paper and adorned with harnesses and trappings. Special colours traditionally greeted the New Year. When these effigies were pierced with sticks, seeds spilled forth. After burning the remains, people gathered the ashes for good luck throughout the year.

The custom is believed to have passed into Europe in the 14th century, when it was adapted to the celebrations of Lent. The first Sunday of Lent became *Piñata* Sunday, derived from the Italian word *pignatta*, meaning "fragile pot". Originally, *piñatas* fashioned without a base resembled clay containers for carrying water. Possibly the Portuguese introduced the custom to India. Certainly Spanish missionaries to North America employed *piñatas* to attract converts to their ceremonies.

Whatever its origins, the ritual so essential to our birthday parties offered a source of employment to numerous skilled makers of *khoia* bags, tailor-made to resemble either various forms of bird and animal, or automobiles, ships, balloons, railway locomotives and aeroplanes. Fashioned from skeleton frames of bamboo strips, covered with layers of thin tissue or crepe, these were filled with puffed rice, in which were buried scores of cheap toys and coins, more than adequate to cater to the numbers of children present.

The birthday celebrant would be blindfolded, armed with a long stick, the length of a billiard cue, and placed immediately under this bag of treasures, which would invariably be suspended from a ceiling fan. The guests would shout deliberately confusing directions until, impatient for the outcome, they would reverse this policy by trying to guide the probing to its desired result. Once the bag was ruptured, rice, toys and coins would spill all over the floor, to be trampled underfoot by excited seekers of the richest pickings. Patient, long-suffering sweepers would stand by with brooms, to clear away the mess once the excitement had abated, and solicitous *amahs* would be ready to console disappointed charges who felt deprived of their rightful reward.

Drowning Pool

It was also at the Jamalpur railway institute that we watched our first movies. Among the latter were old Arthur Askey comedies, including his scary *Ghost Train*, and the first animated cartoon of *Gulliver's Travels*, in which a scene where the sleeping hero is pegged out by Lilliputians left me profoundly disturbed.

Granddad Watson saw little virtue in the invention of the cinema, which trapped us in a darkened theatre when we should have been outdoors, engaged in healthy exercise. He liked to tell of the arrival of silent movies in Tundla, where an elderly resident was entranced by the shifting play of coloured lights on the looped curtains that preceded the performance. When the lights were extinguished, and the accompaniment of live piano music ceased in preparation for the parting of the curtains, this old gentleman assumed the show was over and groped his way through the darkness to the exit, murmuring his appreciation.

But Granddad's jaundiced view of moving pictures was not shared by the rest of the family, who thrilled to epics such as the original *Ben Hur* and the first screen rendition of Jerome Kern and Oscar Hammerstein's *Show Boat*, released a year after my birth. Paul Robeson's rendering of "Old Man River" made a lasting impression.

If I failed my father in his mechanical expectations, I also failed my grandfather in his efforts to encourage a regime of healthy exercise. Sporting activities of any kind were anathema to me, being far better suited to Paul's physique and aptitude. I was doomed to be both inept and effete. Even aquatic pursuits had little appeal, particularly after I came close to drowning at the Jamalpur railway institute swimming baths.

It was my mother's eldest brother Trevor who bore responsibility for this mishap. He had left Paul and myself in the flat shallow end of the otherwise deserted pool, impressing upon us that we must remain there and not attempt to follow him into the deep. Since it was our first visit to the baths, we were unaware of anything deeper than the area in which we stood, and such a prohibition would in any case have served merely as incentive for Paul, who strode recklessly after Uncle Trevor and vanished from sight. Anxious to establish the cause of his disappearance, I followed him over the sheer drop that separated the shallows from the swimming area proper.

Trevor, having completed his traverse of the pool with a leisurely breast stroke, looked back to see both of us missing. Since we two nephews had just recently been measured for our white satin tunics, in which we would serve as page boys for his imminent wedding to our future aunt Ursula, he was understandably panic-stricken. Plunging underwater, he first found and retrieved Paul, administering enough resuscitation to ensure he was still alive. Then he turned back to look for me. I had given up struggling, reaching that stage of euphoria which I have since learned presages a relatively painless death. Before losing consciousness I was mesmerised by a thin but intensely illuminated stream of bubbles; the last air leaving my lungs. Never since have I felt entirely safe out of my depth in water.

The Great Bihar Earthquake

Whatever his lapses, Trevor was easy to forgive. There was always an engaging, self-deprecating smile hovering on his lips, and he had a fund of stories to illustrate how perilous was his bumbling course through life, when in reality he was the least likely candidate to play the role of fate's plaything. He was droll. His mission was to entertain, and he did it with immense charm. I saw him as the most avuncular of my uncles, tall, gangling, soft spoken and slightly absent-minded—though seldom as perilously so as that day at the swimming pool.

In January 1934, during his prolonged courtship of Ursula, who was then living in Jamalpur with her parents, Pop and Esther Cummings, the surrounding state of Bihar was struck by a devastating earthquake that killed thousands. Jamalpur station was torn down, the railway workshops collapsed, and the main line was blocked so that no trains could run through this important depot. The town itself suffered extensive damage and the Cummings family lost their home, being compelled to take up residence in their corrugated iron garage until the bungalow was rebuilt. Snapshots of Trevor and the family, boiling *char* over the fire as they sit outdoors in deckchairs, suggest a safari atmosphere that belies the seriousness of the tragic event itself.

Mahatma Gandhi, who was then deeply involved in the fight against India's caste system, and specifically against untouchability, extracted a positive lesson from the Bihar earthquake. "A man like me," he argued, "cannot but believe this earthquake is a divine chastisement sent by God for our sins".

The following year, on 31st May, 1935, less than a month before I was born in Allahabad, another disastrous earthquake virtually destroyed the distant city of Quetta, at the north-western corner of the Indian sub-continent. It took much longer to rebuild on the ruins of Quetta than it took to restore Jamalpur to normality. Virtually all trace of damage from the Bihar earthquake had been erased by the time my parents moved there.

The Jamalpur *maidan* was expansive enough to land an aeroplane, as was proved one afternoon when I witnessed a lost aviator come down to get his bearings. The descent of his stuttering Gipsy Moth—the first aircraft most of us had seen—attracted a large following, running in its wake as though intent on salvaging an especially valuable specimen cut loose from the kite fights habitually staged during *maidan* evenings.

We encircled the biplane when it came to a standstill, perhaps too close for the helmeted pilot, who waved us back. Keeping his engine running, he summoned one of our number—of dark and clerical mien—to approach, engaging him in a brief conversation before taking off again. Desperate to know what words were exchanged, I presumptuously approached the privileged spectator and asked what the pilot had wanted. The man shrugged. "He is getting himself lost. It is not surprising. On the land, here you are. On the sea, there you are. But in the air, where you are?"

Jamal in Urdu means beautiful, and that is how the outskirts of the colony struck me. There were lakes, waterfalls and groves of trees infested with baboons, liable to leap down and put the unwary to flight with bared teeth. Beyond that wilder periphery stretched enormities of distance, concealing mysteries that would forever be denied me.

It was at Jamalpur that I first became aware of stations in life that had nothing to do with railways, but were imposed by birth, caste and status. There was I first made conscious of my exclusion from the immensity of that greater India outside the narrow confines of my circumscribed existence. Ours was a tiny enclave lost in a great continent. All around were even smaller communities, mere villages dotted across the plains. And I could never explore them, never have anything to do with those other dwellers living their other lives. I was not one of them. That was almost the first lesson I was taught. They were Indian and I was not. I had to stick to our island in their sea.

I would hang upon the garden gate, watching those forbidden other people pass by, dissolving in the heat haze until they became little dancing apostrophes of colour at the edges of my known world. I would wonder at their destinations as they charted their courses across that wasteland; the women walking in columns, pots balanced on their coiled hair, *saris* billowing like sails in the breeze; the men driving and calling to their cattle, coaxing and cajoling them like lovers. Observing high-spirited *chokra* boys wrestling in the roadside dust, helpless with laughter, I would envy them their freedom to roam where they willed so long as they kept their half-starved cattle away from our carefully watered compounds.

Once I was hypnotized by the approach of a troupe of strolling players, drawn from that gipsy tribe of musicians and acrobats who travelled from village to village, living off the land with their songs, their conjuring and their wits. They were a lean, wiry breed, with bundles on their heads, monkeys on their backs, drums and ropes slung from their shoulders and performing bears shambling in their wake.

Catching my stare through the barred gate, one of them paused in his stride and smiled, holding out a hand to beckon me. There was no need of speech. The eyes said it all. *Come with me and you will see what you have not seen, know what you have not known.*

Compound Lives

Servants' quarters were the farthest we were allowed to venture in our familiarity with the natives. These invariably comprised a single row of brick cubicles, occupying the hindmost corner of the back yard of the compound where, if it could be arranged, some strategically located vegetation might screen them from the view of our bungalow's occupants.

It was not our custom to intervene in the affairs of the servants' quarters. We only did so should it become necessary to adjudicate in some dispute among the inhabitants, who arranged themselves according to strict hierarchical structures based on religion and caste. For example a Muslim cook would take precedence over all Hindus, regardless of their caste.

Questions of religion and caste were the first consideration taken into account when recruiting servants, because the unnaturally close proximity in which they were required to dwell created considerable opportunities for friction and stress. Bearers, for example, were in a more lowly position than cooks, and baby *ayahs* took precedence over wash *ayahs*. *Malis*, or gardeners, were only one rank above sweepers, who were lowest of all in the pecking order. It was not an order of existence I would consciously have condoned, but simply one in which I was raised and never came to question until the sheer appalling inequality of it was later borne home to me.

Occupying tiny cubicles in this closely confined domain, some servants had their families living with them, whose children I would befriend as playmates, Paul being at that stage too young—and already altogether too rough—to prove a satisfactory companion. While such fraternisation was not actively discouraged by my parents, it didn't exactly meet with their approval either, particularly because I was oblivious to the ranking structure and therefore to the confusion and even resentment that might be aroused.

I was equally unconscious of the strictures imposed on my playmates by their own parents, who would have been desperately concerned that the disorderly pursuits in which we engaged might lead to some regrettable accident. What, for example, if one of them, provoked into physical assault, should punch me on the nose?

Handicapped by such restraints, my companions from the servants' quarters would prove irritatingly deferential and cautious in their response to my suggestions as to how we should occupy our time. They could tutor me in top spinning and kite flying, neither of which activities exercised any particular appeal to me. They could even teach me to play marbles and their versions of hopscotch and other childish pursuits. But they could never properly view themselves as my equals and would therefore prove vaguely dissatisfying as comrades in arms.

Perhaps my most flagrant, if unconscious, abuse of power and privilege arose when I suggested we should teach local cattle herdsmen not to allow their cows to stray into our property. Ordinarily the gates to our compound would be closed to prevent such an occurrence. Having seen exasperated neighbours emerge from their homes to find whole beds of canna lilies destroyed by masticating bovines, my mother was determined we would not repeat their mistakes.

However on this occasion I got it into my head that the infuriatingly supercilious cattle, casting disdainfully hooded eyes over all they surveyed, needed to be taken down a peg or two and reminded of their proper place in the greater zoological ranking system. So I proposed a scheme whereby, the next time I observed stray cattle in our vicinity, I would leave the gate open and encourage them into our grounds. Equipped with *lathis,* bamboo poles of the kind employed by the herdsmen themselves, we would then lock the gate behind the intruders and inflict punishing damage before releasing them again.

The notion must have seemed so alien to my cow-revering Hindu accomplices that they could only stare at me in astonishment, but presumably it was at the same time so appallingly sacrilegious that it endeared itself to their darker natures, for they eventually grasped their weapons with nods of assent and approval.

We did not have long to wait. Observing the approach of about a dozen strays down the street beyond the gate, I opened that portal invitingly wide and joined those already concealed in shrubbery. Once the sorely tempted cattle were unsafely within our boundaries, I rushed out, closed the gate and set about them with my staff, aiming principally for those lop-sided humps which so strikingly distinguished them from the far healthier and more contented looking cows in my picture books of European origin.

This action provoked a sudden shriek from the servants' quarters, whence I saw my interfering *ayah* bearing down upon us in a cloud of dust and indignation. Her intervention—and the subsequent lecture I received from my parents—put paid to my experiments in cattle chastisement.

Effects of an Encounter With a Tiger

The most memorable landmark in the environs of Jamalpur was a pair of tombstones, adjoining each other but not in perfect symmetry. Both, as I recall, were slabs of either granite or marble, and while they lay more or less in parallel, one was positioned slightly more prominently than the other. The latter contained the remains of a British officer killed by a tiger, while the other contained the tiger. In his *From Sea to Sea*, Kipling writes of "the weird, echoing bund in the hills above Jamalpur, where the owls hoot at night and hyenas come down to laugh over the grave of 'Quillem Roberts, who died from the effects of an encounter with a tiger near this place, A.D. 1864'."

While memory may betray me on the details, it seemed whoever had decided to bury the assailants in so comradely a fashion had also chosen to do so with identical memorials, employing the same lettering and enclosed in the same wrought-iron fencing. I could never pass the spot without pausing to reflect on the manner of their death. I envisaged their corpses, either locked in mortal combat or with the exact distance separating them that was now reflected in the positioning of their graves. Which was the first to succumb? Did the tiger disembowel the soldier and then, fatally stabbed by the latter's bayonet, drag itself off some little distance to die? Or did the soldier survive longest and, with his ebbing reserves of strength, succeed in extending that gap between them?

Though I never made the connection then, I can picture now the discovery of this fatal encounter, just five years after the suppression of the Indian Mutiny. What redolent imagery it would have conjured, back in the days when the Raj had newly returned to the high summer of its glories, all sails unfurled and inflated with poetry and purpose. How fitting a parable that lethal duel must have seemed for the whole experience of imperial India! I only hoped that, when the tombstones were emplaced, each correctly identified the appropriate incumbent. Not that it would matter today, so long after that once potent symbolism has also perished. For if their mismatching bones are to be disinterred, perhaps making way for some pressing urban development, who is there left to care?

I was so prone to daydreaming that my father expressed serious misgivings concerning my sanity. I neither looked nor behaved the way a boy my age would be expected to look and behave. I was perpetually saucer eyed, transfixed in utter astonishment at everything around me. And of course I was extremely, disconcertingly dark; a condition my frequent exposure to sunlight did nothing to allay. The mere passing of a motor car in our quiet streets would cause me to rush outdoors to savour the spectacle.

Yet I displayed no interest whatsoever in how things worked; one of many failings to disappoint my mechanically obsessed father. He could immerse himself in the construction of ever more elaborate model railway layouts—one of which coiled around piles of gravel deposited in an abandoned backyard vegetable garden to look like mountains—and I would merely pause and stare in wonder that he should choose to waste his time in such unproductive diversions.

If my clockwork toys ceased to function, I had no desire to take them apart and explore their springs and moving parts. I would simply cast them aside. When he tried to excite my interest in a huge box of Meccano, I stayed around long enough to observe him embark on an ambitious suspension bridge, and then left him to it, returning to my own diversions, which had nothing to do with complicated assemblies of struts held together with nuts and bolts. The nuts, when he compelled me to try screwing them, hurt my fingers.

Abandoning his efforts to inculcate any mechanistic bent in me, Dad applied himself to the complete overhaul of a secondhand car he had purchased. To do this, he knocked out an entire wall of our brick bungalow and had a concrete ramp built to access the temporary garage he substituted for the dining room. The cumulative cost must have far exceeded that of a new automobile, and for months, while his project was in progress, my mother was prevented from entertaining. "It's Frank," she would shrug. "He does these things." She was learning.

The finished product was a two-seater roadster with a fixed canopy and a dickey-seat that swung open like an inverted boot at the rear. The plan was for my parents to ride in the front with their offspring behind, where we were not readily visible through the narrow back window of the cab. "What if they fall out?" my mother asked. "They will be told *not* to fall out," my father replied.

I enjoyed the occasional drives in the dickey seat as much as Paul did, but was happiest left to my own devices, wandering around in a daze, lost in games of make-believe. It was this tendency that caused Dad the greatest concern. He tried to convince my mother that I was mentally "challenged"—as the present fashionable absurdities of political correctness would term that condition—a belief accentuated when I rotated endlessly around the circular coffee table in the middle of the drawing room, trailing the fingers of my left hand and humming an unrecognizable tune.

"Toodleoomalooma," I would sing, "Toodleoomalooma, toodleay," over and over again. Only later did they discover that the tune was a fairly accurate rendition of Flanagan and Allen's "Umbrella Man", which I had somehow heard before it came to my parents' attention.

The Crashed Aviator and the Haunted Widow

Although he was no more mechanically inclined than I, Paul was reassuringly normal in other respects, given to hectic pursuits of balls in any form, whether designed for soccer, hockey or baskets. No mooning around for him. He was assertively, dangerously active and a cause of constant bemusement and unease for his overly protective elder brother. I endeavoured to restrain him at my peril, for he had little respect for my seniority and no time for my interference. His anger was quick to rouse. He once pursued me with a hockey stick, bent on beating me insensible. Fortunately for me his legs were, at the time, considerably shorter than mine, and a great deal pudgier.

He made it his mission to be better at everything than I was; first to ride a tricycle, first to master the thrill of speed in a pedal car. Seated in the latter, he propelled himself one morning through the compound gates, left open in the immediate aftermath of my father's departure for work in his newly restored coupe. To my consternation, Paul vanished into the midst of a herd of familiar-looking cows, being driven to pasture by a couple of young *chokras* armed with *lathis.* I felt I was being punished in retribution for my relatively recent attempt to discipline those very animals.

Lost in a forest of trampling feet, Paul was clearly invisible to the herdsboys. Unperturbed by his predicament, he pedalled against the current, forcing lowing cattle to step aside like overweight ballet dancers unrehearsed for this particular choreography. Aware something was wrong somewhere in midstream, the boys responded to my quivering finger and urgent, strangulated cries, extricating my brother with a few violent blows on sunken bovine rib cages.

While I became steadily more gawky and even less endearing, Paul remained irresistibly winsome, the kind of deceptively cherubic child people cross the street to coo over. The servants adored him, relations of all kinds made an enormous fuss of him, looking with admiration at my mother as if to commend her on a vastly more successful outcome the second time around. I can't recall resenting this in any way, for I was proud of him myself.

My grandmother's competitive spirit found a new outlet. She was determined the two of us would win the annual Jamalpur fancy dress contest every year, and she spent days dreaming up ideas for infallibly victorious costume combinations. Paul was always the star and I was his foil.

One year he went as a crashed aviator, arms braced Icarus-like in crumpled silver wings bearing Royal Air Force roundels, flying helmet and goggles adorably askew on his chubby little face. I, suitably haunted and haggard, veiled in black muslin with a rag doll of a child cradled pathetically in my arms, went as his widow. Any psychologist might well have detected an alarming rift in sexual identity, but given the general naïveté of the times, no such consideration occurred to Nana Watson. Nor to the judges, who again awarded us first prize.

Paul was meant for centre stage; I was happier in the sidelines, preferring observation to participation. In the shadows I was less conspicuous, afforded the option to dream rather than to act.

A Model Railway Colony

When my father was posted as senior draughtsman to the locomotive shops in Kanchrapara, situated just north of Calcutta on the Assam Bengal Railway, I was transferred from the Jamalpur railway school to its Kanchrapara equivalent. There wasn't much to Kanchrapara. The Bengali poet Isvar Chandra Gupta was born there in 1809, but I didn't know this at the time, and my family had never heard of him, so preoccupied were we with our parochial affairs.

As a poet, Isvar Chandra does not rank very high, but as a satirist he is still held to be one of the best writers of Bengal. Born when Hindu society was in a state of transition, and endowed with a keen sense of humour, he freely ridiculed much that was false and hollow, and much also that was earnest and true, in the movements of his day. I would love to know what he would have made of our narrow little society, but I doubt it would have interested him.

Situated just east of the Hooghly River, Kanchrapara now forms part of Halisahar municipality in the North 24-Parganas district, within the greater Calcutta urban agglomeration. It then embraced—and still does—one of the largest railway workshops in India, and jute milling continues to provide its major industry. A temple is dedicated to Krishna, and a religious festival is held annually. I seem to recall that the latter had something to do with a very large and realistic phallus being transported in procession around the streets; a spectacle my mother did her best to prevent us observing.

Scotland's renaissance man, the celebrated ecologist, town planner and botanist Patrick Geddes (1854-1932) wrote in 1916 a *Report on a Model Colony at Kanchrapara, Calcutta: Eastern Bengal Railway*. Since this was sandwiched between reports on the Madras and Bombay Presidencies, and a town planning report on the city of Lucknow, it is interesting to speculate that Kanchrapara's formal grid layout was dictated by a superior sensibility and a desire to provide a role model for other railway colonies to follow. Geddes had developed a fascination with the organisation of human societies and their spatial manifestation in city and country environments. At the heart of his theoretical and practical interests stood the City, which he considered as a regional, historical and spiritual entity.

Although it could never be described as "pretty", Kanchrapara possessed an undisguised logic and orderliness which other such colonies might lack. It was so rigidly four-square that one could never get lost in it, and its wide roads and shaded avenues seemed designed to convey the impression of being both serenely quiet and charmingly secluded. A stranger would not imagine those who lived there being connected with anything so brutally and mechanically industrial as a railway workshop.

At the Kanchrapara railway school I immediately came to the attention of the headmistress, for entirely the wrong reason. She revived my father's fear that there was something amiss. I lacked powers of concentration, remaining oblivious of whatever my teacher might try to impart, my eyes staring into space, or out through the window, lost in a trance from which I would only emerge if fingers were snapped under my nose. Nana Watson was furious at this woman's verdict that I was "unteachable". Her firstborn grandson, she declared, was brilliant, and a failure to see this only proved the ineptitude of an obviously provincial head-mistress. My grandmother decided my education was too precious to entrust to such a backward institution as the Kanchrapara railway school. She would edu-cate me herself. In fact while she was at it, she would educate Paul as well.

This posed a tough dilemma for my parents. They saw my grandparents as empty-nesters. Having raised five children, all of them now young adults and making their own way in the world, my ferociously matriarchal Nana was suffer-ing severe withdrawal symptoms. She pleaded, she cajoled, but this time she wasn't getting her way so easily. My mother was pregnant again, and not ready to part with her sons until the time arrived for her confinement.

War had just been declared against Japan, following the latter's sneak attack on Pearl Harbour and its simultaneous landings off Malaya's north east coast. Hong Kong, Burma and Singapore had fallen in rapid succession. The Japanese were advancing so rapidly as to bring their bombers within range of Calcutta.

My Aunt as Opera Diva

Hitherto the war for us had meant distant news of Allied defeats and successes in Europe, North Africa and the Russian Front. We had saved silver foil from our chocolate wrappers for "the war effort". When I asked what the silver foil could possibly contribute to the war effort, I was told it was turned into Spitfires and Hurricanes to bring down German bombers over London. I regarded chocolate bars with greater respect. There now seemed to be all the more valid reason for eating them.

The Japanese having suddenly brought hostilities a great deal closer, it was decided that my mother should depart for the safety of Darjeeling—there to deliver her third child—taking Paul and me with her. My father would accom-pany us and then return to his duties in Kanchrapara, which we now understood were also related to "the war effort".

To reach Darjeeling one travelled by train to Siliguri and switched to the nar-row-gauge Darjeeling railway, one of the world's most endearing and enduring toy trains. This battled its way up gradients of one in twenty, via Kurseong and Ghoom, the highest point on a line so twisted and looping, with so many switch-backs where the locomotive must reverse direction, that it resembled the tangled and much tortured cord of a telephone receiver that has never been properly replaced in its cradle.

Unbelievably this ridiculous little train had made its maiden journey along the entire fifty miles to Darjeeling as far back as 1881, so that it was already more than sixty years old when we travelled in it. It is still going strong today, ascending from 146 to 2,225 metres above sea level on a track only two feet wide, which has to be strewn with sand in places, by assistants riding the buffers with their sand buckets, so that the locomotive's wheels can gain better purchase on the rails. My father would have made the trip to Darjeeling even without us, for the sheer pleasure of getting there by this whimsical mode of transportation.

We arrived in Darjeeling so early that year that the spring thaw had not entirely done its work. I found, in the shadowed eaves of our rented bungalow, a six-inch icicle that prompted one of my earliest attempts at poetry:

> An icicle in India;
> How very strange to see.
> I wrapped it in a thermos flask
> And took it down to tea.

Darjeeling brought us back into the opera diva world of Aunt Zena, who I was now informed had been elevated to her considerable heights of self-importance following a meeting with Dame Clara Butt, long before I was born. Zena possessed a voice of such quality that apparently the eminent Dame Clara, undertaking an extensive tour of the "Dominions" with her distinctive form of ballad concert, decided to take her under her wing. Unhappily Granddad and Nana Watson had vetoed the departure of their eldest daughter for uncharted shores of questionable fame and unguaranteed fortune, thereby denying Zena what she felt to be her true vocation. The thwarted prima donna had subjected the family to her histrionics ever since.

Her volcanic temperament had in no way been mollified by her marriage to Leonard Sharp, a member of the Governor of Bengal's band, recruited from Liverpool as a young man and accommodated in the band quarters in Fancy Lane, Calcutta. I liked my Uncle Len. He was proud to call himself a Liverpudlian. He had a cheeky, Liverpudlian grin. His job was not as demanding as it would have been had he served in the band of the then Viceroy, Lord Linlithgow. The latter ruled, from Delhi, a nation largely composed of cow-revering Hindus, yet nightly required his musicians to play "The Roast Beef of Old England" when he escorted his wife into the dining room.

Len, who played the trombone, had plenty of spare time with which to dance attendance on his demanding wife. By the time we met up with them in Darjeeling, Len had taken leave of the Governor's band to teach music at St. Paul's School, the "Eton" of the Himalayas, and Zena had discovered an alternative vocation. Motherhood had become her substitute for an operatic career, and would remain her lifetime mission, long after her two children, Jacqueline and Gordon, were married and raising children of their own. Life revolved around her children, and later her grandchildren, just as—from Len's standpoint—life revolved around Zena. We shared our bungalow with them and instantly entered operatic realms, if only of the "soap opera" variety, long before that term was invented.

Two lessons I quickly learned were that (1) Zena could be the most generous, warm-hearted and loving aunt in the world, fiercely protective of all her kin, and (2) depending on her mood, she was liable to take exception to almost anything one said. She could choose to interpret the most innocent remark as a sly but deliberate insult to her or her children, and would climb into the highest of dudgeons to deliver lightning bolts of recrimination. With Zena one lived on the lip of a volcano, the tectonic plates of her temperament perpetually and unpredictably shifting under your feet. But its sheer, exhilarating, theatrical grandeur made the experience not only worthwhile and memorable but actually treasurable.

Another image etched on the retina of memory: The night sky of Darjeeling made incandescent by a conflagration raging through the marketplace at the foot of the hill on which our bungalow was perched, and Zena, silhouetted on the brink of this catastrophe, more than ever like Brunnehilde, about to plunge into self-immolation in order to save her home and all within. None of us slept that night, but it was Zena who contributed the utmost of its drama.

She had a way of attracting momentous events and unusual phenomena, as though she were a lightning pole thrust into a lowering cloud base. Once a rarely observed sphere of ball lightning actually did fly horizontally through an open window, to explode a fuse box located just behind her head. The truly curious consequence was that she didn't regard such instances as exceptional, but rather as part and parcel of her life. She simply lived on another plane, high above the mundane existence the rest of us pursued.

Dreaded Bread-and-Butter Pudding

Once Mum was admitted to the hospital maternity ward, there wasn't much Paul and I could do. Zena was too preoccupied with her cherubic infant Jacqueline, or Jacqui as we knew her, to spare us adequate attention. So we were sent to a convent school, which Paul loathed with such intensity that spectacular tantrums ensued each morning in the course of preparing him for the ordeal. He was five years old, and this particular convent school, run by an especially forbidding order of nuns, was no kindergarten.

Our school attendance put me in an unfamiliar position of superiority over him, and I would later regret the shameful way I took advantage of this unexpected reversal. To seek refuge from girls chasing him across the playground, intent on smothering him in kisses, he would come running to me, gripping my hand and expecting me to defend him. I would callously disown him, shrugging my shoulders and informing his pursuers that he was not mine, so they were free to do with him what they wished.

Our respective classrooms, divided by a folded partition of opaque glass panels set in wood, backed on to each other. I was in the last row of mine and I knew that he was in the last row of his, sitting more or less directly behind me. Heroic as he was in other respects, Paul was capable of being so shocked, when addressed in severe tones by an adult stranger—and especially one attired in black with a hat like the wings of an avenging angel—that he was in danger of peeing his pants.

On one occasion my concentration on the passage our teacher was reading aloud was broken by the raucous voice of the nun next door. I saw, from the corner of my eye, something moving across the floor, and looked down to see a puddle seeping under the partitioning. This was followed by an even louder yell from the other side. The humiliation of that experience was so great that it sealed Paul's determination never again to let himself be cowed in that fashion, so in that sense the ferocious nun did him a great favour.

When not in school, we were left to the not-so-tender mercies of our *ayahs*, who in turn found they could conveniently unburden themselves for a few hours by entrusting us to the drivers at the pony stables. I dreaded the pony stables; the dank smells of manure, the irritated swish of pony tails engaged in futile defence against the flies attracted there. I was appalled by the whole idea of going for a pony ride, chiefly because my scheming *ayah* found she could bargain for the cheapest rates by hiring the most emaciated and least desirable ponies.

The pony trail was a long, slow circuit of the most exquisite torture. My saddle would slip from side to side across the protruding ribs of my even more hapless animal, perambulated by its driver at a pace calculated to extract the utmost in misery for both rider and mount. Paul, unfailingly set upon the most handsome pony his doting *ayah* could find, would delight in the experience, but I was too preoccupied by the sheer discomfort to appreciate the staggering views of Mount Kanchenjunga from Birch Hill.

Dad returned in good time for the delivery, on 15th May 1942, of his third son, Robert. He took charge of us during my mother's recuperation and renewed his efforts to instil in me a love of bread-and-butter pudding, for which I had acquired an instant dislike which nothing could dispel. So once more I was left at the dining table for hours, staring obstinately at the cold, crumbling remains of this unlovely dessert, which the servants were under strict instructions not to remove until I had consumed it to the last crumb and drop of custard.

My almost equally unlovable *ayah* had succeeded in getting me to eat just about everything else, by threatening that if I didn't, a *kala hati*, or black elephant, would tear down the walls, lift me in its coiled trunk and bear me off on its tusks into the night. But even that threat failed where bread-and-butter pudding was concerned. I was quite capable of sitting through to the next meal time rather than touch the despised concoction. To it was attached the utmost foreboding as to what I might expect in England, where Dad assured me it was a national obsession on a par with tea. I have never much cared for tea either.

The journey back to Kanchrapara became epic in comparison with the outward trip. Firstly Mum engaged a third *ayah* to look after Robert; this time a Nepalese named Jati, of such squat and sturdy dimension as to resemble a brick chicken house. She bore in her waist band a mean looking *kukri*, the curved dagger favoured by Gurkha soldiers, and on her face an expression that signalled her intention to use it at the least provocation. One immediate benefit of her arrival in our household was the departure of my seriously outranked *ayah*. I had now, at the age of seven, learned to fend for myself to the point where I could even tie my own shoelaces!

Halfway down the erratic spirals of the Darjeeling Railway, a worried looking guard approached our compartment, at one of the frequent halts to permit the tiny locomotive to change its tracks or slake its thirst. He urged my parents to restrain Jati *ayah*, who had found sufficient pretext to unsheathe her *kukri* in the third class carriage, where she threatened to behead a drunken Sikh for propositioning her. My parents succeeded in restoring order, and Jati was allowed—against all the rules—to sit with us, so we might keep her under control.

Carousels of Plain and Sky

Arrived at Siliguri, we discovered that trouble had broken out down the line. Imprisoned for a political campaign that was virulently anti-British, Subhas Chandra Bose, former president of the Indian National Congress, had escaped to join the Axis powers, and was now broadcasting from Berlin, on *Azad Hind Radio*, his intention to free India from the yoke of the Raj.

Immensely popular, especially in Bengal and in his home state of Orissa, Netaji, as he was known, stirred up Indian nationalism on a scale not even Gandhi had inspired. "Never for a moment falter in your faith in India's destiny," Netaji told his fellow countrymen. "There is no power on earth that can keep India enslaved. India shall be free, and before long."

The power of his oratory and the thrust of its sentiment had provoked disturbances in Bengal. Passenger trains were being ambushed and boarded by rioting mobs. My father decided we would be safer, and more likely to escape attention, in the guard's van of a goods train. So he made the arrangements and off we set, at a very slow pace indeed, frequently sidelined in one or other goods yard to allow an express train the right of way.

Any train journey was an adventure for me. The greater the distance, the greater the enjoyment; the slower we travelled, the more I could extract from the passing scene. And there was so much to see: forests still dappled with deer and tyrannized by tigers, villages floating like giant lily pads on their tanks of water, accessed by tenuous footpaths snaking tortuously over limitless rice paddies that echoed enormities of sun and cloud, level crossings where cyclists, bullock carts and pedestrians waited patiently in the sun for us to pass, each individual offering cause for speculation as to his or her origin and destination.

And then there were the bridges over which we clattered; crisscross patterns of steel bracing, shuttering fragmented images at the speed of a slow-motion movie projector, and beyond them the flat expanses of dried-up river beds, fringed by distant palm trees. And the little aggregations of huts, wayside stalls, outdoor markets, temples, storage depots, coalescing faster and faster until they merged into conglomerates so large that sooner or later they must surely arrest our progress.

For one who was never mechanically inclined, but who understood the principles of perspective in a fixed landscape, I was fascinated by the mechanics of our motion, hinging upon that visual point on the horizon that moved directly parallel to and abreast of our train. This movable vanishing point served as hub for the cyclorama of scenery that rotated past us. Since the same phenomenon could be observed to be taking place on the other side of the train, I sensed we were being projected forward by the opposing motion of two great discs on either side, whose gigantic radial spokes moved through the heat-flattened landscape to enmesh and then release us, reducing us to an infinitesimal cog in their ceaseless toil

At night I would ask to lie on one of the lower bunks of our reserved compartment, ready to lift the blind and peer out as the train lost momentum in preparation for its arrival at some wayside halt or major interchange. It didn't much matter which, so long as there was something to see; perhaps vendors of *pan birri* or *gurrum char*, hurrying hither and thither with their piercingly monotonous cries, in search of customers at carriage windows, perhaps huddled shapes lying in the shadows, wrapped in cloth and either resting, sleeping or dead, perhaps the stationmaster, impervious to all in his black jacket and cap, flag furled under his arm, consulting his pocket watch for the exact moment to signal our departure.

Long after we left India, I would try to recapture my railway pleasures in verse:

> The lazy vistas cycle by,
> great carousels of plain and sky,
> rotating on their axles pinned
> beyond horizons ill defined,
> spinning slowly past my mind
> and letting memory unwind
> with every mile.
> Don't wake me up if you see me aboard,
> or pull the safety cord,
> but pass me tea, with bread and butter,
> only when I reach Calcutta.

To Paul and myself, on that particular journey from Siliguri to Kanchrapara, the added thrill of travelling in a goods van was adventure writ large, and we were grateful for whatever had precipitated the experience. The fact that this time we would have to lie concealed whenever we rattled through any sizeable human settlement only contributed to the fun. Jati *ayah*, however, found it all very humiliating and unbecoming. Let the mobs dare approach us, and she would deal with them.

Years later my great aunt Esther Cummings (nee Franz), mother of aunt Ursula, described an occasion when a passenger train on which she was travelling was ambushed by a frenzied mob of Hindus, looking for Muslims to slaughter but not too discriminating in their selection of victims. Esther, whose features were so regally aquiline that she might have been mistaken for a fair-skinned Pathan princess, composed herself as she heard the butchers approaching, from carriage to carriage, their progress marked by severed screams and abruptly silenced pleas for mercy.

When they burst into her compartment, she drew herself up to her not very considerable height and demanded to know why they were imposing on her privacy. Removing from her handbag a bottle whose label she hoped would be familiar to them, she brandished this and declared herself the descendant of the Franz whose miraculous antivenin had saved hundreds from certain death by snakebite. Whether or not they recognized the miraculous potion, or had even the faintest idea what she was talking about, they gave her the benefit of the doubt and withdrew.

Manning the Barricades

We reached Kanchrapara to find that the ever diminishing space between us and the advancing Japanese had introduced a much needed element of excitement into our humdrum lives, firstly through the frisson of contemplating the possibility that the enemy might actually succeed in overrunning Bengal, and secondly because of the vastly increased reinforcements committed to our defence.

Our own family had contributed to the manning of the barricades. Uncle Len had left St. Paul's School, within months of his appointment there, to take up a commission as ciphers officer with the Royal Signals, attached to the staff of General Wavell. The following year his duties brought him into contact with the Chindits, brainchild of Wavell and Orde Wingate. Wavell, then Commander in Chief in India, assigned Wingate the task of organising guerrilla activity behind the Japanese lines in Burma.

Wingate has been described as "bearded, covered with eczema and frequently to be seen with an alarm clock dangling incongruously from the belt of his battle-dress". A massively eccentric figure, he attracted as many enemies as admirers. Some thought him a genius, others a madman. Uncle Len was more inclined to view him as the latter, though he retained a considerable affection for his outlandish personality.

During our absence in Darjeeling, Kanchrapara had become an advance air base for the Burma front. The ground crews for No. 27 Squadron of the Royal Air Force, flying twin-engined Beaufighters, became our next-door neighbours—so uncomfortably close that my mother was whistled at from their *atap* huts on the other side of the road. Her response was to plant a thicket of bananas in the compound, to screen the house from "those rude airmen". The banana trees were a welcome enhancement of our environment. Paul and I treated them as a jungle grove, stalking each other through their stems with bow and arrow or picnicking under their broad leaves. They even, in time, surrendered quite edible bananas.

My mother's sensitivity to the advent of airmen at our back door was not helped by the fact that our extremely talented and garrulous Himalayan mynah bird was rapidly acquiring their jargon, their wolf whistles and even their barrack room ballads, snatches of which he would recite at inopportune moments. The mynah was, at one time or other, an irritant to us all. He so perfectly captured the cadence of our gardener's consumptive cough that the man would have loved to wring its neck. Paul and I, frequently summoned to the house by false alarms, mistakenly imagining we had heard our parents calling us, would have gladly aided him in that errand.

One night, when my father was working late on "war related duties" at the locomotive design office (it turned out that he was designing a new armoured car), my mother got it into her head there was a prowler in the garden; almost certainly, in her opinion, one of those RAF boys who'd had too much to drink. She bid me accompany her on the verandah, to see if, between us, we could spot him and scare him away. In the midst of peering out through the latticed screens, we were chilled by a dry cough behind us, followed by "Come here, sweetie", uttered in a particularly coarse and impertinent tone. It was the mynah's closest brush with instant death, but years later, before bidding India goodbye, we were sorry when the time came to donate him to the Calcutta Zoo.

While some of the airmen may have seemed rude to my mother, they were collectively a glamorous bunch, with glossy, well Brylcreemed hair, injecting new blood into social evenings at the Kanchrapara railway institute. They would later be joined by military detachments, including soldiers of the 1st Battalion Royal Lancashire Fusiliers, who were to serve in the Burma campaign with the 3rd Indian Infantry Division. The Fusiliers' jaunty air proved especially captivating to many colony women.

By this time, with that unfailing knack the Watsons had for migrating collectively around the countryside, two of my uncles, Trevor and Denzil, had joined us for brief spells of railway service in Kanchrapara, while Uncle Roland was not far away, studying medicine in Calcutta. Trevor's wife Ursula was a great deal more socially adept than my mother. She was nearly as much fun to be with as her husband and, like him, always had a slightly mischievous smile playing on her lips. At ease in any circle, she prevailed upon my mother to accompany her to Saturday night institute dances Mum would otherwise never have dreamed of attending without Dad.

Ursula convinced Mum it was her duty to entertain the young men protecting us from the Japanese. But in such circumstances my mother was invariably abashed, insecure and given to the most appalling malapropisms. Asked by a young lance corporal what she would like to drink, she intended to request a long John Collins, a cocktail popular at the time, composed of one and a quarter ounces of Bourbon, sour mix and soda, shaken over ice and poured into a Collins glass, garnished with an orange slice and cherry. Unhappily her errant tongue substituted a "long John Thomas". Ursie had the wit and deftness to make light of this, and divert the suddenly silent and incredulous company into nervous laughter, which did nothing to assuage my mother's shame, unmistakably signalled by her scarlet flush, when it dawned on her what she'd said.

Prompted by the same motive, to do her bit for young servicemen so far from home, my grandmother redoubled her efforts at party giving. It was the collective duty of every woman in the colony, she declared, to replace the mothers of those brave lads. If not keeping the home fires burning, we could at least keep the home fans turning.

Not long ago, just before Christmas 2003, I was helping friends to deliver wine to residents of the China Coast Community, a home for ageing expatriate residents of Hong Kong, located in Cumberland Road, Kowloon Tong. There I fell into conversation with Thomas Ovenstone, who had served in India with one of the Gurkha regiments during the war.

When I told him I had spent my childhood in Kanchrapara, and voiced my conviction that he had probably never heard of it, he proved me wrong, describing with great animation how Kanchrapara had proved one of his most memorable wartime postings, principally because of the hospitality lavished upon him and fellow servicemen by the few families residing there. He could not recall any names, but I knew with certainty that my grandmother and my parents would have contributed to that hospitality, for it was commonly accepted in Kanchrapara that none could compete with us in that regard.

The Other Force for Change

Nana remarked on the ability of our new arrivals to drill for hours in the sun without solar topis to keep them from heatstroke. They were making us see with new eyes, she said. She was shrewd enough to piece together her own conclusions about the impact of such people on the social fabric of India. Along with the clamour for independence, heard with increasing stridency from the Indians themselves, the new Britons were themselves a force for change. As wartime conscripts, untutored in its delicate mystique, they burst the bubble of the Raj by refusing to believe, and go along with, all its pomp and circumstance, or indeed its very rationale.

The targets for their rejection ranged far wider than solar topis. This was the generation that would throw out that old battlehorse Winston Churchill, and vote Clement Attlee into power even before the war in the Pacific had ended. Asked why the electorate were so ungrateful as to turn against Churchill, Attlee replied "They didn't turn against him. They turned against the Tories."

Back in 1927, Attlee had come to India with the Indian Statutory Commission, under the chairmanship of Sir John Simon, to investigate the possibilities for local self-government. While to the adults of my family it seemed unthinkable, in 1942, that Britain's Tory-dominated coalition government, in which Attlee served under Churchill as Deputy Prime Minister, would be swept aside by a Labour majority at the next election, we suspected that if and when Labour *did* come to power the disintegration of empire would be one of its first priorities.

And what did they think of us; those young servicemen unversed in colonial ways? Were they sufficiently exposed to the social stratification applicable in India to know the particular place that we Anglo-Indians occupied? Whatever views they held were not expressed in our presence. Perhaps among themselves they debated which of us was darker, which had the more *chee-chee* accent.

I had seldom seen my father so animated as he became in their company. Many evenings he would spend with them, hovering over the snooker tables in the coiling cigarette smoke of the institute billiards room. They rescued him from solitary isolation in the midst of a parochial railway community and restored him to his own kind. Being drawn from the rank and file of the services, rather than the officer class, they reminded him of the qualities of British character absent from those who self-consciously upheld the traditions of Britannia Imperatrix.

To Dad these wartime recruits represented the honest-to-goodness, no-nonsense, take-me-as-I-am charms of the British working class, plunged by war into an alien environment at an age too young to acquire the manners and pretensions of British colonials. Coming from that background himself, even though long out of touch with it, he felt comfortable with them, could talk their language, drink with them and regard them as his "mates". These were men he could point to as the best of Britain, brimming with the barrack room camaraderie he had hoped to find but never really discerned outside the pages of Kipling.

Kipling, I have long since come to recognise, had proved a false prophet for my father, luring him to India in search of imperial adventure only to confront him with a country vastly different, and infinitely more socially stratified, than he had anticipated. His days as a young apprentice draughtsman had afforded him a different perspective on the Raj. Viewed from there, the British seemed less kind, less accessible, less adventurous and less involved.

Fragment of a Rising Sun

At one of our "parties for the boys" Uncle Roland, on leave from his medical college in Calcutta, turned up bearing a shred of silver fabric with the red roundel of the rising sun, removed from the rudder of a downed Zero fighter that had crashed somewhere near the Calcutta *maidan*. Calcutta, he quite unnecessarily informed us, was now within range for both Japanese fighters and bombers.

Roland was a year or so younger than my mother, and the only member of the family to wear glasses since adolescence. If the word "nerd" had been invented then, Roley, as we knew him, would have been a pioneer example. Closest to Nana Watson in intellect, his owlish appearance was entirely in keeping with his owlish mind. If he struck me as old before his years it was not because he looked old, but because he seemed so wise. Yet the solemnity could be dispelled in a moment with a most infectious laugh, and his generosity was unbounded.

Somehow that torn silver fabric he produced at the party, with its fragment of scarlet insignia, brought the war closer than any headlines in the *Statesman* newspaper. Kanchrapara embarked on a furious race to build air-raid shelters; not collective communal shelters—for we decided the colony was too scattered for that—but dedicated family shelters located in individual compounds. We had the considerable work force of the railway labour lines at our disposal, digging deep rectangular pits to be covered with arched sheets of corrugated iron, over which was laid a dense covering of turf. Not satisfied with the crudity of concrete walls, we plastered and whitewashed these, installing electric lighting so that we would not have to endure complete darkness. And then, having gone this far, we decided the result was too bare and forbidding, so we installed furniture, comprising a settee and small dining suite in case the raid might happen to be prolonged, together with a variety of board games, including Monopoly, and of course a bookshelf of reading material to stave off boredom.

It appeared to us a great pity to reserve these shelters purely for use in the event that we might suffer an air raid. And thus began the latest variant in one-upmanship; a round of air raid parties, in which we crowded into the host's shelter and cordially admired his décor, fittings and ability to sustain, if necessary, a prolonged siege in which wave after wave of Japanese bombers might beleaguer us for weeks.

My father and Uncle Denzil were wardens invigilating the colony's Air Raid Precautions, checking to see that when practice sirens were sounded we extinguished our lights and proceeded in an orderly manner to the shelters. Uncle Den was my grandparents' youngest child, and—as his siblings universally agreed—thoroughly spoiled. He never took life sufficiently seriously to give it his earnest attention, preferring to slide comfortably into the easiest of chairs and leave the worrying to others. An affair in his youth, with an older married woman, so alarmed the thoroughly moral Watsons that they intervened and, to "cure him of his ways" as Nana put it, pressured him into marrying a girl of their own choosing. I always felt sorry for the hapless victim of this mismatch. My Aunt Dora was shy and retiring, but tough enough to batten down the hatches for a union that would endure no matter what. She made a wonderful mother to her children, who adored her and were her life. She was also a patient, loyal and long-suffering wife, but her marriage to Denzil lacked the romance that might have offered a more fertile foundation for love.

I can't recall many of those ARP drills, but I do remember one that led to an unexpected outcome. Together with the servants, Paul and I dutifully followed my mother who, despite strict instructions not to, defiantly illuminated our progress across the lawn and down the steps to the shelter, where her torch beam settled on a cobra, rising to spread its hood at our approach. That was it. My mother decided nothing would ever again induce her to visit our air raid shelter.

Between 20th and 24th December 1942, the Japanese launched several air raids on Calcutta and its environs, of which Kanchrapara formed a strategic part. When their bombers first arrived, targeting the rubber dumps at nearby Dum Dum, we forgot all about air raid shelters, crawling under beds and other items of furniture for the duration of the attack. And the following night all our relatives in Kanchrapara moved in with us, bringing their beds with them and clearing out the dining room to serve as a dormitory.

I was running a high fever that night; the latest onset in a series of bouts of malaria that would plague me for years, but for some reason this had the effect of making me even more vividly conscious of my surroundings. I was laid on a mattress under the springs of one of the metal beds lined along opposing walls. Around me were various members of my family, awake and vigilant, listening to the distant crump of falling bombs. Their conviction was that sooner or later the bombers would turn their attention to the strategic locomotive sheds of Kanchrapara, where Dad's mysterious war effort was making good progress. Accompanying the barrage, I could hear my mother mumbling over her rosary beads.

Imaginary Vampire

Ever a sickly child, I was prone to a succession of illnesses, my body temperature capable of elevating itself to the uppermost limits of the standard thermometer, at which point I would hallucinate, hearing voices in the wall or under the bed. There wasn't much with which to combat bouts of malaria in those days, other than bittersweet doses of that old reliable quinine, extracted from chinchona bark. I believe now that my imaginary voices were caused by a ringing in the ears associated with tinnitus, a fairly common side effect of quinine.

Whether due to the cosseting I had been subjected to as an infant, or my mother's concern over my physical well-being, I developed an early tendency to hypochondria. It didn't help that I suffered from low blood pressure, a phobia of hypodermic needles and a propensity to faint at the mere sight of blood in any form, even from a grazed knee. I was also overly impressionable and morbidly suggestible, identifying all too closely with the characters I read about in books. A memorable example was a passage in R.M. Ballantyne's adventure yarn *Martin Rattler*. I vividly recall the effect this produced.

It was an afternoon in the early winter of 1942. I was seven years old, lying on a settee in the drawing room, reading of Martin in his hammock in the jungles of Brazil. A vampire bat had settled on his big toe and was draining him of blood as he slept. Unable to read on, I laid the book aside but found that I couldn't get up. I couldn't even raise the strength to elevate myself far enough off the sofa to examine my own big toe, where I certainly felt needle fangs had been sunk into my flesh. Panic stricken, I rolled off the couch and eventually managed to crawl on all fours into my parents' bedroom, where they were taking their afternoon nap. My mother awoke to hear me cry that I had been attacked by a vampire, at which point I passed out. When I came to, my father was shaking his head as if this latest development was merely taking a stage further what he had suspected all along.

Yet I could cope with genuine crisis as well as anyone my age might be expected to. And when a real fruit bat blundered into the room one evening, so disoriented that my efforts to evict it with a broom led to its impact with a ceiling fan running at full speed, it was my mother who fled screaming from the explosive, blood-drenched aftermath.

Always a doodler, I developed the habit of covering the tiles of the verandah floor with chalk drawings of aerial dogfights, in which pride of place went to barrel-shaped Brewster Buffalos and stub-nosed Beaufighters. The latter aircraft's twin radial engines were thrust so far forward of the cockpit as to seem like pugnacious fists ready to engage any adversary. The enemy were represented by crude looking Zeros, invariably going down in flames, pursued by streams of bullets as large as sausages.

Leading Aircraftsman Jimmy Rushgrove, who had become a favourite with the family and a more frequent visitor than any of the other servicemen within our expanded social circle, was very encouraging of my budding artistic talents, and offered much useful advice. A native of Wigan in Lancashire, young Jimmy was as short and sad faced as a basset hound. When the monsoon broke, he stood wide-eyed on the verandah, watching the water level visibly rise across our flooded lawns. "Eee, it's fair chuckin' it down," he murmured.

One day a wounded vulture, its broken wing rendering it incapable of flight, landed on our flat concrete roof and caused gasps of apprehension. What more fateful omen of impending doom than this gargoyle-necked consumer of carrion? My mother had no one to turn to but the servants, who were ordered up on to the roof to shoo it away with brooms. Paul and I weren't allowed anywhere near this scrawny scavenger, for who knew where it had last feasted, or on what?

The bird was toppled from the parapet in a tangled heap of feathers, and I last saw it shuffling off disconsolately towards the edge of the compound, beyond which it might fall prey to almost anything, including ravenous and possibly rabid pariah dogs. But that was not the end of the drama. My mother read its unwelcome intrusion into our lives as an augury to which she must respond, or repent the consequences. It was high time, she decided, that Paul and I were confirmed in the Catholic faith. She knew just the church where this ceremony should be carried out. Denzil and Dora had been married there, and its miraculous statue of the Virgin Mary surely imparted a special sanctity and significance. Our Lady of Happy Voyage Church in Bandel was the oldest place of Christian worship in Bengal.

Miraculous Virgin

In 1579 the Portuguese constructed a port on the banks of the river Hooghly, which became the origin of Bandel, a centre of their commerce, a substantial part of which was allegedly contributed by a trade in slaves. They enjoyed good relations with the Moghul Emperor Akbar and his successor Jehangir, but not with Prince Harun, who in 1622 revolted against his father Jehangir, commanding the Portuguese Governor of the Hooghly settlement, Michael Rodriguez, to help him with men and artillery. Rodriguez refused, an act the prince would remember with bitterness. When Harun ascended the Moghul throne as Shah Jehan in 1628, he ordered the Moghul Subedar of Bengal to exterminate the Portuguese.

The Subedar took time to prepare his forces but eventually laid siege to the Hooghly fort, at whose walls his large Moghul army proved no match for two hundred well trained Portuguese and their plentiful supply of ammunition. However the Portuguese were betrayed by one of their own officers. On 24th June 1632, the feast of St. John the Baptist, while everyone was in chapel, attending a religious service, the enemy were given secret admission to the fort. Setting fire to the arsenal, they took possession of all the arms and blew up the fortifications.

Panic stricken inhabitants of the settlement were massacred without mercy. The governor was captured and burnt alive, and over four thousand men, women and children were taken prisoner. Of five Augustinian friars made captive, only one aged priest, Father Joao da Cruz, was spared. He and the surviving Christians were carried off to Agra, capital of the Moghul empire, to be thrown to wild beasts.

At Agra a grand Durbar was arranged, and a large arena prepared. Crowds flocked to witness the spectacle of four wild elephants unleashed against the defenceless Christians. But the furious pachyderms became strangely subdued in the presence of Father da Cruz. The largest approached, lifted the priest on to its back, knelt before the Emperor and bowed its head, saluting Shah Jehan with its trunk. The astonished spectators finally found their voice, shouting that the Christians were friends of Allah and should be set free. Shah Jehan ordered their release and sent them back to Bandel to rebuild their mission.

Much else about Bandel was permeated with an equally legendary aura. The statue of Our Lady of Happy Voyage, set in a niche above the altar, atop the façade, originally stood on the altar of the military chapel attached to the Portuguese factory destroyed in the pillage of 1632. On that occasion a Portuguese merchant, Tiago, endeavoured to carry the statue to safety on the far side of the river, but was struck by arrows and sank from sight, along with his burden.

One night following the return of the Christians from Agra, while reconstruction of the church was in progress, Father da Cruz saw a strange light on the river bank and heard a voice like that of his old friend Tiago calling out to him. Early next morning a group of villagers approached the church, shouting that "*Guru Ma*", the Blessed Mother, had returned. Father da Cruz was led to a spot where the statue lay in the mud, and where a concrete cross stands today.

There was more to come. While celebrations were in progress for the blessing of the rebuilt house of worship, a Portuguese ship cast anchor alongside. The vessel had survived a terrific storm in the Bay of Bengal. The captain, a deeply religious man, had made a vow of thanksgiving to the Blessed Virgin which entailed removal of one of the ship's masts for presentation to the church. Not knowing quite what to do with it, the parishioners erected it in the grounds in front of the main façade, where it can still be found.

All told, Bandel was going to be an awe-inspiring venue for my confirmation into a faith whose dense and convoluted dogma I was struggling hard to accept. The setting alone was pretty dramatic. The church, which by this time had been invested with the honorific of "basilica"—albeit a minor basilica—stood on the far shore of the Hooghly, commanding a sweeping view of a river down which a great many waters had flowed since the ancient image of Our Lady of Happy Voyage had resurfaced from its bosom.

Tapestry of Fallen Empires

I had never before seen the Hooghly at this point, even though Kanchrapara was located but a few miles away. My acquaintance with the river stemmed from those occasions when we crossed it in Calcutta, to change from one station to another. In Calcutta it seemed a river tamed; subordinated to the city's sanitary needs. But viewed this far upstream it was a wide river; so wide that the opposite bank was a coastline glimpsed across a minor sea. And its waters were of such an unappetising shade of brown it seemed all India was voiding itself through this one outlet.

An offshoot of the sacred river Ganges, and held to be its principal route through the many-mouthed delta that conducted that mother of waters to the sea, the Hooghly swept past vast tracts of land linked to the earliest incursions of competing colonists from the west. Its starboard shore scrolled downriver in an immense historic tapestry of bygone settlements that bravely staked their ephemeral claims in the name of one or other European power, in the days before the East India Company rose to ascendancy over all rivals.

Bandel was among the earliest, but others included Chandannagore, whose gate still bore the motto of the French Republic *"Liberte, Egalite, Fraternite"*; Serampore, a Danish settlement from 1699 to 1845, and not much of a success as a trading centre, though its cultural contribution included the establishment of a printing press and publication of the first vernacular Bengali language newspaper; Chunchura, site of a Dutch factory built in 1656, which later passed into British hands; and finally Murshidabad, well known for its silks, for the Hazardwari Palace, seat of the Nawabs of Bengal for some three hundred years, and for the nearby battlefield of Plassey, where Robert Clive laid the foundations of British rule in India.

Ignoring all that heritage, as if it were of no more consequence than the silted debris of its last floodwaters, the Hooghly's languidly spiralling currents floated serenely by, bearing stately barges under threadbare, empty-bellied sails, starved of so much as a breeze across that haze-edged hinterland of the Bengal plains. The hulls of these vessels were weighed down to within inches of the water by stacked bales of jute, leaving crews straining at their oars to achieve a semblance of progress. Some staggered like floating barns under bulging mattresses of hay, as if large chunks of agricultural land had been carved off from adjoining fields and set adrift on the torrent.

To cross to the far bank we entrusted ourselves to a narrow rowboat, shaded with an arched roof of bamboo matting, whose two-man crew stroked us transversely against the grain of the flow, compensating for its momentum by aiming slightly upriver.

The architecture of the church proved, on closer examination, every bit as strange as its legends had implied. It constituted a miniature rococo theme park of religious experience. One moved from tableau to ornate tableau, from painting to multi-coloured painting, in wonderment at the fervour that inspired them.

Paul and I were dressed in silk satin tunics, Paul looking typically angelic while I appeared gauntly apprehensive. Although well rehearsed in the liturgy of the service, I was afraid of being distracted by all its trappings so abundantly displayed on all sides. Most of all, I was afraid I would fail to achieve the desired state of ecstasy that would make my first communion and confirmation a transcendent experience. I was proved right, although I did manage to simulate an appearance of ecstasy that convinced my mother the trip had proved worthwhile—if not my cynically dubious father, who had come along for the ride.

The other decision Mum had reached, in the aftermath of our cathartid visitor with the broken wing, was that Kanchrapara was too close to the Burma front for comfort. Her parents were about to be posted to Tatanagar, much farther removed from the potential danger zone. She decided to submit to Nana's entreaties and entrust to her care her two elder sons, while she stayed by her husband's side in Kanchrapara, nursing her newborn infant—or rather overseeing Bob's nursing by his highly competent Jati *ayah*.

Far Titanic City and a Near Fatal Thunder Box

At the dawn of the twentieth century, one of India's earliest and greatest business entrepreneurs, Jamshedji Tata, laid the foundations of his country's steel industry in southern Bihar, on a site named after him. Jamshedpur was to India what Pittsburgh was to America or Sheffield to England. But when we arrived there it was still raw, still new, and the suburb of Tatanagar, to whose railway works my grandfather was posted, was rawest and newest of all. So rapidly has the megalopolis subsequently expanded that Jamshedpur and Tatanagar have now become one, both names serving to identify the conglomerate whole. In 1942 nocturnal Jamshedpur was a glowing reminder of the contrast between the two entities, its blazing foundries lighting the night for miles around and plunging into greater stygian darkness we of Tatanagar who lay outside that orbit. Our horizon was perpetually illuminated by the seductive glow of the far titanic city.

Tatanagar was the closest I have lived to the cutting edge of human habitation as it scythes into the vulnerable flanks of hitherto untouched wilderness. The jungle began at our back yard, and from it emerged varieties of disturbed creature capable of driving my grandmother to hysterics. Black bears were common, and easily put to flight by servants armed with dustbin lids and other noise producing aids, but the occasional leopard was another matter. Panicked by noise, it could turn unpredictably on its pursuers if it sensed itself cornered. When there was a leopard around Nana would gather her grandsons and retreat with them into the bungalow, locking all the doors and windows and instilling a sense of siege. In vain did I point out to her that Kipling's *Jungle Book* portrayed both Baloo the Bear and Bagheera, the black panther, as friends of Mowgli, the "man cub".

She had a particularly morbid fear of snakes; more so than Granddad, who had lost an aunt to snakebite when she was still in her teens. It was one of his most chilling stories; of how the girl, living in a newly settled area of India just as remote as ours, was in the habit of swinging from the bamboo rafters that extended over the edge of the verandah. One morning a krait, lying in a hollow trough of bamboo, sank its fangs into her finger. There was no time to take her on a frantic search for medical treatment, for the poison was spreading too rapidly. Her father used a penknife to carve her finger to the bone, but it was too late even for that.

Nana's nightly ritual, before retiring to bed, was to stuff rolled newspaper under every door and window frame, so that the entire hot and airless house was hermetically sealed as assuredly as a bank vault. It was useless to plead suffocation. Rather we should die of asphyxiation than the venom of some intruding reptile.

She never succeeded in infecting me with her dread of snakes, despite countering with her own selection from Kipling by urging me to read his *Rikki-Tikki-Tavi*, despite my grandfather's tale of his aunt, despite the episode in the air raid shelter and despite one other close encounter in the compound at Kanchrapara, when the servants discovered and dealt with a nest of young cobras, which scattered in all directions, one of them passing between my legs. I was fascinated by snake charmers, and suffered no qualms when allowing them to drape pythons around my neck and across my arms. However I had more sense than to go near their cobras, even though I knew their venom had almost certainly been milked beforehand. And following an experience of my father's, I took care to examine the thunder box before seating myself for my morning defecation.

In Kanchrapara, as in Tatanagar, there were no flush toilets, or septic tanks, so that we were dependent upon the dawn patrol, a team of specially untouchable men in that heinous caste ranking that continues to plague India's rational development as a civilised country. These were the nightsoil removers, or "night shite shifters" as Dad affectionately termed them. He even invented an anthem for them, sung to the tune of *Colonel Bogey's March*: "We are the night shite shifters; we shift shite by night".

Travelling by slow creaking bullock carts, whose unlubricated wheels seemed deliberately calculated to ensure the maximum disturbance of our slumbers, our nocturnal visitors would, with much clattering and banging, collect and dispose of the contents of our commodes, or thunder boxes, doubtless to be used as fertiliser for distant vegetable gardens.

We had about half a dozen thunder boxes ranged down one side of the bathroom, the other side of which was occupied by a low-walled bathing area with a shower head and a bucket one could dip directly into the adjoining metal drum for one's ablutions. The practice was to leave unused thunder boxes with their seats and lids up, to indicate which were available, and then close them after use. One morning Dad went into reverse, to position himself over what he thought was an unused thunder box, when he glanced down and found, to his annoyance, something dark and coiled deposited below. He was about to move on in disgust when he saw the object uncoil, and realised it was a krait that had somehow scaled the metallic legs of the commode to clamber in.

At Tatanagar my closest brush with danger came from a scorpion on my wrist when I withdrew my arm from a pile of bricks that had not been removed following construction of our house. To me it was an unfamiliar insect with a rather whimsically upended tail and I proffered it for examination by our gardener. He warned me not to move, sweeping the edge of his broom across the back of my hand so accurately that I hardly felt the bristles as he dislodged the scorpion, which he then battered to a pulp with his slipper.

At the Forest Edge

Nana set about turning the verandah of our newly built Tatanagar bungalow into a semi-alfresco classroom. She invested in a set of children's encyclopaedias, together with an assortment of books on poetry, geography, history and mathematics. She engaged a carpenter to construct two small school desks and chairs, before which she would place a blackboard and the table where she would sit to direct our studies. While the carpenter applied himself to his task, she taught herself to teach; a skill she had never before found it necessary to acquire.

All her children had been educated at Oakgrove, the alma mater of those Anglo-Indian children whose fathers manned the railways. Situated at Jharipani, a wayside halt on the steep, winding road between Dehra Dun and the hill station of Mussoorie, Oakgrove was still in existence when I called there in 1979. The staff of both the boys' and girls' schools were delighted to show me around, and to point out to me the plaque bearing the names of distinguished old boys, including that of my uncle, Roland Watson. Jharipani's only other landmark, which vanished many years ago, was a restaurant opposite the school gates, owned by a German couple, the Ungeforans, who sold Beck's beer at twelve annas a bottle.

It had caused Nana great distress to see her offspring depart for that boarding school at the end of each summer and winter vacation, and I now believe that her insistence on teaching us herself stemmed from that loss, as an insurance that she would never be similarly deprived of her grandsons too. She proved a stern taskmistress. We were kept to a strict timetable, only interrupted by incursions of animal trespassers in the garden, or crises in the servants' quarters. Especially vigilant for spelling mistakes, she would rap the palms of our hands with a ruler and then retire to her bedroom to recover from the shock of what she had done. When sufficiently rallied, she would return to her desk to continue our instruction, her features recomposed but her voice betraying a slight quaver.

I owe my firm grounding in education to my grandmother. She taught me, above all, a love of poetry and literature, which were unmistakably her favourite subjects. I already shared her pleasure in reading, having become an ardent fan of Ballantyne, Robert Louis Stevenson, Jack London and the faraway places they described. She also introduced me to Dickens, Jules Verne and Edgar Allen Poe, and tried, without success, to win me over to Sir Walter Scott. The legend of King Arthur was a particular favourite with her, and the very idea of Camelot would make her misty-eyed. Perhaps it was from her that I acquired my florid literary style, my heavy dependence upon simile and metaphor. One of my earliest short stories began: "His arms flailed across the surface of the swimming pool like twin tin-cutters".

My reading preferences did not always meet with her approval. Our nextdoor neighbours possessed a complete set of Richmal Crompton's "William" series—at least as complete as it could be at the time—for the author was to continue writing these until her death in January 1969. I borrowed them and was immediately converted. For a classics mistress at Bromley High School for Girls in Kent, Crompton displayed an amazingly perceptive grasp of a boy's world. When stricken with polio in 1923, she had already published *Just William*, which would be followed in quick succession by *More William, William Again* and *William the Fourth*. The illustrations to those early books, by Tomas Henry, perfectly captured the flavour of Crompton's narrative.

Two especially vivid images stand out from our sojourn in Tatanagar: the explosive incineration of a forest giant at the edge of our property, which I happened to be watching at the moment it was struck by a lightning bolt, and torrential floodwaters sweeping down a narrow, densely wooded valley, which put paid to our plans for a picnic in the hills. The swollen brown river was savage in its destruction, uprooting trees and employing them as battering rams with which to bring down others that left a trail of debris in their wake.

Living close to nature also meant living close to its elemental forces, which in minutes could leave our garden battered into submission, destroying weeks of patient cultivation. Nana was convinced the especially violent thunderstorms resulted from the high incidence of iron ore in the ground, acting as lodestones with which to pull down and discharge the electrical mass of any passing rain clouds.

The arrival of Aunt Barbara, latest addition to the family through her marriage to Uncle Roley, was a welcome respite from the routine into which our lives had fallen. Born into the Mercado family in the Burmese hill station of Maimyo, which had now fallen into Japanese hands, she met Roley in Calcutta, where she was a nursing cadet and he was completing his stay at medical college. In order to marry him, she became—as often happens in such cases—a fanatical convert to Catholicism, but this did nothing to dissipate a puckish sense of humour that made her seem more a big sister to us than an aunt.

She won our respect and gratitude by defying Nana's prohibition on the opening of windows at night, convincing her it was unhealthy to sleep in airless rooms and that, despite whatever rudimentary climbing skills they might possess, snakes were unlikely to scale blank walls of raw brick. Nevertheless Nana insisted the barriers of newspaper remain under the doors.

Massacre of Egrets

Granddad's mysterious and war-related railway assignments called for a great deal of mobility. Having seen Arthur Askey in *Ghost Train*, discovering behind that nightly apparition a secret railway schedule that shunted German gun-runners down an innocuous British branch line, I wondered if it was my grandfather's responsibility to protect us from similar incursions by Japanese infiltrators.

Hardly were we settled into Tatanagar than we were on the move again, this time back to Jamalpur, where we rented a house with a walled garden, plagued by flocks of cattle egrets cacophonously roosting in its immense pipul tree. It wasn't just the noise, exacerbated whenever nocturnal predators such as civet cats were prowling among them. It was the mess they made of everything beneath, their toxic lime deposits preventing even grass from growing under the fairly substantial span of branches stripped bare of leaves by their competition for roosting space.

The Hindu god Vishnu is said to have been born under a pipul tree, while Buddha allegedly spent six years meditating under another. I can only assume that in neither case was the tree infested with egrets. The snowy plumage of these birds—so white we called them *dhobi*, or laundry birds—belied their noxious habits. I have seen them perched on the stern ends of buffalo, impatiently pecking under an upraised tail before the unfortunate beast has had a chance to properly discharge its waste. They were equally irreverent in their attitude to villagers squatting in the fields for their morning evacuations. An apt Malay proverb I was to come across in later years provided a colourful equivalent to the adage of pride before the fall: No matter how far and high the egret flies, he always ends up in the shit.

Our egrets were most decidedly—and collectively—heading for the shit. Granddad decided the civet cats weren't doing a good enough job of keeping down their population, and since no other repellent appeared to work—neither smoke, air-guns nor, least of all, firecrackers and other loud noises—the time had come for a more drastic solution. He found and engaged a team of egret exterminators.

The method employed was memorably extreme, and one that would give me nightmares for weeks to come. The task was carried out under cover of darkness, when the birds were restlessly asleep, by some half a dozen men armed with torches and with extremely long and slender poles, assembled by binding together lengths of bamboo. The final segments of these poles ended in steel tips, sharpened into spear heads. The entire assemblage would be elevated with infinite, wobbling care until, steered by torchlight, the tip lay directly under the breast of a sleeping egret, at which point it would be thrust up with great force.

I was as transfixed by the spectacle as the birds by the spears. Standing in the darkened garden, craning my head back to watch the torchlight playing on the leaves, I picked out the huddled white shapes of dream-rapt egrets, frozen in stillness and blinded by the glare. It was a long, slow business, interrupted by raucous shrieks and the fluttering feathers of dying birds. Because of the height at which they roosted, and the odds against achieving perfect aim with those trembling spears, some birds were skewered through their wings and other body parts instead of their breasts. The pure whiteness of the feathers made the blood seem more intensely red. I wished that they would all wake up and spare themselves the horror by flying blindly into the night, never to return.

When the monsoon broke shortly afterwards, it seemed the heavens were bent on washing away all trace of the massacre. The garden filled rapidly with flood water, high enough for Paul and I to set sail in our metal bath tub, out through the gate and into the street, where the populace were celebrating the arrival of the rains with fervour and enthusiasm.

More than those of the Western calendar, the many and colourful Indian festivals were always our favourites. Best of all for Paul was *Holi*, the feast of colour, which we celebrated by throwing coloured powder or squirting coloured water at fellow celebrants. For *Holi* we would be permitted out in our "dispensable" clothes, so it didn't really matter in what polychrome condition we might return. My preference was for the five-day feast of *Diwali*, and especially the night of the new moon, ending the "dark fortnight". Known as *Laxmi Pujan*, this was the night when Lord Vishnu, in his fifth avatar as Vaman, defeated King Bali and liberated Laxmi, whose freedom signified the triumph of light over darkness, when night became day.

Preparations for *Diwali* were as demanding as any prelude to Christmas. Although my grandparents paid them no heed, they permitted the servants to observe them to the full. The servants' quarters had to be cleaned, washed and whitewashed. Their children were taken out to buy crackers, candles and a *hatri*, or small house-like structure made of mud, where a tiny idol of Lakshmi was seated in the middle. A pair of earthen Lakshmi and Ganesh statuettes were essential for the *Diwali Pujan*, and invariably I would be able to scrounge a Ganesh for myself.

Ganesh was my hero. His elephant head, with only one tusk, sat wisely and amiably on the rotund body of a dancing child, seeming the epitome of contentment. He was the god of wisdom and learning, as well as the remover of obstacles. In his four hands, he held a shell, discus, club and water lily. Like most Indian gods, he had a "vehicle"; in his case a rat, usually shown at his feet. With his protuberant belly and a twinkle in his eyes, Ganesh was unquestionably the most lovable, mischievous and accessible of the Hindu deities. But much as I cherished him, I knew better than to admit this to Nana. One of Trevor's more memorable anecdotes concerned an occasion during his childhood when he persuaded his sisters Holly and Zena to eat the sweetmeats placed before the shrine of a *sadhu*. When Zena reported this to her parents on their return home, Nana was so horrified she took her progeny directly to the local priest, who was asked to wash out their mouths with holy water.

Paul had no truck with earthen statuettes. His interest in *Diwali* was purely incendiary. He loved the fireworks; the onion-shaped ones ignited simply by throwing them against walls, the rockets one stood in bottle necks, lit and hurriedly retreated from and, best of all, the firecrackers that leapt so unpredictably they kept you dancing out of their errant path. But of the numerous rituals associated with *Diwali,* the defining image for me was provided by the myriad tiny oil lamps that decorated and delineated houses, garden walls, entire villages islanded in their lakes of darkness. It was as if night had remembered the shapes of day, sketching them in pointillist outline and paying brief homage to the delicate and impermanent imprint of a humanity ever at the mercy of its gods.

Call of the Brainfever Bird

From Jamalpur we were posted to Asansol, of which I remember little other than the fact that my mother had been born there and that it was one of the older, larger and more important railway colonies, almost on a par with Jamalpur. Located some two hundred kilometres west of Calcutta, Asansol lay in one of West Bengal's major industrial and urban regions, having sprung into existence largely because of its value to the railways as a supplier of fuel. The quality of coal deposits in the surrounding area was regarded as exceptionally fine, as was the quality of its education. Constituted a municipality in 1896, Asansol had several colleges affiliated with the University of Burdwan.

Certainly it was large enough to possess a far better railway school than Kan-chrapara had boasted. Nana knew the town well, from the time when she deliv-ered my mother at the local hospital. She decided she could safely entrust us to the care of the local headmistress, but hardly were Paul and I installed in our respective classrooms than we were on the move again, this time to Lilloah.

Built around its carriage and wagon works, Lilloah was held, by those who lived there, to be the loveliest colony on the East Indian Railway. There were only three roads, which between them perfectly exemplified the stratification of social rank and caste. The first, as you entered off that famous Grand Trunk Road that connects virtually every city of consequence in India, was Gardiner Road, consisting of mini-manors in the English county style, housing the col-ony's top "*wallahs*", including the managing director and upper management. Next was Pearce Road, accommodating those just slightly less elevated in the pecking order, and finally came Jenyns Road, a mixture of homes for middle and lower management and, at that time, the only street with multi-storey apartment dwellings.

We ended up in one of Jenyns Road's first-floor apartments, from which, when I lay in bed, racked with malaria, I could gaze out through the windows at a view engulfed by a solitary flame-of-the-forest, its branches so laden with scarlet blossom that it seemed the sky was on fire. With it I associate the raucous call of the brainfever bird, boring into my skull like a dental drill.

When not bed-ridden, I would be out in the garden playing with my brother—and sometimes the neighbours' kids—until, our singlets drenched with perspiration, we would be summoned indoors to change into something dry.

The Lilloah railway institute had the reputation of being the best for miles around. It boasted the customary bar and library, plus badminton and tennis courts and an impressive ballroom with a handsome stage for plays and recitals. But the setting, and the quality of architecture, were especially fine, and the insti-tute dances attracted attendance from many neighbouring colonies, including Howrah, Bandel, Burdwan and even Asansol.

During the brief time we spent in Lilloah, our railway school presented a play on the institute stage, based on the Arthurian legend. Whether or not this choice was influenced behind the scenes by Nana I shall never know, but I do know that she threw herself into the task of designing and assembling the costumes. Paul was to play Lancelot and I was to play Merlin, and again the contrast between us was as marked as sunlight against shadow. Paul was radiant in his silver-painted chain mail, with a convincing cardboard shield, helmet and visor he could swiftly close if threatened with backstage kisses, while I crept about in long, black, sinister looking robes with a pointed hat better suited to a witch than to Arthur's trusted adviser and confidant.

Knowing my brother was set to steal the show before he even so much as uttered a syllable of dialogue, a spirit of rebellion possessed me. I was not going to be overshadowed again. Reserving the full extent of my unsuspected talents for the actual performance, when it was too late for me to be reined back by anxious teachers, I squeezed every last ounce of theatricality from my lines. I hammed it up unmercifully, and reduced the audience to helpless laughter in all the places where there shouldn't have been any. I turned what should have been a solemn and dignified recapitulation of one of England's most enduring legends into a one-man comedy show, with supporting cast. Whatever the reaction of the producer and school principal, I received the bulk of the applause.

I went through a particularly sickly period in Lilloah. If it wasn't malaria it was, in Nana's opinion, anaemia, compounded by a lack of calcium. I was forced to consume some form of tasteless blood tonic, and once a week she accompanied me to the clinic for a calcium "fix". The calcium gluconate was injected intravenously, and painfully, so that I would have to sit around the clinic for a long time afterwards to avoid fainting.

It was also in Lilloah that I became aware something was amiss with Nana. She would spend longer hours in bed, and would frequently summon me to her bedside to read her to sleep. She would do this on the pretext of checking my comprehension, and discussing a book's literary merits, but I know now that my grandmother was soothed by the sound of my voice.

Her particular favourite was Franz Werfel's *The Song of Bernadette*. We had both seen and enjoyed the movie in Calcutta, with Jennifer Jones in the title role, but the book was more satisfying. I would look up from the page to see her turned sideways, half sunk into the pillow, gazing at me in a strange, disquieting way, as if she were about to lose me rather than simply slip into slumber. Her fingers would stroke the pillow in front of her face. It was a habit she never lost. Seeing that my attention had strayed from the text, her eyes would widen to stare at me the more intently.

On one such occasion she unexpectedly asked "Will you come and visit my grave when I'm gone?"

"Nana, what are you talking about?" I protested. "Who says you're going anywhere?"

"Just supposing," she murmured, and then, with her eyes closing, as if about to fall asleep, she added "Will you bring flowers? Will you place just one flower beside my headstone? Or will you forget I ever lived?"

I squirmed uncomfortably in my chair. "I will come and read you *The Song of Bernadette*, just as I'm doing now. If you'll let me get on with it."

But my attempt to turn it into a joke was ineffective and unconvincing, for both of us.

Intimations of Mortality

Initial acquaintance with death should come by degrees, starting perhaps with the loss of childhood pets. It should not be thrust upon us without warning, to catch us entirely unawares. I was not yet nine years old. It was unthinkable that I should lose the one person around whom my whole life, to that point, had revolved.

But Nana was getting too tired, and her grandsons were becoming too much for her to manage. My mother came to Lilloah to take us off her hands. Our younger brother Robert was almost two years old, and we had not been around to watch him grow. In later years Mum would ask me "How could I have been so insensitive as to surrender you to my mother, knowing I would see so little of you?" In later years I would tell her "Perhaps you had some presentiment that she was not long for this world. You loved her so much you entrusted your own children to her, because you knew how badly she needed us."

We returned to Kanchrapara to find a colony steadily more immersed in the atmosphere of a wartime supply and support base for operations in Burma. Adjoining our little community was a staging area for troop movements to and from the front-line defences. We even had Americans with us, including the 19th Liaison Squadron, US Army Forces, flying L-5 Stinson Sentinels. The unarmed Sentinel, with its short field takeoff and landing capability, was used for reconnaissance, removing litter patients from front line areas, delivering supplies to isolated units, laying communications wire, spotting enemy targets for attack aircraft, transporting personnel, rescuing Allied troops from remote areas and even as a light bomber.

Earlier arrivals were 893rd Signal Company, Depot Aviation, who reached Kanchrapara in March 1944, to handle telephone, teletype, and airborne/ground radio communications to and from all parts of China, Burma and India. At war's end, in late 1945, Camp Kanchrapara would process American servicemen returning to the United States, among them the men of 858th Engineer Aviation Battalion, the first engineers to work on the Burma Road and the only black battalion in all of the China theatre during the whole course of the war.

Paul and I also found on our return that much of our bungalow's surrounding compound had been converted into a chicken farm, with the result that the unattractive four-square brick edifice had now almost wholly disappeared behind even less attractive wire mesh. Hundreds and hundreds of yards of it were stretched between and across steel poles seven feet high.

My father was ever a man whose latest hobby possessed him to the exclusion of all else. Having destroyed our dining room in Jamalpur, to make way for a garage, he successively carved out his territorial claims from our various Kanchrapara bungalows to pursue other interests, ranging from increasingly ambitious model railway layouts to the construction of crystal wireless sets and an early attempt at ham radio. Bursting out from behind locked doors, he would excitedly announce that he had tuned into some station or other that had previously been beyond audible range, and he would insist that Mum drop everything and don a pair of cumbersome earphones to appreciate his achievement.

She would resign herself to these guinea pig endeavours with good grace, listening solemnly for a moment or two and declaring that yes, she could hear voices, speaking in Bengali or some other dialect. But what was the point of eavesdropping on something one shouldn't, when she would much rather listen to Zena or Roley? The latter, both gifted with good voices, could sometimes to be heard singing on All India Radio from Calcutta, where Zena was performing in a production by the Calcutta Amateur Theatrical Society (CATS).

Mum suspected, from what she understood of the language, that the rather heated Bengali speakers were stirring up anti-British sentiment. On Hitler's personal recommendation, Subhas Chandra Bose had left Germany by submarine, in February 1943, to seek Japan's help in the liberation of India from hated British rule. In Japanese-occupied Malaya and Burma he recruited to his Indian National Army thousands of his disaffected fellow countrymen scattered by the diaspora that had taken place as a result of the cavalier colonial practice of shipping the cheapest available labour to where it was most needed, no matter what the consequences for indigenous populations.

Rallying to their Netaji's cry "Delhi Chalo" (onwards to Delhi) INA troops had marched with the Japanese through Burma, and early in 1944 had crossed the frontier into India to besiege Imphal, capital of India's easternmost state of Manipur. Where such an undertaking might have succeeded when Allied forces were in retreat and at their weakest ebb, it proved, in 1944, a push too far, and a year too late. Orde Wingate's airborne troops began to cut off Japanese supply lines, and British reinforcements were airlifted into Imphal faster than the Japanese could retaliate. Their forces at the gates of India were compelled to withdraw, commencing a long, humiliating and casualty-ridden retreat during which untold scores of Japanese and Indians died of disease, compounded no doubt in the latter case by heartbreak.

Uncle Len, whose role as ciphers officer had placed him, if not in the thick of the action at Imphal, at least close enough to observe at first hand, was for a long while out of touch with us and a cause of concern to all the family.

News that Netaji and his army of liberation had come so close before being foiled by belated Japanese planning, and superior Allied air power, was not well received by his myriad supporters in Bengal and elsewhere in India. The ground-swell of anti-colonial feeling became more palpable and impossible to ignore. Incidents of riotous assembly grew in number, and we began to hear, in conversations not intended for the ears of children, mention of the hitherto inadmissible possibility that "we" might be forced out of India. That we should instinctively align ourselves with the threatened Raj was a measure of how far we Eurasians saw ourselves as "Anglo" rather than "Indian". If the British went, we went. Any writing on the wall intended for them was intended for us too.

White Leghorns and Rhode Island Reds

Dad's sudden decision, at this point, to become a poultry farmer was possibly motivated in part by his belief that the occupation would provide both a thera-peutic diversion from growing uncertainty and an emergency food resource should we—God forbid—be compelled to dispense with servants and all the other comforts of the railway colonial lifestyle. Whatever prompted it, the chicken mania played havoc with that lifestyle, which became very uncomfort-able indeed. Enormous hen "runs" devoured formerly well maintained lawns and play areas that Paul and I saw as our private domains.

Not content with White Leghorns and Rhode Island Reds, Dad began look-ing farther afield for rarer varieties to breed and cultivate. We watched in dismay as the chicken empire made inroads into hitherto sacrosanct preserves like the badminton court, and the long abandoned air raid shelter was turned into a repository for grain and other avian foodstuffs. While Mum abstained from any-thing to do with all this, on the grounds that her husband was not to be thwarted in whatever absurd new enterprise might seize his fancy, she could hardly ignore its effects. The condition to which the garden had been reduced made it impossi-ble to organise any further parties on the scale to which we had been accustomed. Was this too one of Dad's conscious or unconscious motives?

Nor could any of us ignore either the arrival of a growing range of subscription magazines, treating every fowl aspect of this latest obsession, or the construction of an enormous metallic incubator alongside the bungalow, in which literally hundreds of eggs would be carefully maintained at their correct brooding temperatures. Such investments were costing a great deal of money, not to mention the fact that we were becoming tired of the recurrence of chicken on the menu. Despite ourselves, Paul and I had inevitably developed a fondness for certain individual birds that displayed some character trait or other distinguishing feature that would single it out from the flock. Every time we heard the squawking of some unfortunate fowl destined for the table, we would rush out in the event that we must protect one of our favourites from insensitive servants who, in desperation, would catch what they could.

Then there were the predators to contend with; flocks of kite hawks wheeling overhead by day and packs of jackals attempting to burrow underneath the fencing by night. Expenditure on rolls of wire meshing had to be doubled, in order to provide raptor-proof ceilings for all the seven-foot-high enclosures, and sheets of corrugated iron had to be sunk at least five feet into the ground around the perimeters to discourage nocturnal excavators. Finally there was the noise factor; how to cope with scores of cocks and cockerels greeting each dawn long before we were ready to do so. Mum fervently wished that Dad would rediscover the delights of wireless telegraphy or something as innocuous as stamp collecting.

It would have been helpful had he developed an efficient marketing system that would permit him to recoup part of the outlay, but profit wasn't the motive. The amassing of large stocks of poultry became an end in itself, affording him a degree of satisfaction quite beyond our comprehension. If in nothing else, this satisfaction resided in the fact that he had *proved* it was possible to rear several varieties in adverse circumstances, including an uncongenial climate and predators of great tenacity and endurance (eventually the equally chicken-crazed jackals found a way to burrow *through* the sheet metal by destabilizing the sheets and pushing them aside).

Arrival of Chuldum

The next "Dad fad", when the poultry palled, was photography. So another room had to be surrendered as a darkroom and studio. This time the pretext was our passport photographs. We had to be prepared for any sudden evacuation of India, and a lot of time could be saved if we had our passport photographs ready, instead of having to depend on some overcrowded, overworked commercial studio (of which there were not very many in Kanchrapara anyway). Since natural lighting would be cheaper and more reliable than investment in studio lighting, the laundry shelves were ransacked to supply sheets as backdrops, appropriately strung and pegged on washing lines so that not too many wrinkles appeared. All of us took turns to sit on the piano stool in the blazing sun, trying, if not actually to smile, which would have been asking a lot, at least to appear calm and composed while he fiddled with the angle and the focus.

It was particularly galling to me that among those from the servants' quarters observing our discomfiture was Jati *ayah's* son Chuldum, who had come down from the hills to spend a brief holiday with his mother and to whom I had become devotedly attached. Somewhere around fifteen years old, Chuldum was thick-set like his mother, and had also acquired her air of supreme self-confidence, devoid of any sense of servility towards others who might regard themselves superior to him in station.

Was it for what Chuldum could teach us of the manly pursuits that had hitherto proved so alien to me, or was I devoted to him merely for the pleasure of his company? Paul clearly valued him for his skills in kite flying, and in constructing and using extremely accurate catapults, while I unreservedly adored him. If I had had found it necessary to explain this infatuation at the time I would doubtless have argued that it stemmed from Chuldum's independence and willingness to suffer our attentions to the point of taking on the role of mentor. More likely however, it was at this point that I became aware of disquieting effects on my metabolism, induced by his mere presence in my life.

We would follow him on catapult hunts, imitating his example in dispatching toads as they skittered across the nearly dried-out bottoms of monsoon ditches. I could even smother my distaste at the accuracy with which he contrived, at extreme range, minor amphibious explosions that spread little blossoms of entrails across the mud. When I took aim myself, I was careful to miss by the closest of margins, so it wouldn't look as if I deliberately intended to. At least Chuldum wasn't needlessly killing birds, presumably because he was nominally a Buddhist, with his own interpretation on its edicts, in which toads ranked so low in the animal order that to him they hardly warranted inclusion in the hierarchy of species capable of reincarnation.

I would later discover that Chuldum was well named, for the Nepalese appellation signifies self-assurance, independence, and confidence. It also denotes depth of mind, power of concentration and the ability to follow a line of thought to its logical conclusion. The character reference for Chuldums goes on to say: "Your strong characteristic of individuality qualifies you as a leader. Although you do not tolerate interference in your own affairs, this characteristic does not prevent you from interfering in the affairs of others. You are usually either telling or showing someone how to do something properly."

Kite fighting was his particular vocation. The small, lightweight, square-shaped paper kites favoured for this purpose really came to life in his hands, swooping like raptors upon the more fitfully nervous acrobatics of others bold enough to take him on. Paul would be permitted to grasp the bamboo rod, on which the free-rolling drum of kite thread could be played out like a fishing reel, while Chuldum would allow the thread, coated with finely powdered glass, to run through his bare hands, gripping and tugging on it to effect the precise manoeuvres required to cut through the threads of his assailants.

His efforts were more often than not quickly rewarded, for the opposing kite would suddenly stall, like a spent Albatross vanquished by a Sopwith Camel in some World War One dogfight. It would then spiral downwards out of control, growing smaller and smaller in the distance as the breeze carried it far beyond the bounds of our tiny railway colony, pursued by bands of *chokra* boys bent on recovering it no matter how many rice fields they might negotiate en route.

His mission accomplished, Chuldum would turn to us with a broad but grim smile of satisfaction, rubbing his palms together to smear fresh blood flowing from the finely incised patina of scars, worn with the pride of old war wounds. The sight was almost enough to make me swoon.

Unlikely Fishing Expedition

Fishing was one of very few activities I can recall pursuing in my father's company. This latest in a string of passing, and often ephemeral, interests came as a surprise to me because Dad was not by nature a hunting and fishing sort of man. His only hunting expedition I was ever aware of had proved neither distinguished nor productive. It had been undertaken, with Denzil for company, during that period when Mum was away with Paul and myself in Darjeeling, awaiting the arrival of Robert.

On that occasion things had gone wrong almost from the start. He and Denzil had set off in Dad's little Ford economy saloon for the foothills of the Assam ranges, taking care to keep well away from the war. However they mistimed the undertaking and were caught by the onset of the rainy season, as a result of which they were frequently compelled to turn back by the condition of the narrow and steeply inclined mud roads. At one juncture they found their way across a raging river impeded by the absence of the substantial part of a wooden bridge. Alongside this torrential scene they discovered a group of loin-clothed Nagas squatting on their haunches, smoking pipes and gazing silently and impassively at both the damaged bridge and the travellers seeking to cross it.

Dad was inspired to negotiate, for an agreed sum of money, their help in replacing the missing timbers from the bridge, which were found conveniently trailing in the waters below. This operation took a while, at the end of which the Ford set off again, rounded the corner of a hill, where the road kept abreast of a horseshoe bend in the river, and came upon a second bridge reduced to the identical state of disrepair. Squatting alongside, awaiting their approach, were the same Nagas with their pipes and phlegmatic expressions. They had simply crossed the crest of the hill to makes preparations for the Ford's arrival, and this time the cost of restoring the bridge was substantially higher. Dad correctly surmised that inflation would boost it further for the return journey.

Game proved scarce, so that Dad and Denzil succeeded in shooting only a few wood pigeon and, at one stage, a peacock. However in its death throes this bird screamed such piteous and incriminating cries as to attract the attention of a local tribe that happened to revere peacocks as sacred. Firing bows and arrows, the tribesmen raced after the rapidly retreating Ford, which Dad desperately endeavoured to keep from bogging down in mud puddles.

By comparison with that excursion, fishing would seem to offer a less stressful diversion. Dad had been informed, by his colleagues in the railway workshop, of a lake some miles from Kanchrapara that could only be reached on foot or by bicycle. He invited Paul and myself to accompany him there, and even provided us with fishing rods for this purpose. Armed with an ordnance survey map, sandwiches and thermoses, we set off on our bicycles, across a maze of narrow earth bunds between freshly planted paddy fields.

The paths were so slender that I became hypnotized by the task of keeping my tyres aligned on them. And the water in the fields so perfectly reflected the cloud-pillowed sky that I felt I was riding a tightrope across a boundless blue firmament. Should I lose my balance, I must surely fall through endless space. Meeting farmers and their wives heading on foot for their fields, we would be compelled to dismount and sidle past them, holding our bicycles out of their way. Here was that prohibited "other India" I had yearned to discover and was now experiencing at a considerable disadvantage, so preoccupied with steering along the straight and narrow that I had little opportunity to take in the view.

Arrived at the lake, we found a scene of haunting desolation; a large grey body of water surrounded by dead and dying trees. Those leafless trunks waded out into mirror-smooth stillness like the skeletal forms of an army smitten by some fearful apparition that had instantly petrified them in their tracks.

The fishing was bountiful, and entirely to Dad's satisfaction, although I had to request his assistance to remove the hooks from those few specimens that I landed myself. I kept hoping he would never ask us to come back to this place again. The fervency of this prayer was considerably amplified when my front wheel slipped off the embankment on the return journey, plunging me into freshly planted paddy stalks from which I emerged covered in mud. Endeavouring to wrestle my bicycle out of the cloying embrace of the submerged rice field, I was made aware that I had attracted the attention of a grazing water buffalo, which began moving towards me, lifting its feet from the swamp with prodigious sucking noises that accelerated in frequency as it approached. I threw the bicycle up the slope, where Dad grasped it and then extended his spare hand down to me.

Not to be discouraged by the fact that its sheer weight prevented it from ascending after me, the buffalo maintained its pursuit below, and parallel with, our anxious little convoy, now and then launching charges that caused bits of the embankment to crumble beneath our wheels. It was a situation that I believe discouraged even Dad from venturing along this path again, for he never suggested any further fishing expeditions.

Of Rescue Dinghies and Victory Magazine

When Chuldum wearied of our adulation, and Dad of his fishing, Paul and I headed for the railway institute, to compete with growing numbers of servicemen for space in the swimming pool. Provided I kept to the shallows, and "swam" only in inverted commas, such aquatic pursuits had lost their terrors for me. There we were introduced to the pleasures of inflatable RAF rescue dinghies, with which Beaufighter aircrews equipped themselves to assist their own fishing expeditions, in their case angling for Anglo-Indian girlfriends.

These swimming pool excursions were followed by matinee cinema screenings in the main Institute hall, where I greatly admired Leslie Howard in *Spitfire* and *The Scarlet Pimpernel* ("they seek him here, they seek him there") and then felt let down by his role in *Gone With the Wind*. At this stage Dad was institute secretary, which meant free admission to all showings, but without guarantee of a seat. The wooden benches were so overcrowded that Paul and I would happily sit on the floor in the front row, craning our necks to gaze up at a screen whose immediacy compensated for its acute inclination.

A rare example of live entertainment (Kanchrapara couldn't match the amateur theatrical talents Nana had mobilized in other colonies earlier in her career) was a visit by a touring troupe from ENSA (Entertainments National Services Association) who were presenting variety shows to soldiers and airmen based in different parts of India. I couldn't recall any of the performers, but years later, when I got to know the late Geoffrey Weekes, Director of Radio Television Hong Kong, I happened to mention Kanchrapara and he immediately recollected taking part in an ENSA concert at the railway institute there. It did little for his ego to learn that I was one of the brats in the front row.

A favourite retreat for me was the institute reading room, where I eagerly sought out the latest issue of *Victory* magazine, lightheartedly chronicling the turning of the tide that produced Allied advances and Japanese reversals on the Burma front. Inevitably the cartoons portrayed the "Japs" as racial stereotypes; small, squint-eyed men with pinched faces, glasses and enormously protruding teeth. But as so often happens, this crude caricature backfired, for it begged the question as to how they could come so far, achieve so much and generally scare the pants off us if they were such silly looking dwarfs. Best of all were comic strips illustrating the trials and tribulations of those who worked with mules transporting rations and equipment along the Burma Road.

Dad was concerned to find me poring over a journal intended for servicemen. Having forbidden me to read the paperback novels of an author writing lurid war accounts under the pseudonym "Gunbuster", simply because these contained words like "bloody", he was anxious I might chance upon language even more robust in the pages of *Victory* magazine.

Meanwhile, our education was in danger of being neglected now that Nana could no longer undertake that task. It was the Kanchrapara railway school's inability to teach me that had led to her mission in the first place. Nothing had happened there since that would make it any substitute for her self-taught instructional skills, and there was nowhere else close at hand that offered better prospects.

Uncle Roley was now also in uniform, as an officer in the Royal Army Medical Corps, and he and Aunt Barbara had been posted to Lucknow, where they would be living some distance out of town. If we were looking for a good school, St Francis College in Lucknow was reputedly one of the best in India. However, they cautioned, it was a residential school, and though they might be able to visit us at weekends, and take us home with them perhaps once a month, we would have to be admitted as boarders. This was not something Nana could willingly endorse, but she resigned herself to the fact that there was no available alternative.

Furthermore, at least one branch of the family would be at hand to ease the strain of separation from the eldest and hitherto closest of her grandchildren, of whom there were now increasing numbers.

The Wrong Train

I cannot recall why it was left to Jati *ayah* to see Paul and myself aboard the train for the start of our journey to Lucknow. I can only guess that my father was working and my mother too indisposed, or preoccupied with Robert, to see us off herself. Whatever the reason, it removed parental control over my habitual panic at the thought we might be late, we might be left behind or, due to some unforeseeable calamity, all train services had been cancelled. This travel phobia had remained with me ever since, at a very early age, I was left alone at the window of a train compartment while my parents were on the platform outside, saying goodbye to relatives and friends. The carriage had lurched from the recoil of the locomotive shunting into its coupling, prompting me to assume I was about to depart without them.

No amount of reassurance on subsequent occasions had led me to entrust any confidence in long-distance travel plans. Now that I saw myself effectively in charge of marshalling our embarkation (for Jati *ayah*, however redoubtable, was no expert in this area) I also saw myself responsible for quickly responding to any setbacks.

To reach the railway station, with our prodigious quantities of baggage, we boarded an open-deck trolley. Consisting of a single bench on a square wooden deck, set on four wheels with buffers fore and aft, this engineless contraption was propelled by two runners who balanced themselves barefoot on the narrow and blisteringly hot rails, which they grasped between their toes. Once sufficient momentum was achieved, the runners would leap aboard the buffers, dismounting again for further exertions when the trolley began to slow.

The trolley rails ran parallel to the main line, and I could see in the distance that a train was already stationary alongside the Kanchrapara station platform. Hardly had I urged our breathless trolley runners to redouble their efforts when the train began to move, slowly heading southward towards us, in the direction of Calcutta. Nothing if not quick-witted when under the mistaken impression that things were going awry, I commanded that the trolley be stopped—no easy matter at the speed we had achieved—and leapt off, to land on hands and knees, well before it could adequately decelerate. Picking myself up, I hurried over to the main line with anxious Jati *ayah* in pursuit, and stood defiantly between the rails, directly in the path of the oncoming locomotive, waving my arms.

Because of its considerable mass and velocity, the locomotive experienced even greater difficulties slowing down than had the trolley from which I so clumsily dismounted. In fact it was soon evident there was no hope of it stopping before it reached me. Jati *ayah* grabbed my hand and dragged me aside as prodigious quantities of metal thundered past, brakes screaming and sparks flying. Only half listening to our heroic little Nepalese retainer, busy upbraiding me for my hysterical attempt to stop the wrong train, I watched the enraged features of the driver glaring back at us from the running board as the locomotive continued on its way. In its wake went the coalescing blur of countless other curious faces at carriage windows, wondering what had caused this brief hiatus.

Jati *ayah* urged me to consider what would have happened if I had succeeded in stopping a train I had absolutely no reason to delay. The rebellious train driver was quite possibly a unionist looking for any excuse to contrive an "incident". This would almost certainly have led to my father being summoned from the workshops to appease an angry mob. We lived in sensitive times, when anti-British feeling was at flash point. Where would it have ended?

In appropriately chastened mood, I continued the trolley journey to the station platform, arched over with metal sheeting, under which we waited with our considerable luggage for the correct train to arrive. But my neurosis had not entirely abandoned me. In the midst of loading our suitcases and hampers, with Jati outside on the platform supervising the coolies engaged in this task, the carriage again lurched from some minor hiccup involving the coupling system. Without pausing to think, I flung myself at the emergency cord and hung there. Paul contributed his share by clinging to my waist, and between us we managed to effect whatever process was involved in ensuring the train would not move until the controlling mechanism was released.

This time I managed to bring about virtually all of the alarming consequences that Jati had earlier forecast. It took a fairly heated stance on her part, with one hand poised on the hilt of her unmistakably lethal *kukri*, to discourage the stationmaster, guard and engine driver from taking the issue any further. We were just excitable children, she explained, not used to travelling on our own and anxious that we were going to be separated from at least half our possessions by the abrupt departure of our train ahead of schedule.

Peripatetic Beggars' Opera

The journey to Sealdah station in Calcutta, terminus for the Assam Bengal line, was not considerable, covering approximately twenty six miles. But it was fraught with possibilities for further misadventures involving two relatively young children travelling unaccompanied—Jati *ayah* having fulfilled her responsibility by delivering us to the train and now, doubtless with considerable relief, heading homeward by trolley.

We had to be on our guard against beggars thrusting hands through open windows in mid-journey. How such hands would materialise, apparently from thin air, was accounted for by the fact that their owners were riding the footboards lining both sides of the carriage, clinging to door handles and whatever other protuberances might offer sufficient purchase. It was not unusual to see Indian trains—particularly local commuter trains—travelling through the countryside like bloated caterpillars encased in ragged clothing and human flesh. There were freeloaders all over the roof, even lodged on the buffers between carriages, transforming such conveyances into peripatetic beggars' operas.

Deprived of adult escorts, Paul and I felt particularly vulnerable to importuning itinerants. Their gestures of feeding cupped hands to gaping mouths looked more threatening than beseeching, as if at any moment the fingers would become talons, reaching in to grasp us by our collars, perhaps by our throats.

I had been taught, at an early age, that charity was a misplaced impulse when faced with the enormity of need one encountered in India. I would seldom be in a position to perform a charitable act and escape its consequences. Appeasing one mendicant would only bring others, more insistent, to take his or her place. In India I learned to turn a blind eye to suffering, hardening my heart to an extent that may have permanently impaired my capacity for compassion. So great was the want that if I had a pocketful, even a suitcase full of change, it would be exhausted in minutes.

It became easy to accept poverty and hunger as permanent fixtures in the landscape. They were so extensive, so endemic a condition that they no longer registered on my conscience. They simply disappeared from the periphery of my vision, as if they weren't there. Not until those hands were thrust in my face was I reminded of the potent reality; the imminence of something unappeasable, something ravenous and unstoppable that would always be lying in wait until I awoke from my reverie to concede its claims. Only by closing the window and pulling down the blind could I erase its palpable presence. I had already forgotten my grandfather's story of the *sadhu* evicted from the train, and the curse that killed his oppressor dead on the tracks.

Arrived at Sealdah station, trains would disgorge such streams of passengers, both from within and without their carriages, that they resembled the abandoned husks of disembowelled insects, vacated by infestations of entozoa. The huge volumes of traffic turned Sealdah itself into the cavernous interior of a wasp hive, whose teeming inhabitants milled about the latest trophy hauled in from the sunlight.

Here was a fertile economic arena for street children. The platforms were home to many urchins who had run away from their families or had migrated there along with them. The empty carapaces of stationary trains were immediately filled by swarms of these youngsters, clambering aboard and foraging through compartments on the lookout for discarded tins, bottles, newspapers and magazines, anything that can be resold, if only for a pittance. To negotiate a path to the station exit, one stepped cautiously over the meagre belongings of a refugee encampment, seemingly so permanently installed it was unlikely ever to be dislodged.

It was with some relief that we spotted Aunt Barbara, waiting to accompany us to Lucknow. She took charge of the arrangements to transport our baggage to Howrah. Where Sealdah handled all the local train traffic in Calcutta, Howrah was the terminus for most long-distance rail routes. In 1854, Eastern India's inaugural train ran from Howrah to the ruins of Pandua. Situated on the opposite bank of the Hooghly, the station's imposing, many turreted façade dominated the river frontage and served as the most prominent landmark of Calcutta's twin city, a sprawling industrial metropolis cluttered with jute mills. To get there we had to catch a taxi through the heart of Calcutta.

City of Unremitting Joylessness

Calcutta even then looked like a gigantic version of Miss Haversham's wedding cake, a blackened, mouldy, crumbling ruin of a once great city overlaid by the ghostly presence of its better days. Afflicted by the peculiarly English nostalgia that clings to wreckage of the past rather than seeking out portents of the future, I saw—and still see in Calcutta—a strangely reassuring unwillingness to relinquish the grip of history. The city had arrested death, holding it at arm's length and bearing triumphant testimony to the possibilities of sustaining the processes of decay so as to extract, from a doomed but still lingering corpse, its last iota of usefulness.

Much more than Delhi, which reflects the apogee of empire, much more even than its forerunner, Madras, Calcutta preserved the traces of Britain's fascination with the *idea* of India. It was here that the dreaming, irrational Celtic blood, asleep in British veins since the Roman and Norman conquests, stirred to the poetry of Byron and battened upon a landscape which, even though Byron never visited it, was practically of his own invention. Inspired by a romantic idealist, notorious for his passionate and disastrous love affairs, the British fell passionately and disastrously in love with India.

Disastrous because it led each to expect more from the other than their marriage could consummate. Britain bedded with a veiled houri and awoke to discover a painted whore, diseased, hungry and desperate with poverty. India pillowed with a pale-skinned conquering hero and found the only thing white about him was the pigment of his skin. In all other respects, he was no better than the best of his predecessors, of whom there had been many. Which is why, more than any other image that springs to mind, I continue to associate Calcutta with Miss Haversham's wedding cake; in the last throes of staleness and decomposition, held together by cobwebs and the power of memory.

The memory of that particular journey through Calcutta is of buses and trams clattering and rattling by us, and scraping past each other, so crowded it seemed impossible for anyone to collect fares from those within, so close they almost sloughed off their burden of extraneous passengers clinging to the loose panels of bodywork. Pedestrians threaded perilous courses through traffic lanes and tramlines, girding their *dhotis* to avoid being splashed by waterlogged potholes. Their hazards were further complicated by stray cattle, wandering at will in the thoroughfare and relying upon their sanctity to protect them from harm. The look in their voluptuous and scornfully bovine eyes suggested that Calcutta should bow down in the dust to give thanks for their condescension to grace such extremities of squalor. All of this was accompanied by a ceaseless blaring of car horns, a monotonous threnody of anguish delivered up from the streets against the travails of living in India's largest city. The sheer hopelessness of Calcutta bred its own grim determination to persevere. It was a city that had made both an art and a virtue of unremitting joylessness.

Until 1943, the year before our journey to Lucknow, the Hooghly River was crossed by a pontoon bridge that swung open at its central span to let river traffic through. That structure suffered major damage during a cyclone which came close to putting an end to Uncle Roley's budding medical career. Called out at night in ferocious weather for an emergency consultation, he discovered, as he started driving across the bridge, that the pontoon sections were breaking apart.

Flinging his car into reverse, he managed to escape unscathed, only to be caught on the wrong side of the river.

There was considerable opposition to construction of a replacement bridge, due to fears that it would affect the river currents and cause silting. This problem was eventually solved by crossing from shore to shore with a single cantilevered four hundred and fifty metre span, avoiding any requirement for pylons in the river itself.

My father was immensely impressed by the design of the new Howrah bridge, which he regarded as a triumph of engineering. It rapidly became the busiest in the world, choked with traffic during the morning and evening rush hours to the point where it might take forty five minutes to get across, in a flow so glacially stagnant that bullock carts made the better progress. Through the bridge girders, the turrets of Howrah station loomed tantalizingly close.

I was familiar with Howrah from many previous journeys. Once released from the taxi into its dark, cavernous, reverberating zeppelin hangars, it seemed every bit as big, noisy and teeming as I remembered. In the clinker between the tracks, stained with spittings of blood-red betel nut and the residue of ancient faeces, were buried the earthenware shards of generations of disposable *gurrum char* bowls and an entire archaeology of rail travel. Venerable wooden sleepers carried the burden of the waiting trains, while disorderly human ones sprawled comatose across the platforms, oblivious to the passing flow of pedestrian traffic under high girders where pigeons flew and crows added their harsh, plaintive cawing to the general cacophony.

Canvas bed rolls, each containing two crisply starched bedsheets, a blanket, pillow and pillow case with a hand towel, had been ordered in advance and installed in our bunks. Vegetarian meals were similarly booked for delivery somewhere along the line. With Aunt Barbara in attendance, we were ready to leave. Our express train began, infinitely slowly and soundlessly, to gather momentum, shedding like the strands and fibres of a discarded chrysalis that vast aggregation of disparate and desperate humanity that seemed never to have left, since I first set eyes on it, the echoing empyrean of Howrah station.

Maleficence of Monkeys

Aunt Barbara was seldom lost for a story to tell, or a devastatingly funny observation to voice regarding the oddities of the passing scene. Her nursing career had brought her into contact with others whose anecdotes she avidly collected and delighted in recounting, until I began to see that she had personally lived through all those escapades herself.

One of her fellow nurses had served in a sanatorium for mental patients, located in the Himalayan foothills, where one morning she witnessed from a kitchen window a baker's delivery man approaching on foot along the drive, a basket of loaves balanced on his head. A movement in the bushes behind this visitor betrayed the fact that he was being stalked by one of the pyjama-clad patients. Awareness of his pursuer soon dawned upon the delivery man, who quickened his pace in a futile effort to outstrip the chase. Eventually, casting discretion, the basket and all his loaves to the wind, the baker's man broke into a run, rounding the corner of the building overlooked by a second window on the other side of the kitchen. Hurrying across to observe the outcome, Aunt Barbara's colleague saw the hapless quarry trapped in an enclosed garden, against the far wall of which he flung himself in a despairing heap, resigned to his fate. Dashing across the intervening space, his stalker tapped him on the shoulder, declaring "Last touch! You're it!" and then took to his heels again.

Another colleague had been transferred to a posting every bit as remote as Tatanagar had proved for us, where she found her bungalow plagued by a maleficence of monkeys, entering the premises at will and making off with anything they could get their hands on. Deciding that the cure lay in providing the intruders with a feast too tempting to resist, she purchased quantities of bananas, which she peeled open and laced with castor oil before replacing their skins. Arranging these on the dining table, she withdrew to watch the monkeys descend en masse and help themselves to everything in the bowl. The following morning there wasn't a monkey to be seen, but the garden was draped with banana skins and substantial deposits from the interiors of painfully departed simians.

Castor oil was also a handy remedy for inquisitive bystanders intruding upon my aunt's spells of duty in the outpatients' department of her Calcutta hospital. She administered this purgative as "free medicine" to those hangers-on who arrived in the company of accident victims and other casualties, driven by mere curiosity as their only pretext for being there.

Towards animal victims of human neglect and cruelty, Aunt Barbara was infinitely more compassionate. And waifs and strays elicited tolerance beyond the point of absurdity. Her homes were always filled with menageries of dogs, cats, parakeets and sundry other creatures, and the chief danger of travelling anywhere with her lay in her impulse to immediately adopt any she found en route. Only the ever-present threat of rabies would discourage her from stepping out of our railway carriage to hoist under her arm some miserable looking cur scavenging in a platform rubbish tip, so we could bear it away with us to a new life beyond the limited powers of canine imagination.

La Martiniere

Lucknow was formerly the seat of the Nawabs of Awadh or, as the British pronounced it, Oudh. It is now the capital of Uttar Pradesh, the most populous state in India. Situated on the banks of the river Gomti, the city is famed for styles of art and literature peculiar to Lucknow, and also boasts some of the finest Moghul architecture in the country, including the Bada and Chota Imambara. The name can be traced to the epic Ramayana, in which Lakshman, brother of Lord Rama, is alleged to have settled here.

Here too, in 1800, the British built a handsome Residency for their imperial representative. Set in beautifully landscaped gardens, this was beleaguered for twelve weeks in 1857, when their forces held out against mutinous sepoys in what would later be known as the first Indian War of Independence. The Siege of Lucknow became one of the great epics of empire. Of the three thousand British inhabitants who took refuge in the Residency with Governor Sir Henry Lawrence, only a few score survived, half-starved, sick or dying, when Sir Henry Havelock broke through the Indian lines eighty seven days later. Havelock's forces proved inadequate to lift the siege, which lasted another twenty three days.

The Residency, still in ruins, looks much as it did in the immediate aftermath of its prolonged resistance. The pock marks of cannon-shot can be seen embedded in those walls that remain standing. The heroic defenders earned, between them, four Victoria Crosses and, for the ruins of the Residency itself, the right to fly the Union Jack night and day, without the customary ritual of lowering it at sunset. An image that would linger in my mind, from India's independence the year after my family left its shores, was a photograph of that flag being finally lowered over the ruined hulk of a building that had come to symbolise the whole imperial ethos.

There was one especially historic school in Lucknow, whose students had fought side by side with the soldiery defending the Residency. This chateau-like structure was erected by a Frenchman, Claude Martin, who arrived in India in 1752, as an ensign with the French army. He was taken prisoner by the British at Pondicherry in 1761 and, after the decline of French influence on the sub-continent, served under the British East India Company, rising to the rank of Major-General. Taking up residence in Lucknow, he occupied an important position in the court of Nawab Asaf-ud-Daula, as a result of which he amassed an immense fortune. The major portion of his monies and estates were left for the founding of three institutions, in Lucknow, Calcutta and Lyon, his birth place in France.

Constantia, the central portion of the main building at Lucknow, was originally designed and built by Martin himself as his country residence. Constructed in an extraordinary mixture of styles, it incorporated gothic gargoyles and massive heraldic lions. Martin decreed that after his death it should be converted to a school, to be known as La Martiniere. He lies buried in the crypt under the central room of the building.

Rudyard Kipling's Kim supposedly attended this distinguished institution. but sadly, it was not the school for which Paul and I were bound.

Bloodier than Red Brick

Our school, St. Francis College, was run by Franciscan Brothers, a Catholic order much given to producing such educational establishments. Named after St. Francis of Assisi, it boasted an enormous oil painting which depicted Christ, half suspended on the cross, his right arm released from its nail to clasp our founder around his shoulder. I remember a lot of blood dripping everywhere. The saint, with his right foot placed on what looked suspiciously like a representation of planet Earth, gripped Christ by the waist with bleeding hands, that also bore the sacred stigmata, and gazed adoringly up at him with a glint of unmistakable ecstasy in his eyes. Aside from being historically inaccurate, the portrayal struck me as alarmingly ambitious in terms of the Franciscans' global aspirations.

The predominant colour of the school buildings was a bloodier than brick red, trimmed with white edging around all the arches, balustrades, porticoes and pillars. Their architectural style seemed inordinately dependent upon such embellishments—arches in particular—leaving rooms open to the four winds, if only there had been the merest breath to indicate the approach of even so much as a zephyr.

Our brothers were, for the most part, a stern lot, swishing around in their dark brown robes. Even in "civvies" they managed to look severe. Discipline was extremely strict, and entailed corporal punishment for fairly minor offences. When one boy was reported to have bitten another, in a playground fight, he was chained for a day out on the verandah, with a dog collar around his neck.

Subjects taught included Urdu, whose written form followed the Arabic alphabet. Although I could speak the language well enough, and found the script aesthetically appealing, I could never master the correct sequence of symbols and consistently got low scores in tests. This delivered me into the vengeful hands of our Anglophobe Urdu master, a cadaverous man with an uncanny resemblance to Muhammad Ali Jinnah, future mastermind of the partition that sundered Pakistan from India. His preference was for a ruler applied both to the palm and the back of the hand.

Meals were taken canteen-style in a large refectory at the rear of the college "campus", alongside a bakery where a team of sweating bakers, stripped to the waist, would smash slabs of dough against stone benches with the same vigour displayed by the *dhobi wallahs* flogging our clothing into submission in the laundry not far away. Both industries would send missiles flying with sufficient force to put out the eye of some hapless passer by; pellets of dough in the case of the bakery and buttons in the case of the laundry.

I never seemed to get enough to eat, but the twist to my "Oliver" was that I sought for more outside the school grounds, spending all my pocket money on foodstuffs sold from baskets and trays by wayside vendors who listlessly fanned off clouds of flies. To me the fruits of the forbidden tree were always the most delectable, and never more so than prohibited sweetmeats like *jelabies, halwa, barfi, rusagullas* and, best of all, *kulfi* ice cream, packed into metal cones and sealed with wax.

Although I may have been prone to malaria, anaemia and all the standard tropical ailments in my childhood—compounded by extreme hypochondria—I owe my subsequently hardy constitution to such early gastronomic adventures, and to the fact that indulgent servants didn't necessarily see eye to eye with my mother on what I should be permitted to eat. I believe it did me more good than harm to have been exposed, as I was, to dirt and germs, flies and other unsavoury hazards of Indian life. It helped me develop immunities that would later fortify my travels, unscathed, through remoter and less health-facilitated corners of the world, from the Solomon Islands to Swaziland.

Baiting the Rhinoceros

The entire school slept in a vast dormitory hall, rectangular shaped and flanked along three sides by rows of arched doorways, left open for the ventilation that never came. My bed was located pretty much in the middle of this immense space, so that I would lie sleepless, surrounded by gentle sibilants, subdued ululations, murmurings and outright snoring of my far less insomniac schoolmates. Also, at various points around the floor, I would become aware of the curiously mechanical motions of those older boys who had unaccountably chosen to withdraw beneath their sheets, and I would wonder what curious form of ague might have taken temporary possession of them.

In the almost unbearably hot pre-monsoon months, the obligatory midday siesta was additionally imposed upon us, guaranteeing afternoons in which I could sit up in bed and read some unauthorised work of fiction smuggled under my pillow. Usually it would be the latest *Tarzan* adventure by Edgar Rice Burroughs, and indeed the only time I can recall initiating an act of aggression was prompted by my determination to recover one such novel from a schoolmate disinclined to return it.

In those summer months too, classes would resume in the evenings, after supper, followed by one last, riotous bout of exuberance on the darkened lawns in front of the school, when we would don bedsheets, knotted around the neck, and run about trailing capes in the style of our comic-book heroes. I endeavoured to recruit Paul's cooperation in the role of Robin, cast as accomplice to my Batman. I proposed a variant of the partnership entitled "Man Bat and Wonder Brat". But he could never see himself as my subordinate. And perhaps as a result of early over-exposure to fancy dress contests, he had developed a distaste for dressing up.

My younger brother's courage and recklessness showed no sign of diminishing. Invariably he would be a principal contender in those playground fights I so carefully shunned. At the Lucknow Zoo, to which we were marched in procession after Mass on Sundays, he found a low-slung branch along which he would descend into the rhinoceros enclosure, to bait the short-sighted and bad-tempered occupant into charging, whereupon Paul would leap into the foliage and narrowly make his escape. His companions wagered their pocket money on the outcome of these exploits, while I would run in search of a zoo attendant to put a stop to his foolhardiness.

Taking a shortcut through an alley intended for cleaners to service the cages, I was caught up sharp when a tiger hurled itself at the wire meshing narrowly separating us. The crash of this unexpected impact preceded, by a split second, its thunderous roar of frustration so that I stood petrified until rescued by a justifiably annoyed cage sweeper.

Infinitely preferable for me, but boring to most of the others, were the Sundays we spent marched in procession to the ruined Residency. Finding some pretext to break away from the rest, I would set myself down beneath a tree, with a map of the Residency walls spread on my knees to indicate the various strongpoints and the manner in which they had been defended eighty-seven years earlier, together with the ammunition expended and the casualties suffered. I would recreate in my mind the epic engagements, closing my eyes to listen to artillery bombardments and the explosion of mines the enemy had succeeded in placing under defensive positions. One of the first shells crashed into the billiard room, where it felled governor Sir Henry Lawrence, the man who had elected to defend the Residency in the heart of the city rather than retreat to a position that might be more readily secured. On being asked if he was hurt, Sir Henry replied, "I am killed." He wasn't just then, but he died two days later.

The siege of the Residency had all the ingredients of high drama in the grand imperial tradition; a "thin red line" holding against overwhelming odds, heroism in the face of adversity, the stoicism of English ladies living in appalling conditions, the death of a gallant commander, finally the skirl of bagpipes on the wind and the unmistakable sounds of a relief column marching with flags flying and kilted Highlanders leading the way. News of the relief was reputedly sent in the form of a Latin sentence that, when translated, read, "I am in luck, now." But its imminent arrival had already been famously dreamt by one of the beleaguered women, Jessie, who awoke to declare she had heard the approach of bagpipes. There was even a plaque in the ruins marking the spot where this vision had occurred to her. I felt sorriest for those sepoys who remained loyal to the defenders. The lead troops of the relief force were Highlanders, and in their furious push into the Residency they bayoneted a few of these unfortunate faithfuls by mistake.

The British had needed their mythology to remind them of their appointment, by no less an authority than God himself, to fulfil a sublime destiny. Their mission was to civilise the uncivilised, educate the ignorant, exploit the hitherto imperfectly exploited and bring all unclaimed areas of the known world within the sphere of British influence and commerce. They were good at it, so long as they could continue to believe in it. But it needed an effort of will, reinforced by conviction of their mystical racial superiority.

When the time would eventually come for that effort to flag, the collapse would be almost as total and immediate as a subsiding house of cards. It would be as though a little boy in the crowd called out "But the king isn't wearing anything!", sending the rudely awakened monarch fleeing naked from the parade, piteously clutching his privates.

But that time was not yet. Or at least if it was upon us, I wasn't aware of it. I too needed that mythology to lend its focus to my own existence, which I saw as a chance by-product of that predestined order of things. I needed those quiet, meditative moments in the Residency to reflect how fortunate I was to have been—no matter how insignificant—a beneficiary of that divinely ordained history, and to hope that, with its other more abiding consequences, we could continue in this way forever.

A Last Farewell

We saw Nana for the last time when she visited us in Lucknow in the autumn of 1944. Accompanied by my mother and Robert, now well into his third year, she surprised me by wearing an overcoat with a fur collar, which looked highly inappropriate for Lucknow in any season. She also looked drawn and tired. We all stayed for the weekend at Roley and Barbara's bungalow, *Dinki Kot*, where the family had just been enlarged by the addition of Robin (though not, as Paul and I were disappointed to learn, named after Batman's accomplice). It was a brief visit, of which I recall very little. Since it was a Watson trait to weep copious tears when parting, even for a matter of months, I paid no special heed to Nana's display of grief on this occasion.

Some weeks later Roley arrived at our school, in uniform, to tell us that Nana had died in Calcutta. She was fifty two years old. It had been a kidney infection of the kind which today can be cured by a brief course of antibiotics. I remember that Roley was sensitive enough to adjourn with us to a less frequented area of the school, on the verandah enclosing the assembly hall, before breaking the news. But there was no good or easy way of breaking it. Paul burst into tears but I was too stunned—as I generally am even now in such circumstances—to react immediately to such unacceptable information.

I waited until Roley's departure, taking Paul by the hand for the walk to his car while I stayed behind. Then I circled the assembly hall to the far side, immediately adjacent to the perimeter wall where I was unlikely to be disturbed. I let the full implications of my uncle's news sink in, and wept as I have never wept since. She had known, I decided. Of course she had known. Why else had she, in that momentary lapse, posed that impossible question as to whether I would visit her grave?

We had to see out the rest of the school term, culminating in sports day, when Mum would return to Lucknow to collect us. Paul and I went down with measles, sharing quarantine in the sick ward with two other measles victims. It was quieter there, and I would have slept better were it not for the erratic gyrations of an overhead electric fan I felt convinced would fly apart at any moment, sending its blades scything lethally in all directions.

Roley and Barbara paid more frequent visits, with Robin in tow, bringing treats including tins of condensed milk, which we loved to lather on raw slices of bread, clumped together in tightly held sandwiches to minimise spillage.

For Evensong every day we would file up the stairs to the crowded little chapel, where our liturgical chant would reverberate too intensely within a tightly confined space, needing more room in which to expand and breathe. It was not a setting from which I gained the solace and consolation I sought, not an enclosure from which my prayers could ever break free.

There was a serious infestation of lice in the dormitory, which required all of us to queue up in front of a visiting team of barbers, to be shorn bald. It suddenly became a pleasure, rather than a trial, to wear our solar topis for weekend excursions, especially if we had the misfortune to encounter boys from La Martiniere marching, similarly single-file and remaining pointedly aloof from us on the opposite side of the street.

I had developed a passion for cinema foyer posters of forthcoming attractions, and especially for the smaller-sized leaflets handed out at the door, containing essential information in miniature, together with full colour photographs of selected scenes. I collected these in the way that other boys might collect stamps or cigarette cards. Unhappily the delousing programme called for the upturning and spraying of all mattresses and bedding, which led to the discovery of my concealed stockpile of cinematic treasures. Brother Felix thumbed through these distastefully, considering them pornographic. I lost everything.

I was not unhappy at the prospect of leaving Lucknow. Granddad was not adjusting well to his role as widower. It had been too close and loving a marriage for any hopes of a swift recovery. His loss would remain with him for the rest of his own relatively short life. He needed as much distraction as possible, and Paul and I were the grandchildren who had been closest to him. Since Nana had died in Calcutta, and was now buried in its suburbs at Tollygunge cemetery, he refused to leave the city, despite the growing threat and increasingly frequent reality of communal riots there. Places had been found for us at St. Xavier's College at 30, Park Street.

"Nothing Beyond"

Run by Jesuits, an altogether more thoughtful and intellectual order than the Franciscans, St. Xavier's was one of the premiere institutions of Calcutta. Rabindranath Tagore had briefly studied there, but according to a biographer had "found the conventional system of education uncongenial". The school motto was *Nihil Ultra* which meant "nothing beyond"; one which I thought laid itself open to entirely the wrong interpretation. It was considered a matter of great prestige to be associated with this institution, whether as student or as teacher. And the atmosphere was palpably more earnestly academic, and distinctly more collegiate, than it had ever been at St. Francis's.

"St. Xavier's," I was told, "is not merely a centre for learning; it is a place where one grows up to become a complete human being." While I hoped this would prove true in my case, I felt I had a long way to go. There was something distinctly wrong with my libido, and I was being made more frequently and inconveniently aware of this fact by developing hopeless, unrequitable and incommunicable desires for older schoolboys. Since nothing at St. Xavier's was designed to encourage or even comprehend, leave alone tolerate, such impulses, I began to withdraw into introversion and secrecy, struggling with inner demons like those assailing imperiled saints portrayed in the throes of tempestuous temptations.

Established is 1861, the college premises on Park Street stood at the busiest business hub of the city. Yet its gothic structure was entirely of a piece with much of the rest of Calcutta, which is to say that its faded imperial elegance was even then rich in nostalgia but largely unsuited to contemporary needs. At least its ancient classrooms were capacious enough to circulate the air, quite unlike the cramped accommodations in other colleges.

St. Xavier's greatest jewel was its library, which stored a collection of more than seventeen thousand six hundred volumes and periodicals, inherited by the Jesuit Fathers in 1908 from the then Archbishop of Calcutta, the Most Rev. Dr. Paul Goethals, SJ. These were extremely rare and precious books, filed in sixty one sections ranging from voyages and travels to flora and fauna, anthropological and archaeological works, bibliographies and dictionaries. With the library went a reading room where I spent every moment of my free time.

Introversion seeks seclusion, in retreats and sanctuaries where silence and contemplation provide defence against the rough-and-tumble unpredictabilities of social immersion. For some reason I could not discern, I suffered a serious psychological impairment that made me uncomfortable in the presence of both my own and the opposite sex, and no book that I knew enough to lay my hands on could explain why. If I was condemned to bluff my way through life, as detached observer rather than involved participant, I could at least choose to expose myself as little as possible to situations where my defects would be apparent to others. What better substitute for the realities of a life experienced than the virtual realities of lives perceived through the medium of literature?

With his quite opposite temperament, Paul of course was busy enjoying the college's many other facilities, which encompassed an expansive playground, where football and cricket were played according to their season, and where he could develop his budding taste for athletics. St. Xavier's also accommodated a political students union for senior boys, a hotbed for debate in those troubled times. Plays were staged in the college auditorium, drama workshops were regularly held, and films shows were organised by the cinematic society.

Hindi was the preferred optional language in the curriculum, which struck me as strange considering the prominence, if not predominance, of Calcutta's Muslim community, creating a precarious communal balance that was giving rise to considerable strains even within the college enrolment. On one occasion a playground argument between Muslim and Hindu factions led to two young assailants duelling with penknives. On a personal level, Hindi was giving me as much trouble as the Urdu I had been forced to study at St. Francis. Instead of sailing elegant little boats, like sequences of musical notation, across the sheet from right to left, I was having to string characters on laundry lines, with as little success.

It wasn't far from the college gates in Park Street to Marquis Street, where Granddad was renting his apartment. We could have walked it in a few minutes, and sometimes did. But it was easier, and almost as cheap as the cost in shoe leather, to hire a rickshaw. We thought nothing of it then. If anything, we supposed we were doing the rickshaw pullers a favour by offering them our custom. We weren't particularly heavy; even the two of us side by side, with our satchels of school books.

But just occasionally we might find ourselves alongside our schoolboy neighbour, Leslie Maidment, heading in the same direction, and then our capacity for unwitting cruelty would know no bounds, for we would bribe our puller to outrun our rival, and the chase would be on. Dodging and weaving against the grain of never very accommodating traffic streams, our undernourished, thin-flanked haulers would strain their utmost to earn their few extra annas, and possibly knock years off their lives in the process.

Imperial Banyan

Also resident in Marquis Street, in an apartment on the far side of the intervening circular driveway, was Aunt Zena, made a grass widow by Len's prolonged preoccupation with strategic cipher duties on the Assam front. Her children, Jacqui and Gordon, were younger than Paul and I but not so much that we couldn't find diversions of mutual interest, such as trips to the nearby household of a wealthy Calcutta merchant who had opened his garden and its menagerie to the public.

More to my taste would be a visit to the Hogg Market, now known as the New Market and lying just around the corner from Marquis Street. If the contents of Aladdin's cave were distributed through the maze of the Minotaur, the result would but palely reflect the excess and extent of the labyrinthian Hogg Market. Much of it was so far removed from sunlight that it seemed subterranean, and almost all of it was impossible to trace again unless one laid, like Theseus, a careful thread of remembered signposts.

For matinee screenings of such movies as *National Velvet, Anchors Aweigh, The Bells of St. Mary's, The Keys of the Kingdom* or *A Song to Remember,* we might savour the air-conditioned delights of the Lighthouse Cinema, followed by milkshakes at Firpo's Restaurant. Or we might stroll across the green acres of the Calcutta *maidan,* created in 1773 when the jungle was cleared to allow free range for the guns of Fort William. Dominating that expanse was the domed white splendour of the Victoria Memorial, gazing with magisterial impartiality upon barefoot young *chokra* boys kicking a football around in the vicinity of a group of polo players in full gymkhana regalia.

Farther afield, we would voyage downriver by ferry, from the piers of the Howrah waterfront to the Calcutta Botanic Gardens, among the world's classics of the genre, on a par with Kew, Missouri, New York, Berlin, Sydney, Peradeniya in Ceylon, Singapore, Calcutta and Bogor in Indonesia. Founded in 1787, the Calcutta Botanic Gardens boasted the world's largest and oldest banyan, so large that this single tree constituted an entire forest, so old that the original trunk had rotted away and the remains of its hollow shell were supported by rooted branches that spread outward in every direction. The banyan is a parasitical fig tree that may grow independently or may germinate from a seed dropped by a bird into the branches of another species, which it then envelops until, with its own roots firmly established, it destroys its host. Hence it is also known as the strangler fig.

I stood in awe of the Calcutta example, which had conceivably not only long ago destroyed its host but had, in turn, destroyed itself to give life to its myriad successors. Years later I would view it as a paradigm of the British empire. Only when I saw the diminished condition of the country that had brought that empire into being did I recognise the parallel. The fate of the ancient banyan tree was the fate of empire. The main trunk had withered and died of old age. Only the branches had taken root and survived, so far removed from the stem that gave them birth they still thought of it as their source of sustenance. They remembered the vanished trunk at the heart of their existence, much as India would long remember the Raj.

End of the Line

Once a week, bearing lilies purchased from flower stalls outside the Hogg Market, Paul and I would accompany Granddad on a crowded tram to the end of the line, for a visit to the Tollygunge cemetery where Nana was laid. It was a well maintained cemetery, where gardeners were always at work, watering and cropping, cutting and trimming around the headstones with the care and precision of barbers. Little sound intruded, save for the clatter of trams and the cawing of omnipresent crows.

Remembering her as she lay on her pillow, gazing at me while her fingers stroked the sheet before he face, I would remove from its vase a single lily and place it at the foot of the cross inscribed with her name. The ordeal was greater for Granddad. He, who had loomed so large and indomitable in my life, now seemed depleted, all his strength spent, unable to focus on anything but his loss of that diminutive woman in whom virtually all of his own life had been concentrated.

He would stand for minutes with his solar topi under his arm, gazing into the distance, still and statuesque as a soldier bearing vigil by a catafalque. And I knew what was in his thoughts. How could he survive this? How could he allow his children to tear him away from India while she still lay here, abandoned by those she had loved and nourished? But the parting was inevitable, and its imminence unmistakable.

Bengal had the largest concentration of Muslims in India. It also had one of the country's worst histories of communal riots. The first recorded instance occurred in an industrial suburb of Calcutta in May 1891. These were followed by the Bakr-Id disturbances in 1896 and the Tala outbreak in 1897. In the year 1925 alone—a decade before I was born—there were over forty communal riots in Calcutta. Communal and caste politics were initially expressed in elite conflicts, in job recruitment preferences and in political concessions. The British pursued divide-and-rule policies, discriminating in favour of or against particular communities to suit their political interests. They evinced little interest in eradicating communal violence.

When it became apparent the British were preparing to leave, such violence gathered momentum, and nowhere more so than in Calcutta. In the name of religion, newspapers wrote provocative editorials inciting violence. The war cry of "*jihad*" was heard on Muslim lips, and Hindu revivalist and fundamentalist organisations did not lag behind. Calcutta was on the brink of fulfilling Kipling's description of it as "city of dreadful night".

There were days when it was not safe to go to school, when we kept our Muslim servants with us overnight to prevent them coming to harm in the streets. Uncle Len, reunited with his family after a prolonged absence, was riding his dispatch motorcycle down Chowringhee one evening when he came upon a mob looting and burning. He had to draw his revolver to deter a group of thugs barring his path.

Gathering of the Tribe

This was a time of gathering, a coming together of all the Watsons and their progeny under one protective roof at Marquis Street. Although we knew we were not the primary targets of the agitation, we might be caught in the crossfire. For us of the younger generation, the implications were too much to grasp. We were simply happy to be reunited in the largest tribal assembly we had ever witnessed. We posed for photographs, lined up in order of height and age, myself in front, followed by Paul, Jacqui (from Len and Zena), Diana and Michael (Trevor and Ursie), Gordon (Len and Zena again), Robert, Brian (also from Trevor and Ursie), Robin and Kim (Roley and Barbara) and Keith (Denzil and Dora).

Never before and never again would we all be captured in the same scene. We would be dispersing, to go our separate ways, perhaps eventually to end up in Britain, or one of its dominions, but who knew precisely where? Our parents were anxiously pursuing whatever plans and travel arrangements there might be time to make before it became too late.

The contingency for which we had long prepared, hoping it would never arise, that it might yet be averted, was now upon us—and clearly unavoidable. Gone were those conversations that politely skirted around the subject. Now, in our social evenings with neighbours, and in our communications with friends and relatives whose links with India had already been severed, we approached the subject head on. What were our options? All those postcards and photographs, passed around to show how well our forerunners had settled in, depicting quaint little cobbled streets and Norman churches, looking as prettily miniaturised as something from a model village; how much closer that world seemed now, and how ineffably alien and strange.

Had these been "wish you were here" holiday snapshots, the prospect of joining our cheerfully encouraging precursors would have seemed immediately attractive. Who would not wish to satisfy curiosity as to what life in that never before visited "homeland" was *really* like? But this would be a one-way journey, from which there was no coming back. It would require us to take everything we could salvage, in order to fit in with whatever awaited us at the other end. We would need a great deal more than warm clothing to insulate us for that acclimatisation.

All over India, in scattered railway colonies once lived in, visited or merely seen in passing, similar agonies of decision-making were, for the most part, giving rise to the identical conclusion—that we had no other choice. Plans were afoot for a massive diaspora of the Anglo-Indian community, heading west to Europe, south to Australia or perhaps east to Canada. Few had opted to remain and take their chances.

India seemed ever more impatient to see us go. Increasingly one ran the risk of encountering in the street large numbers of people marching in procession, with banners and placards, shouting "*Jai Hind!*" Three nights in August 1946, from the 16th to the 18th, were given over to "The Great Calcutta Killing", when untold numbers of Hindus and Muslims were slaughtered outright or left to die in the gutters.

The same fear that possessed us during air raids by Japanese bombers returned to haunt us now, but this time with greater immediacy and more lasting impact. We were besieged and helpless, islanded within a city gripped by mayhem. Behind the locked doors of our crowded apartments, we felt it dangerous even to venture out to replenish essential food supplies. Calcutta was losing its head. After what happened there during those terrible days and nights, India was a country where we could never again feel entirely safe.

Bye-Bye Blackbird

Dad secured passages for us on the *Brittanic*, sailing from Bombay at the close of August 1946. Although we didn't know it then, this was almost precisely a year before the date to be set by Lord Mountbatten for the country's headlong rush to split into three geographical regions, which would leave the remains of India sandwiched between the bifurcated halves of Pakistan, and each political entity claiming the hollow victory of independence from the other.

Farewells were predictably harrowing. The lyrics of the ballad "We'll meet again, don't know where, don't know when" kept recurring in those last few days, and were sung around the piano at one last family gathering, when we stood in a circle, arms on each other's shoulders, the adults choking and stumbling over the words. What was going to happen to India was already happening to us.

Of all that leave-taking, the scene that remains most vividly etched on my mind was my mother's parting with Jati *ayah*. I had never seen that stony faced little Nepalese cry before, and hadn't thought her capable of it. I had never seen my mother cry as much.

The journey across country, east to west, from one seaboard to another, was the longest we had ever undertaken by rail. Even for me the scenery eventually palled. What little we saw of Bombay, en route to the docks to board our waiting ship, suggested a city more vibrant and less jaded than Calcutta, but also lacking the latter's curiously imperishable imperial panoply. Certainly the Gateway of India, and the famous Taj Mahal hotel, directly alongside, were impressively grand, but they seemed imposed on their background, more in the manner of a theatrical façade, best viewed from the sea. Furthermore if one had seen the real Taj Mahal, whose gardens had at one stage provided a frequent picnic setting for my parents, how could one be swept away by a mere hotel under that name?

The lyrics of another contemporary song, carrying quite a different implication, drifted up to us from the troop decks below as our ship cast its moorings. There was no mistaking the fact that the little bevy of Eurasian girlfriends, waving tearfully from the dockside, were the target of the chorus. "Pack up all my cares and woe. Here I go, swinging low. Bye-bye blackbird."

Save for the disappointing lack of ceremony attendant upon my gesture with the solar topi at Port Said, the voyage was pleasant enough, offering the customary ship's diversions but essentially uneventful. While Mum and Dad relaxed with Robert in canvas deck chairs, Paul and I exhausted the possibilities of deck games and peered over the sides to watch for flying fish or see who could count the most sea snakes swimming by. After leaving the Suez Canal, we never touched land again until we sailed into Liverpool docks.

In Lilliput Land

Years before, the animated movie of *Gulliver's Travels* had scared me by portraying Gulliver's predicament, enmeshed in the ropes of his miniscule Lilliputian captors. Now a word I overheard from a fellow passenger, as the *Brittanic* slipped into its berth at Liverpool docks, brought back that sense of unease. He said we would shortly be surrounded by "Liverpudlians" by which he meant the inhabitants of Liverpool. I mistook this word for "Lilliputians".

The towers and turrets, domes and cupolas had been the first to catch my eye. In these I had seen reassuring familiarity; the caparisons of a great mercantile city that looked fitted for its role as one of the more vital cogs in the engine that drove an empire. But now closer examination revealed the unexpected; what I should have been prepared for, but wasn't, in the form of white stevedores labouring on the dockside. Together with something else I couldn't have anticipated because it contradicted all my expectations, and would become increasingly apparent as we travelled by train to Barnstaple in Devon, where we were to stay with Nana and Granddad Moss.

The smallness, the narrowness, the Lilliputian scale of everything.

Ex-Regimental Sergeant Major William Moss was at the dockside to meet us, reviving my last memory of him in India, when the tables were reversed, and we were looking up at him in his railway carriage. Here it was he who looked up at us as we crowded the railings along with our fellow passengers while the ship manoeuvered itself alongside the wharf. When we disembarked, his greetings were affectionate enough, but he soon made it clear who was in charge by brusquely taking control of the situation.

One of the other many things I had not foreseen was the extensive damage Liverpool sustained during the recent wartime air raids, the scars of which were especially visible in the area around the Victoria Monument in the city centre. Granddad took grim pleasure in pointing out that nothing we had experienced in India could possibly compare with the privations Britain had suffered—by unspoken implication on our behalf. He led us with great efficiency through formalities and procedures that rapidly deposited us aboard what I saw as an absurdly small compartment of an absurdly small train belonging to an absurdly small railway. And from there on the disillusionments began to pile up.

Much of what I viewed on our journey is now recalled, in hindsight; with my subsequent interpretations overlaying the original impressions. Even so, the seeds were planted that day of the disquiet which would dictate, through all the years ahead of me in England, my inability to see this as my fatherland rather than as my father's land. The overriding surprise was not so much the drabness as the confinement of the view, the limitation of the vista. I was used to sweeping panoramas and distant horizons that gave me a proper sense of my microscopic place in the greater order of things, but here the impression was reversed. Here I felt more like Jonathan Swift's hero in the kingdom of the miniscule. The passing landscape was undeniably pretty and absorbingly interesting, but somehow confined and carefully contrived, as if it were manicured and miniaturised scenery, shoehorned into a Hornby model railway layout of the type so dear to my father.

I could see now where he had derived his inspiration for backgrounds that had nothing to do with the spaciousness of the Indian plains.

The conviction would grow that, much as I might be indebted to the stimulus of rich literary and cultural traditions that had shaped my attitude and outlook, I could never physically adapt to the restrictive environment that had inspired them. I was intended for a greater breadth and scope, unfettered by narrow concepts dictating the pivotal English sense of "home" as foundation for one's being. Increasingly I would be forced to recognise that my formative years in India had abruptly ended. A door had closed that could never be reopened. Although the admirably succinct phrase had yet to be coined, that was then and this was now. Denied the English sense of home, as foundation for my own being, I was cast in the role of misfit and drifter, a person of no fixed abode.

What had been pivotal in my life was already dying and would soon be extinct. I was a product of the greatest empire the world had known, a phenomenon that would be rapidly translated from unforgettable glory to barely remembered shame. The roots of my existence were being eaten away in a headlong rush to withdraw, to retract, to erase all of that as though it had never been. It was this dawning discovery that would make me increasingly cynical of the speed with which Britain was losing its right to call itself Great, the haste with which it was divesting itself of all the trappings that had earned it that right.

Could this be the much vaunted "sceptred isle"? A counterpane country better suited to illustrate a *Child's Garden of Verses* than a history of imperial destiny? Where the sceptre? Where the majesty? I was like Dorothy in the Emerald City, discovering the Wizard of Oz had deceived me with a megaphone.

Those first negative and heavily biased impressions were exacerbated by the sheer austerity of postwar Britain. I was failing, of course, to make allowance for the fact that this country was emerging from one of the most traumatic passages of its eventful history. Standing alone off the coast of a continent enthralled by Hitler's dreams of Aryan supremacy, it had provided the last bulwark of resistance in the name of sanity and freedom. And the effort had demanded much courage and greater sacrifice. Britain was exhausted, its vitality and optimism drained, a glorious Technicolor saga now leached to monotones of black and grey.

Barnstaple would serve to reinforce these disappointments. My grandparents' home, a tiny terraced house in a thin side street of a narrow provincial town, was *reductio ad absurdam.* Even allowing for the privations that Britain had suffered in order both to win and to survive the war, what I witnessed in Barnstaple could not have been entirely a consequence of postwar asceticism. This was not just littleness of place but small-mindedness of those inhabiting it, with their shrunken horizons and their disinterest in what lay beyond.

Admittedly Devon, as a county, packed a lot into a small space, and assuredly it did look prettily contrived for maximum picture postcard effect. But if not here, where else in these islands would one find the birthplace of those architects of the grandeur that had so stirred my imagination? Where else would one seek those conquerors of half the world? Perhaps they had to leave England, and set eyes on India and other such enormities of landscape, in order to acquire that greater vision. Imperial ambition was perchance a fever that could only possess and inflame the cool English temperament in the heat of that moment when horizons expanded and the vistas stretched far, far beyond these shallow shores.

William the Conkerer

Paul and I were enrolled in a primary school, to which we walked each day through a maze of alleyways and back lanes, satchels on our shoulders. Our classmates were the sons of farm workers and shopkeepers, who had lived far from vulnerable urban concentrations targeted by German bombers, so had not qualified for the massive wartime evacuations of schoolchildren that might at least have instilled awareness of a world beyond gently rounded Devonian hills. On learning I was born in India, one classmate asked if I had lived in a wigwam and carried a tomahawk. He wasn't joking. And my familiarity with English, not to mention my near BBC intonation, invited curiosity. Where had I learned not only the language but that manner of speaking it? I wearily replied that even in my wigwam, I had tuned into the BBC World Service.

In point of fact the BBC Light Programme provided abundant other pleasures for which my brother and I would hurry home, so as not to miss the next episode. Chief of these were the serialized *Dick Barton, Special Agent* and *ITMA: The Tommy Handley Show*, whose nonsense rhymes and absurdly loveable characters had us converted from the first time we heard them. I was also delighted to find Arthur Askey and Richard Murdoch alive and well on the airwaves.

Still living at home with her parents was Dad's youngest sister Vera, barely out of her teens and somewhat bemused to find herself cast in the unaccustomed role of aunt. She was slim, petite, attractive and—since her essentially sweet but browbeaten mother Rose was too intimidated by her husband to assert her own good nature—repository of the only discernible geniality in that household.

She took very seriously her duties as kinswoman to two young initiates into the manners and customs of England, appointing herself as our companion and invaluable tour guide on many walks through the Devonian countryside. She tried hard to inspire our interest in our newfound home, more successfully with Paul than proved the case with me.

A proposed excursion to Westward Ho aroused my curiosity—until I learned, upon arriving there, it was arguably the only place in England named after a book, and a fairly recent book at that, being Charles Kingsley's novel of the same title, written less than a hundred years earlier. I had read *Westward Ho*, and assumed it took its name from the setting, rather than the other way round. It came as a considerable disappointment to learn that a group of investors, in a singular example of life imitating art, had seen money to be made from catering to those so charmed by Kingsley's mightily successful work that they would want to visit its location. About the only feature recognizable from his pages was the pebble ridge overlooking three miles of flat sandy beach.

We pressed on, visiting in the course of similar weekend excursions other Devonian resorts including Torquay, Ilfracombe and Bideford, where we found a statue of Kingsley, whose *Water Babies*, I was now equally disenchanted to hear, were inspired by his campaign to improve working conditions for child chimney sweeps.

Paul immersed himself in what was for him the newfound extramural activity of "conkers", requiring selection of the largest and most promising horse chestnut seeds, through which holes were carefully bored to thread them on string. These were then swung at opposing "conkers" in the hopes that the adversary would suffer the greater damage. Some exceptionally good "conkers" could survive several such engagements before being vanquished themselves. Paul became quite a skilled exponent of conkering, to the extent that when classmates learned his other Christian name was William—one he hated and had never employed—they dubbed him William the Conkerer.

Finding little satisfaction in this pursuit, I looked for fresh reading material, and was rewarded by Mark Twain's *Tom Sawyer* and *Huckleberry Finn*, together with W.E. Johns' *Biggles*. Mostly I would go for solitary walks to try and discover things to love about Barnstaple. Perhaps if I had tried harder, I might have found them. Historically at least, Barnstaple had much in its favour. It was an ancient town, granted its original charter in 930 AD by King Aethelstan, grandson of Alfred the Great, and it had prospered through many centuries, its port eventually becoming a major trading link to America. Its traditional Pannier Market and Butcher's Row, even its absurdly narrow High Street, could arguably be described as picturesque.

Barnstaple featured many fine buildings and attractive alleyways, remnants of an original Norman castle wall, the ornate Queen Anne's Walk and the 13th century "Long Bridge". All it lacked was anything remotely familiar to me, even the merest trace of a stray whiff of a vaguely recognisable scent that might conjure up something of my past. I was desperately, agonizingly homesick, and Barnstaple was about as comforting for that ailment as a severely starched matron greeting me on the doorstep of a horrifyingly uninviting boarding school.

Reversal of Fortune

None of us were happy in my grandparents' overcrowded terrace house, least of all our elderly hosts, whose patience was strained when they learned we might be staying a great deal longer than we had at first intended. The problem was that Dad had suffered a massive loss of self-confidence within weeks of our arrival in England. He had been offered—while still in India—a well-paid job as senior draughtsman in an engineering firm in Newcastle. His prospective employers had even footed the bill for our passages to England. But he returned from Newcastle after barely a fortnight to tell Mum he couldn't possibly subject her to the conditions he had found there. Straight out from India, where servants had spared her the necessity to perform any domestic chores, leave alone learn to cook, she could never manage in that harsh environment.

Mum rightly wondered what could be so much harsher about Newcastle than we had already encountered in Devon, but she accepted his decision. Consequently I was denied the opportunity to see an area of England where I would have found friendlier, more receptive people of less taciturn and insular disposition. Only many years later, in my middle age, would I explore the north country for the first time, and succumb to its superior charms. Ever since I have seen the map of England as a tankard of ale, with the froth at the top and the lees at the bottom.

In turning down his job offer, Dad set himself back considerably farther than the proverbial square one. The labour market was saturated with ex-servicemen seeking any employment, anywhere, and this fact further exacerbated his new-found inferiority complex, so at odds with the self-assurance he had consistently displayed in India. He tried, unsuccessfully, to explain the reversal. No matter how important his wartime work for the Assam Bengal Railway, he believed he had failed his country by not enlisting in its armed forces, and was therefore "unfit to sweep the streets" walked by those who had.

Granddad Moss, far from coaxing Dad out of his misery, reinforced it by pointing out that he would have to forget all about the grand colonial lifestyle he had pursued in India. He was back in England, and he'd better roll up his sleeves to rediscover what real work was all about. It was around this point that Mum developed a serious dislike for her father-in-law. This aversion escalated into a flaming row one evening at "high tea" where, still unaccustomed to the dietary restraints imposed by ration books, Mum thought her growing sons were not receiving sufficiently nourishing fare on which to retire for the night.

The underlying reserve, and slightly strained atmosphere, that invested those ritual evening gatherings of the family around the dining table were in keeping with the restraint I had detected in the English people as a whole. But they represented a marked departure from the easygoing camaraderie of the troops we had met in India during the war, particularly those from the northern counties who comprised the bulk of the Lancashire Fusiliers. Not just in Devon, but elsewhere in the south of England, I would find myself surrounded by people sparing in their speech, reticent in the emotions and undemonstrative in their enthusiasms. Whatever warmth one might hope to find was as safely conserved, and outwardly undetectable, as hot tea in a well insulated thermos flask.

Could it be that reluctance to aid the enemy, by divulging too much, had become so deeply ingrained that it lingered on along with those wartime posters whose tattered remains one could still find here and there in post offices and railway waiting rooms? The message had been dinned into the populace that "Loose Lips Sink Ships". All around me, those lips had yet to be properly loosened again.

It was time to leave. Trevor, Ursie and their kids, who had followed us to England within a matter of weeks, were just about to vacate a rented house at Leigh-on-Sea in Essex, in order to move to the Midlands, where Trevor had secured employment. They suggested we take over their lease. Once again we played Watsonian leapfrog. Where others of the family went, we followed.

Trials and Tribulations

Our first experience of snow soon palled in the seemingly endless winter of 1947, one of the harshest on record. There was a limit to how much enjoyment Paul and I could derive from snowballs. It was a winter of particular trials and tribulations for my mother, trying to keep some semblance of warmth in a fairly large semi-detached by feeding coal to a solitary fireplace, into whose embers my father would stare for hours, watching his whole life crumbling to ashes. Had we known the symptoms of a nervous breakdown, or even that such a condition existed, we might have done something about it. But we didn't, and he got progressively worse, to the point where he would run upstairs to hide if he heard a knock at the door.

Most of all he was sorry to have inflicted on his wife the worsening situation in which we found ourselves. He had been obliged to repay, to his would-be Newcastle employers, the cost of our fares from India, and what remained of his Indian savings was fast evaporating. Mum gave him her unstinting sympathy and support, never grumbling, ever reassuring him that the right opportunity would come along and that all he needed was faith and patience. Having spent relatively little time with her in India, where my grandmother had monopolised so much of my childhood, I now came to see my mother in a new light, heroically getting to grips with the hardships of a life for which her own upbringing had left her so hopelessly unprepared.

Since Dad could not summon the courage to appear outdoors, I would be sent on errands to purchase his cigarettes, migrating from tobacconist to tobacconist in the hopes of finding something other than Turkish, but invariably forced to return with nothing but "Abdullahs".

Meanwhile Mum set about teaching herself to cook, starting with the simple things like learning how to make toast and fry an egg. Since ration coupons didn't stretch very far, the range of ingredients available was in any case adequate for only the most basic of menus. As her experiments progressed to the occasional roast, pastry or steamed pudding, I was the appointed guinea pig on whom to try out the results. I never flinched, assuring her that even the most stubbornly resistant of soufflés, clinging tenaciously to the floor of the pan, were delectable. My reaction was probably more soothing to her ego than helpful in terms of analyzing her mistakes, but I think I correctly deduced which was more important to her at the time.

It was frustrating to discover that nowhere could one buy rice, except in cans of precooked, sickeningly sweet rice pudding. Indeed, no shopkeeper we met appeared to have heard of it in any other form. As for ingredients required to make the least ambitious of curries, what, they asked, was a "curry"? In the austerity of postwar Britain it seemed to us that, despite uncounted generations of Englishmen who had spent the greater part of their lifetimes in India, none appeared to have brought back with them a craving, even a desire for curry. It would be left to much later immigrants from India, Pakistan and Bangladesh to spread the contagious curry fever throughout the British Isles. How could we have known, back in 1947, that within the next half century curry would come to be voted England's most popular dish?

Mum came close to breaking when Robert, Paul and I all went down with whooping cough, but once that was over, and signs of a belated spring were setting in, she recovered her characteristic optimism. Even Dad gained sufficient confidence to embark with us on an excursion to neighbouring Southend-on-Sea. So grim had been that winter it was our first actual sight of the sea since arriving on the Essex coast. It was also our first experience of a typical English seaside amusement park and a not-so-typical English pleasure pier. Southend boasted the longest in the world, long enough to require a train ride to reach the end of it. And it was that railway, of course, that had lured Dad out of seclusion.

"The America Ground"

When we moved again, in the summer of 1947, it was once more to a seaside location. Having begun our coastal habitations at Barnstaple, on the river Taw, so near the sea as to have served as a naval port in the reign of Edward III, following this with our spell at Leigh-on-Sea, we were now moving to Hastings, on the English Channel. The fact that we had not ventured very far inland might suggest we had elected to pursue a peripheral existence, rather than one that would commit us irrevocably to our new home in the British Isles. But in fact once again the move was prompted by family considerations—albeit this time of a more distant family.

My great aunt Norah was Nana Watson's younger sister. Although she bore some physical resemblance to the woman who had loomed so large in my life, she was quite unlike her elder sibling in every other respect. And she had married Gerald Kelly, a man whose only link with Ireland lay in his name, which seemed entirely at odds with his swarthy features and his unmistakably Anglo-Indian accent. In the best traditions of making the most of one's connections, no matter how tenuous, the Kellys—including their children Clifford, Bertie, Mavis and Olga—revelled in their assumed Irishness, seizing on every pretext to gather round the piano and belt out sentimental Irish ballads as if they had been weaned on them.

None of the family, to my knowledge, had ever set foot in Ireland, but that didn't stop them from looking over four-leaf clovers, taking Kathleen home again, extolling Galway Bay and Mother Machree, following MacNamara's Band, inquiring into the state of things in Glocca Morra or smiling with their allegedly Irish eyes. To that extent at least, they were exuberantly, even defiantly Irish.

We occupied the top floor of their terrace house in Linton Crescent, damaged in one of the first air raids by the Luftwaffe, on 14th September 1940. There mother cooked on a small gas ring and tried to make the best of her meagre housekeeping money. Trains rattled past the bottom of the back garden every half hour or so, plunging into or out of the tunnel separating Hastings from the next station at St. Leonards-on-Sea. But Dad had at last found work, as a lathe operator with a small engineering company producing safety equipment for coal mines.

Hastings was probably the least likely place in the British Isles to house light industry of any kind. It was essentially a hoteliers' and shopkeepers' town that had seen better days, and was unlikely to witness their return. Its single historical claim to fame was the bestowal of its name on the Battle of Hastings, where the troops of Duke William the Conqueror of Normandy had roundly defeated the Saxons and killed their King Harold the Second with an arrow in his eye.

But the battle, on 14th October 1066, had in fact taken place several miles away, at a spot which was later, and appropriately, entitled Battle. Although many others, including Napoleon and Hitler, subsequently attempted to emulate the Norman victory, the Battle of Hastings remained the last occasion on which Britain was conquered by a foreign power. With only its Norman castle clinging to a cliff edge as reminder of that epic occasion, Hastings had largely retired from historical view, limping along as a minor fishing port originally included in the *Cinque Ports,* first mentioned in a Royal Charter of 1155.

In exchange for certain privileges, the *Cinque Ports* ("cinque" being derived from the French for five) maintained ships that could be called upon by the Crown in times of strife. Often the ships and men from these royally chartered ports got away with what amounted to open piracy around the Kent and Sussex coast, enjoying a status one writer has described as a "legalized mafia". As in any contest of this kind, Hastings was not as successful in smuggling as its rivals. To my mind it was the *Cinque Port* that had long ago sunk without trace. As if in recognition of that fact, there had been an extraordinary period, in the early 19th century, when rebellious squatters declared independence from municipal authority, occupying what was then undeveloped land and now comprises the bulk of the present town centre.

Living in rotting hulks of abandoned boats, or in remains of former smuggling vessels captured by excise men and sawn in half, these renegades demonstrated their independence from the Hastings Corporation by hoisting the American flag and announcing that "The America Ground" had become a self-governing town-ship in its own right. Served notice in November 1834, to be off the land by the following Michaelmas, the failed secessionists finally migrated, according to one observer, "with their houses on their backs!". It is unclear just how many structures were transported in their entirety to new sites, but shortly thereafter no less than twenty-eight buildings in central St Leonards, just next door, were identified as having been moved bodily from the America Ground.

Once that problem was resolved, efforts in the Victorian era to elevate Hastings to the status of a genteel watering place, on a par with infinitely more successful Eastbourne, led to the inauguration, in 1891, of two lifts up the cliff face to the West Hill, entailing funicular cars riding steeply inclined rails and attached to steel cables. But Hastings never really attracted the refined patronage that Eastbourne received, appealing more to day trippers from the East End of London with their kiss-me-quick hats and taste for naughty postcards.

School for Scandal

Thanks to the educational grounding I had received from Nana, in our semi-alfresco verandah classroom, I secured a grammar school scholarship by passing the entrance examination while attending primary school in Leigh-on-Sea. I gained admission to Hastings Grammar School, one of the oldest in the country. A fellow schoolboy too senior for me to fraternize with then, though I would come to befriend him in Hong Kong many years later, was Peter Godber. As commandant of the Hong Kong Police riot training school, Godber would work wonders in preparing anti-riot squads to handle the spillover of China's cultural revolution. But he was subsequently destined to become the most celebrated target of Hong Kong's Independent Commission Against Corruption. I had a knack of consorting with people whose reputations would fall into disrepute.

A more celebrated, but much earlier graduate of our school was Archibald Stansfield Belaney. Born in 1888, Belaney was entranced from childhood by the already disappearing culture of the North American Indian. Leaving Hastings Grammar at the age of sixteen, and remembered as an indifferent student of solitary disposition, he worked briefly for a local firm of timber merchants and then headed for the Canadian wilderness. There he eventually divested himself of his English persona and stepped into the wholly invented but long sustained role of Grey Owl, wise Indian hermit of the woods who campaigned as one of the world's first conservationists.

An even earlier association with my alma mater was that of the infamous Titus Oates, born in 1649 and expelled from every boarding school he ever attended. At a loss for a career to pursue, Titus set his eyes on a mastership at what would later become Hastings Grammar School, founded by William Parker senior in the early part of that century. William Parker junior, who had succeeded his father as school principal, must have been unimpressed by Titus' credentials, for the latter set about discrediting him by confiding to the Mayor of Hastings that Parker junior had committed an unnatural act with "a young and tender man-childe" in the porch of All Saints Church. When Parker junior was arrested, and bailed to appear before the magistrates, Titus further accused Parker senior of uttering words of high treason, for which the punishment was to be hung, drawn and quartered.

Witnesses came forward to prove that neither father nor son could have committed the crimes of which they stood accused. Both were exonerated, much to the relief of Hastings residents, who celebrated by lighting bonfires and ringing bells. Charged with perjury, Titus was bound over to appear at the next Sessions, but managed to make good his escape. Joining the navy as a chaplain, he was soon discharged for misconduct. Later he would launch a wave of persecution against Catholics all over England by maliciously inventing a completely fabricated "Popish plot", describing it as a Jesuit plan to assassinate Charles II. His finely woven tapestries of falsehoods led to many being burnt at the stake. The reputations of the earliest recorded victims of his calumny fared better. William Parker's name remained proudly associated with the school he founded, and has since been restored as the name of the school itself, which years ago dropped the word "grammar" from its appellation.

My favourite teacher at Hastings Grammar was the highly popular and much loved Tom Cookson, husband of author Catherine Cookson, who lived for forty-six years in Hastings, far longer than she had lived in the northern counties featured in her copious and hugely successful novels. They had met in the thirties, when Catherine left her spiritual heartland to move into a large old house in the Hastings town centre. There, to help the mortgage payments, she took in lodgers, one of whom was Tom, who to my mind strikingly resembled Arthur Askey. Though his mannerisms were different from Askey's, they were equally endearing.

Tom would arrive in his racy looking Rover saloon, which he parked outside the school entrance. He had a way of moving about which was simultaneously self-effacing, in his unwillingness to draw attention to himself, while being strikingly conspicuous because of the peculiar, almost furtive manner in which he sought to avoid that attention. He also had a way of impatiently spurning the duster to erase his notations on the blackboard, preferring to use the sleeve of his academic gown. If a larger surface of chalk needed to be cleared, he would reverse into it and gyrate like a friendly bear enjoying a back scratch on a favourite tree. Popular as he was, staff and students avoided physical contact for fear of contamination with powdered chalk.

Our music master, affectionately known as "Bimble" Batts, conducted lessons from a grand piano on the stage of the assembly hall, the only room large enough to contain instrument, instructor and initiates. With the sun behind him, streaming through high windows, his more frenzied passages at the keys turned his academic gown into the taloned wings of a vampire much too late abed, and liable to disintegrate before our eyes. The fact that his head was entirely bald, and of a smoothness that bounced sunbeams around like the gyrations of a scintillating ballroom globe, contributed to his bizarre but intensely intriguing appearance.

"Bimble" made it his mission to demythologize the great conductor Leopold Stokowski, perhaps the only name familiar to us from the musically illustrious of our time, largely because we knew him from the Disney film *Fantasia*, for his much publicised love affairs with such celebrities as Greta Garbo and for his famously aquiline profile and flowing mane of white hair. "Bimble" dismissed Stokowski's alleged Polish-Irish ancestry, and untraceable middle European accent, as pure invention, declaring he had known "Leopold" as plain Albert Stokes, a struggling musician in London who needed a gimmick on which to found a legend. Whatever his origins, "Bimble" could not deny that the self-invented man was a genius, despite the enormous liberties Stokowski took with his transcriptions of compositions by such greats as Bach and Beethoven.

Although I had dutifully read the classics dictated by Nana Watson's emphasis on serious literature, I preserved a secret passion for comic books. In India, these had invariably been of American provenance, portraying the fantastic adventures of super-heroes such as Batman, Captain Marvel and Superman. In England I had reverted to more juvenile fare, such as *Dandy* and *Beano*, rife with characters like Big Eggo the Ostrich, Biffo the Bear, Korky the Cat and Desperate Dan. By the time I entered grammar school, I had outgrown these, graduating to *Champion* and *Hotspur*, and becoming a particular fan of Rockfist Rogan, World War Two fighter pilot, who exemplified the flying aces I had idolized in India, even if he operated in a different theatre of war.

Less involving, although I read each issue from cover to cover, was cowboy Clint Morgan, for whom a typical predicament would read: "Clint Morgan was robbed of his gold-dust by the notorious Grey Mask and his gang. Grimly determined to recover it, Clint captured Grey Mask and forced him to lead the way towards the gang's hide-out but suddenly they spotted a redskin, trapped by his foot, being attacked by a grizzly bear. If Clint went to the redskin's aid, Grey Mask would escape!"

Learning of my addiction to comics, generous old Uncle Roley, arriving with Aunt Barbara and the family on another of those surprise visits so dear to his heart, came laden with a cardboard carton full of the same secondhand comics I had just sold, in part-exchange for others, to the very supplier from which he obtained them. My face must have betrayed what courtesy forbade me to reveal, for he accompanied me and the carton back to the shop, where he invited me to select anything I hadn't read.

The "Daily Mirror" Crisis

A calamitous conflict with the Kellys once again demonstrated how prolonged proximity can tax familial ties. On this occasion the trigger was a thoughtless and inopportune remark from a great nephew already establishing a reputation for bad judgment and rotten timing. Great aunt Nora came to us at breakfast to inquire if we had seen her *Daily Mirror*, the only newspaper to which she sub-scribed and one which Dad, if he was up early enough, was known to borrow before others were out of their beds. Unable to resist the opportunity for a crude pun, may God forgive me, I asked if she was in the habit of looking in her mirror daily. Since Nora never looked fit enough to address her reflection in any kind of mirror before about eleven in the morning, this remark was at first received in icy silence, followed by a torrent of invective. It was again necessary to urgently sum-mon the moving van.

We transferred ourselves to a smaller terrace house at 95, St. George's Road, on high ground behind West Hill. If Hastings could be said to have another side to its tracks, this was it. St. George's stretched on either side of our front door, as if some rupture in the earth's surface had unexpectedly exposed the cave mouths of troglodytes. It would grow in our affections through the simple fact of its seeming inescapability so that, when we did eventually break free of its tenacious embrace, we would subsequently come to look upon it with the nostalgia that ex-prisoners are known to develop for their erstwhile incarceration. I know that my brother Robert, whose formative years were spent there, now loves it with the affection I feel for Kanchrapara.

Here our circumstances became so reduced that Mum would occasionally find herself unable to continue cooking our meal because she had used up her last pennies for the gas meter. Here the bathroom would double as combined kitchen and dining room, its chipped enamel tub topped with a chintz-covered board when not in use, but denying the possibility of anyone cooking or eating while it was. Here we were all dependent upon a single outdoor toilet, which must be reached by walking through the exposure of our sunken front yard, where one was briefly visible to every passer-by. So fearful was I of being caught with a chamber pot in my hands that I would hesitate with my head around the door, listening for footsteps. Here too, Dad's hobby den was a converted boot cupboard under the stairs, where he was forever giving himself electric shocks from his close proximity to exposed wiring. And here we would finally learn to put away our photograph albums and memories of India, because India had become too painful to remember.

Dad's idea of a Saturday afternoon outing was to take the family on the top deck of a double-decker bus all the way to Cooden Beach and back. It was an exercise in daydreaming, playing the game of what house my parents would buy if they won the football pools. The quality of the average residence bordering the roadside would improve markedly after the bus had passed the Glyne Gap gasworks. From there on, for the long haul through Bexhill-on-Sea and then via the seafront to Cooden Beach, the scale and ostentation of the dwellings would be enhanced in proportion to the distance they were set back from the road, until some of them assumed manorial pretensions. At the end of the road, the bus would revolve full circle, and for the return journey we would be afforded a view of the houses we had missed on the opposite side.

Among the Troglodytes

Ironically other families of the Watson tribe, who had moved to England progressively over the years, invariably occupied larger houses than ours in different parts of the country for far shorter periods of time. Over the course of frequent visits, they came to look upon 95, St. George's as their beacon, their touchstone, holding it in some esteem, as if it were their one dependable constant in life. With the exception of my maternal grandfather, Arnold Watson, they never had to live in it for any prolonged duration.

Granddad found it small, narrow, dark and cold, which was a fairly accurate summary. He particularly disliked the steep flights of stairs, sandwiched so narrowly between rooms that they seemed an afterthought, as though the builder only remembered to put them in at the last moment. Paul and I shared a front bedroom with him on the top floor, where we would lie in bed listening to the stairs creak so slowly under his weight that we could almost imagine he was deliberately overdramatizing the ponderousness of his approach.

Whatever love he once had for healthy living and fresh air had not carried over to the English climate, which Granddad felt was of such dubious quality that it must be kept at bay. He insisted on locking all the windows at night, as if preserving, for very different reasons, the ritual Nana had practised in Tatanagar. I saw it as an unconscious effort to lock out not just the climate but England in general. Next he would light a large circular paraffin stove by his bed, which would be left burning until morning. My mother was beside herself with anxiety that the fumes would kill us all in our sleep. She dreaded the prospect of climbing the stairs to wake him with his cup of tea, only to find us asphyxiated from lack of oxygen. But nothing would induce him to desist, and if she persevered in her efforts she would be accused of turning against her own father. It was the first cause of tension between them I had ever observed.

Granddad's only newspaper was the *News of the World,* whose more bizarre and salacious items he would read aloud to us at breakfast, enjoying the pleasure of reminding us, yet again, of the appalling nature and unspeakable customs of the people among whom we had chosen to live. My curiosity would be lasciviously aroused by his recital of headlines such as "Scoutmaster Found Guilty of Indecent Behaviour" and "Vicar Defrocked for Conduct with Choir Boy". Eventually he would move to Bristol, to join the family of his youngest son Denzil, and there, not too many years later, he would die, still in his sixties, more of a broken heart than of any clearly definable physical ailment. His tombstone in the local cemetery was virtually identical to the one over his wife's grave in distant Tollygunge, even down to the lettering and the inscription.

Paul had by now also gained admission to the Grammar School, and would accompany me for the walk there and back each day. Robert was admitted to a technical school backing on to a view of the Hastings Old Town. I can never remember, in all my schooldays, catching a bus or trolleybus anywhere in Hastings. I walked everywhere, even to the other end of St. Leonards-on-Sea in search of the secondhand bookshops that used to absorb almost every moment of my free time. When I walked myself out of shoe leather, I refused to allow Mum to spend money resoling my footwear, whose bottoms I would stuff with cardboard to cover the holes.

I also vigorously refused to see her spend money on football boots for me. I had no interest in football; even less in cricket. Let the boots and other sporting accoutrements go to Paul, who excelled in both pursuits. For my non-compliance with such activities, I was condemned, while my schoolmates were at play in midfield, to run round and round the football pitch or cricket turf, whichever the season happened to be. To me this was no punishment but a boon, for I was left to my own devices, ruminating as I ran. It was as if I was inflicting self-punishment for allowing myself to be removed from India and planted on this alien soil.

Yet I loved Hastings Grammar. Its single-turreted eminence, atop a hill over-looking Queen's Road, seemed entirely suited to its scholastic antiquity. Steady expansion of its intake had necessitated the addition of ugly, prefabricated class-rooms in the grounds, and the creeping inroads of surrounding residential devel-opment had robbed it of the spacious sports fields it had once overlooked. The sports meetings I so despised now required excursions to a site more than a mile away, presently occupied by the school which long ago replaced the one I attended. I would rather be left to my own devices in the quietly dignified school library, poring over reference works or mugging for my next dreaded geography test.

Geography was a puzzle. I yearned to travel to the places and peoples illus-trated in its text books, but the descriptions supplied were appallingly uninviting and downright uninformative. Why should I be interested in primary products and economic levels, population distributions and gross annual rainfalls? And his-tory was no better. None of it brought the participants to life or explained their motivation. One might as well be bent over mathematical equations. People made geography. People made history. Why weren't the people in there? Why couldn't I get a feel for their characters and personalities?

Literature was more to my taste. People were what literature was all about. Lit-erature breathed through them and they breathed through literature. Literature gripped the imagination. Literature was the only subject that held my attention even after school.

While we had been close as brothers, to the point where each would fre-quently comment on our shared telepathic ability to anticipate what the other would say, Paul and I remained divergent in temperament. He was never short of friends; I neither attracted nor sought them. He was unfailingly in the thick of whatever the action might be; I was as far from it as I could distance myself. It wasn't that I had consciously *chosen* not to conform; it was just that I felt no par-ticular desire to do so. Since I did not seek acceptance into any of the cliques or coteries around me, I didn't see that the rules of conduct which determined such acceptance had any relevance to me.

My detachment allowed me to observe the processes involved in the evolution of social groups. There were those, like Paul, around whom such groups naturally gravitated, like gaseous cloud seeking to form new planetary bodies, and there were others who must make the effort to enter their gravitational orbits. For me such groups exerted an opposing, almost centrifugal force, repelling rather than attracting me. I wanted to remain a free roaming particle in the farthest regions of my given space.

Nicholas Thomas Nicholas Carter

Inevitably, however, my singularity attracted a kindred spirit, whose eccentricities were sufficiently intriguing to arouse my curiosity and lower my defences. His name was Nicholas Thomas Nicholas Carter. The second Nicholas in his nomen-clature, he insisted, served a quite separate and distinct purpose from the first. He was the same age as me, but from a different class and—as I quickly deter-mined—even odder than I was. He would take me to his vastly larger home at the other end of town, where his mother, who I gathered was either separated from her husband or recently divorced, fretted in the background like a nervous house-maid, uncertain as to what was required of her role towards her son, leave alone his visitor. Nicholas Thomas Nicholas largely ignored her.

His father, wherever he might currently happen to be in this world or the next (for I was never so bold as to inquire), had left behind a considerable store of pho-nographic albums, all of them storing shellac disks that rotated on a wind-up turntable at seventy eight revolutions per minute (or thereabouts). At those speeds they could accommodate only four minutes play per side, so that Beethoven's Fifth Symphony required sufficient disks to fill a hard-covered binder the thickness of a municipal ledger. Nicholas Thomas Nicholas, whom I addressed simply as "Carter", would take the process of listening to an approved piece of music very seriously indeed, exercising extreme care to change the needle of the wind-up gramophone each time he changed a side. To hear an entire sym-phonic movement, leave alone the complete symphony, would require much fussing at the turntable, exhaust the best part of a tin box of needles and consume most of an afternoon.

If a work passed the listening test, it was deemed to be worth retaining and preserved on a separate shelf. If it did not, it would be ceremoniously conveyed to the back window of the study, on the third floor of the semi-detached, and hurled to destruction. The trick was to spin it horizontally, with a flick of the wrist, aiming for the doorway of the deserted dog kennel at the foot of the gar-den. We found disks bearing the Red Seal label of The Victor Talking Machine Company tended to be more accurate in flight than those bearing the Columbia or Brunswick roundels. Occasionally an entire binder, its glossy and cheerfully coloured cover failing to sway his purpose, would be flung contemptuously as far as Carter could find the strength to hurl it, spilling its subordinate disks en route, like saucers deserting a doomed mother ship.

Carter was an accomplished performer on the piano, and excessively fond (or so I thought) of Schubert. I would have preferred something more red-blooded, a rhapsody by Liszt perhaps or even a Chopin polonaise, but I was content to listen to anything he chose to play, for I had never before encountered playing of that quality in anyone my age. But it was an accomplishment he took for granted, and one that never held his attention for long. I envied him his gift, and wished that my parents could afford a piano, or even find the room in our crowded home in which to accommodate one. He had opened my ears and my appetite to serious music, and for that I would ever be grateful to him.

When tired of music, Carter would return to his task of assembling his pedal-propelled limousine. He refused to have it referred to as a mere pedal car and claimed that he was filing a patent on the design. It was a two-seater, its occupants being required to pedal side by side, boxed into an assemblage of planks nailed together and covered with metal sheeting. Its appearance was one of unsurpassed ugliness, but Carter insisted we must test its roadworthiness on the actual road. I acquiesced only with the greatest reluctance, pointing out that to do so we would (a) probably be required to have it registered and (b) were too young to be behind the wheel (there was a steering wheel of sorts, which both of us were expected to share). He dismissed my reservations, pointing out that there was nothing to prevent us pedaling a tandem bicycle on the road, so why shouldn't we be allowed to pedal his limousine?

The effort of doing so proved hazardous in the extreme, for the pedals refused to function synchronously. Either I would be more forceful, in which event we would turn almost directly at right angles to collide with the kerb, or he would counter with a burst of energy that would propel us the other way, into the path of whatever traffic might be rapidly approaching from the rear. Outraged blasts of car horns eventually attracted the attention of a police constable, who held up his arm and brought us to a standstill. Carter's protestations were overruled. We were not to proceed further.

The great petrol-less limousine project abandoned, Carter turned to building a model of the Bristol Brabazon, then under construction at Filton aerodrome in Bristol, whose runway had been specially extended to accommodate this giant. Although technically innovative, and declared a triumph of British engineering, which would serve as a great morale booster to drab, postwar Britain, the Brabazon would never go into production. It was then the largest airliner attempted in Europe for the transatlantic service, but it was based on faulty commercial judgement, designed to a costly 1930s standard of luxury, and achieved a cruising speed of a mere 250 miles per hour. Carter's interpretation of it, based on an artist's impression, fell hopelessly short of how I hoped the prototype would look on completion.

At around this stage, Carter's interest in me declined. I felt I had fallen short of his expectations, that I was perhaps lacking in reverence for his achievements, his creative intellect, his unique vision. Invitations to accompany him home suddenly ceased. Weeks went by when we would either take pains to avoid each other at school or nod cursorily in passing. And then, unannounced, he turned up one day at our front door in St. George's Road, wearing jackboots, a German Army greatcoat and a Nazi helmet with a swastika so crudely daubed on its front that I imagined he had painted it himself. All of this apparel was at least one size too large for him, and presumably had been acquired by his father as war souvenirs.

The effect was so unexpected, and so ridiculous, that I could think of nothing to say. The thought that he had marched across town in that garb, causing consternation and irritation to scores if not hundreds, left me speechless. He clicked his jackboots together, thrust out his hand in a savagely frowning Nazi salute, turned on his heels and was gone.

Ladies of Claremont Steps

On the opposite side of the street from the Brassey Institute, housing the Hastings Public Library at the foot of Claremont Steps, was my favourite secondhand bookstore, run by two extremely dignified old ladies who might have been sisters, friends or even lovers but were, first and foremost, very good at running a bookshop. Their shop was small and the corridors between cabinets oppressively narrow, but the shelves were stacked with the best selection of books in town. Furthermore their contents were meticulously arranged so that they could place their hands immediately on whatever the customer might require.

What the premises lacked, in the way of space, they more than made up in opportunities for serendipitous voyages through uncharted waters, aided by their occupants' ability to interpret the vaguest of information and identify the most elusive author or title hovering on the tip of a client's tongue. Both women possessed a sixth sense for books, which eschewed catalogues and depended seemingly entirely on memory. Furthermore they were catholic in their tastes, and as liable to stock some early bound volume of the *Boys Own Paper* as a rare edition of *Paradise Lost*. Finally, they would happily permit a barely adolescent teenager to spend hours buried in some corner, poring over whatever might currently take his fancy, without interruption except to inquire if one might like some tea. I like to think they were secretly delighted that I loved books as much as they did.

When I consider the demise of the secondhand bookshop in Britain, I remember with special affection the two old ladies and their bookshop at the bottom of Claremont Steps. There was much competition for them at the time, most of which has now vanished, except in the field of antiquarian booksellers, where you need to know what you're looking for and have what it takes to pay for it. The days of untroubled browsing, suspended only to partake of the occasional cup of tea, are long gone. As is the almost psychic ability of an experienced bookseller to sense exactly what one wants but cannot quite remember. To me, the ladies of Claremont Steps were the female equivalents of Moses, coaxing, guiding, directing rather than forcibly leading me into the interior of a promised land which, I now discovered, I had hitherto merely glimpsed from a vestigial peninsula. Beyond those mountains, towards whose peaks they gently nudged and steered me, stretched a vast hinterland of literature whose extent and abundance I had barely begun to grasp.

The Brassy Institute, on the other side of the road, was a dignified building in much the same architectural style as Hastings Grammar School. There I would bury myself for hours in the reading room. Its well-stocked reference shelves would stand me in good stead when I later came to be employed as a reporter with the *Hastings and St. Leonards Observer*, whose offices and presses were located less than a hundred yards distant.

The Boys Own Paper was by now my magazine of choice, obtained weekly from W.H. Smith's bookshop by the Memorial. It was no longer the exemplar of boyhood's literary ideals it had set out to be at the launch of its considerable career in 1879. Nor had it remained the paragon of imperial endeavour, now that there was no empire left to exalt. So one could not expect it to continue inspiring its readers to perform acts of irrationally selfless and unquestioning heroism, as once it did with Henry Newbolt's grandiloquent lines:

> "The sand of the desert is sodden red—
> Red with the wreck of the square that broke.
> The gatling's jammed and the colonel dead,
> And the regiment blind with dust and smoke.
> The river of death has brimmed its banks,
> And England's far and Honour a name,

But the voice of a schoolboy rallies the ranks—
'Play up! Play up! And play the game!'"

One particular service *The Boys Own Paper* continued to perform was to encourage its pubescent readers to submit their own literary contributions, thanks to which I won first prize in the under-fourteens category of a short story contest. This required me to provide a satisfactory explanation, and a convincing ending, for an incomplete scenario entailing the discovery of a mysterious aircraft on an abandoned airfield. The prize money was a princely five pounds, but the satisfaction mattered more. And the theme was right up my runway.

The Man who Duelled with Göring

By this time my bedroom on the top floor of 95, St. George's Road was a shrine to aviation. Thanks to W.E. Johns, and *Biggles*, I had ventured into the wider realms of aeronautical history, and was exhausting my meagre pocket money on anything that could contribute to my knowledge of the subject. My heroes were the aces of the Royal Flying Corps, Edward "Micky" Mannock, with sixty-one victories to his credit, James McCudden, with fifty-seven, Albert Ball, with forty-four, and reputedly the highest-scoring RFC ace of all, Canadian Billy Bishop, who claimed he had brought down no less than seventy-two enemy aircraft, and who earned the Victoria Cross for single-handedly attacking a German airfield on the Arras front.

Another RFC ace, with a lesser tally of sixteen victories, but with a Distinguished Flying Cross and Distinguished Service Cross to his credit—not to mention a wonderful way with words—was American flyer Elliot White Springs, who summed up the life of a combat pilot in his subsequent writings, such as *Warbirds: The Diary of an Unknown Aviator*:

> "The heavens were the grandstands, and only the gods were spectators. The stake was the world. The forfeit was the player's place at the table; and the game had no recess. It was the most dangerous of all sports—and the most fascinating. It got in the blood like wine. It aged men 40 years in 40 days; it ruined nervous systems in an hour. It was a fast game—the average life of a pilot at the Front was 48 hours. And, to many, it seemed an age."

My own private flying ace may not have survived that war with a distinguished service record, but survive it he did, to become the only man I personally knew who had encountered Hermann Wilhelm Göring in aerial combat. George Lush

was in his sixties when I met him. He owned a garage, to provide for his retire-
ment, and the fourth oldest aircraft on the British Aircraft Register, to provide for
his amusement. I had in my possession a copy of the complete register of *all* individual aircraft in operation, whether privately or commercially owned, anywhere
in the United Kingdom, and there, number four on the list, was George's pride
and joy, his Klemm monoplane, registered in 1928.

The initial prototype was equipped with a Harley Davidson motor cycle
engine, but George's had a rotary Daimler which gave it a top speed of about sev-
enty-six miles per hour. Born of a design for gliders, the Klemm boasted the largest wing span of any light plane of its period, measuring eighteen metres from tip
to tip. Its low engine power and glider-like temperament made it difficult to
manage in high wind conditions, so that George only took it up on perfectly
windless days. The result was that every time I sensed the merest possibility of a
perfectly windless day, I would dash down to Pebsham airfield and wait in hopes
of an appearance by George.

Pebsham has long been replaced by successions of vegetable gardens, light
industrial parks and housing estates, but in my days it embraced sufficient
expanse of greensward to allow for light aircraft to land or take off, provided there
was someone around to lend a hand—if need be—with the ritual swinging of the
propellor to provide ignition. On most weekends, I was the hopeful stand-by,
ready to offer just that service, and for my pains I might be invited aboard for a
brief trip to Brighton and back, or an aerial sightseeing tour of the Sussex downs.

Swinging the prop was the aeronautical equivalent of cranking the engine of
an automobile. In the latter case you could break a wrist if you didn't let go in
time. In the former you could lose much more if you fell forward into the propellor blades. I was always very careful to lean back. Most owners of Tiger Moths
and other pre-war biplanes would still require that service, in reward for which
nothing could better compensate me than a ride in an open cockpit with the
wind whipping my ears. I became such a fixture at the airfield that even owners of
some of the postwar models, like Austers and twin-engined Miles Messengers, fitted with electrical ignition that didn't need them to shout "contact", would take
pity on me and invite me aboard.

My real quarry though was George Lush who, if the windsock by the solitary
Quonset hut hung as limp and lifeless as a used condom, would sooner or later
turn up in one of the many cars from his garage. He was a loner, was George,
used to handling things on his own and reluctant to seek help. I practically had to
thrust myself upon him, by asking irritating questions as he set about preparing
the elaborate rituals for his departure.

Flying Motorcycle

In its disassembled state, the low-wing Klemm monoplane was stored in the Quonset hut, from which it had to be removed like a dagger from its sheath. The centre wing section and fuselage had a fixed connection, while the outer wings were dismantled after each flight and stacked alongside in the hut's narrow confines, in which George would trust no one else to follow him, for fear of them stepping on vital parts in the semi-darkness. I would wait until George emerged into the sunlight, dragging the fuselage backwards by its tail wheel. Then I would ask the superfluous question as to whether he would need any help with the rest of it.

At first he would shake his head, but eventually my persistence paid off, and I was allowed to assist him in carrying out the port and starboard wings, balancing these while he affixed them to the centre wing-section with four screws. The tail unit could also be separated from the fuselage for better transportation on the ground, but George never needed to do that. When the whole assemblage was completed to his satisfaction, he would stand up, cast a calculating glance in my direction, as if determining how much I weighed (which wasn't very much in those days) and then incline his head towards the rear cockpit.

After the first time, I knew the routine backwards. I would clamber aboard, being careful to put my hands and feet in the right places, don the helmet and goggles left in the dashboard, strap myself in with the lap belt and then sit perfectly still, touching nothing at all, until he had personally managed the rest. He didn't place sufficient reliance in me to entrust any more than that. What he accomplished on his own was complicated and considerable. He would do something in the front cockpit which I presumed involved priming some kind of pump, then he would set the ignition, then he would dismount, being careful not to step on the wing fabric which his cockpit immediately overlooked. This meant he would have to walk all the way round the port wing to reach the propellor, which he would swing himself until the engine fired. Then he would pull away the chocks.

Now came the tricky part, because the Klemm would immediately start to roll forward. George, running as fast as he could to retrace his course around the port wing, would also have to keep pace with the moving plane, climb, rather than clamber aboard his cockpit (for clambering might have entailed putting a shoe through the fabric) and take command of the controls. At his age I sometimes wondered if he would make it and, if he didn't, what I might do about it. I could picture him, left winded in my wake, shouting after me some instruction I would not be able to catch. Should I ease back the throttle, and if so where was it? Should I apply the brakes, and if so where were *they*? Or should I throw discretion to the winds and, once the tail wheel had lifted from the forward momentum, pull the joystick towards me and kiss the grass—and possibly the world—goodbye?

The prospect of my worst/best expectations being realised was simultaneously tempting and terrifying. But having pursued this ritual for more than twenty years before I ever got to meet him, George never put a foot wrong. And once in the cockpit, he restored our ability to communicate, albeit only via a rubberized voice tube through which he shouted at me and I shouted back. The Klemm's glide angle was so shallow that it required a fairly severe tilt of the joystick to get the nose away from its alignment with the back windows of fast approaching terrace houses, over whose roofs we barely skimmed en route to the Glyne Gap gasworks.

George used the gasworks chimneys as a fairly reliable altimeter. If he hadn't gained sufficient altitude to clear them, he would have to bank sharply to the right. If he had, he would use the chimneys as a pivotal point on which to execute a much shallower and more leisurely turn to the left that would carry us in an eastward direction, following the pebbled coastline of the St. Leonards and then the Hastings seafronts. Leaning over the side, I would see an unfurling carpet of upturned faces on summer beaches, eyes shaded to observe the passage of this relic from another age, popping above their heads like an airborne motorcycle. Ian Fleming's *Chitty Chitty Bang Bang* could well have found its inspiration in George's elderly monoplane, but to me it was the very embodiment of flying; affording an unrivalled sense of superiority over all I surveyed, combined with a progress sufficiently leisurely to drink it all in.

Landing was even more critical than take-off. George had a standing agreement with the farmer owning the adjoining field, at the back of Pebsham, that he should keep his gate open at the crest of the ridge topping its shallow inclination. George would trail his narrow-based undercarriage through the open gate, sometimes his wings just brushing the top of the hedge on either side, and would then follow the contours of the slope to the field below. To ensure his path to the gate was clear of cattle, he had the bulb of an antique car horn affixed to the side of the fuselage just below his cockpit, swearing that the sound of this carried louder than the subdued puttering of the engine.

It was a relief to discover there were seldom cattle in the way to test his theory. But in any case the approach was maintained at just above stalling speed, slow enough for any necessary bovine evacuation to precede our arrival. I would watch the radial cylinders popping in rotation, only to be cut dead halfway down the slope, allowing us to glide serenely and silently for the final hundred metres or more until, to ensure we didn't interminably carry on doing so, George would again jerk the nose skyward and force a soft pancake on to the grass.

Then of course would come the sad process of dismantling and putting it all away, until the next time.

Tale of a Dogfight

During one of these protracted aftermaths to another brief afternoon in the air, George finally volunteered the story of how he met Hermann Göring "face to face" over the Western Front in the final months of World War One. Face to face in the sense that, in those days, aviators circled each other close enough to identify who they were up against.

There was no mistaking Göring, who had just taken command of the late Baron Manfred von Richtofen's JG 1 squadron, better known as the Flying Circus. Göring flew a white Fokker D.VII, with the standard black crosses of the German Air Force. I was thrilled to learn his Fokker was white. The very first adventure of flying ace James Bigglesworth, penned by ex-W.W.I Pilot Officer William Earle Johns, had been entitled *The White Fokker*. Göring was one of the first pilots to fly the D.VII in combat. Richthofen had tested the D.VII in trials at Adlershof, but was shot down and killed just days before it entered service.

When introduced, the D.VII was not without problems. On occasion its wing ribs would fracture in a dive, and high temperatures might ignite its phosphorus ammunition or cause its gas tank to explode. Even so, it proved durable and easy to fly, with "an apparent ability to make a good pilot out of mediocre material". Equipped with a BMW engine, it could outclimb any Allied opponent. Highly manoeuvrable at all speeds and altitudes, it was more than a match for any of the British or French fighter planes of 1918.

George was in an SE5a, powered by a Hispano-Suiza engine, affording him the advantage of a freely manoeuvrable Lewis .303 gun mounted on the upper wing, directly above his cockpit. Whenever he and his adversary found themselves locked in another tight spiral, he employed his ability to angle the Lewis gun so that it fired across the intervening space. The trouble was, George didn't have much ammunition left in the radial drum, so that the next time they circled each other he lifted off the by now empty canister and hurled it defiantly, but of course ineffectually, in Göring's direction, as if daring his adversary to do his damnedest.

To George's surprise, and relief, Göring signalled disengagement, grinning under his goggles as if to suggest "Let's do this again some other time". Göring at that point had twenty-two kills to his credit. George had none. He would have been a sitting duck had his adversary sought to follow through. George's account of the engagement was laconic, matter-of-fact. Göring's gallant conduct on that occasion explained why George could never subsequently see him as the bloated morphine addict who founded the Gestapo and then went on to command Hitler's World War Two *Luftwaffe*, leave alone the convicted war criminal of the Nuremberg Trials who swallowed cyanide two hours before he was due to hang.

Göring was not Richtofen's direct successor as head of the Flying Circus. That position had gone to Wilhelm "Willi" Reinhard, who assumed command of JG 1 on 22nd April 1918. In July 1918, Reinhard attended aircraft trials near Adlershof. After Göring had finished test flying a Zeppelin-Lindau D.I, Reinhard replaced him in the cockpit and took it up for a further trial. He was killed when a strut broke and the top wing collapsed. Göring stepped into his shoes as ringmaster of the Flying Circus. Years later I would watch the movie *Blue Max*, and wonder at the curious coincidence of its ending.

Göring penned his own account of what it was like to be caught in a dogfight. There were, he said, perhaps a hundred planes contending in limited airspace, flying at less than three thousand feet under a ceiling of thick cloud. Antiaircraft fire, particularly threatening at that altitude, was constantly arching up from below. On the ground the German and British armies were locked in combat. The pilots caught occasional fleeting glimpses of the battlefield, with its drifting clouds of gas and the bright streaks of light made by flame-throwers. Above, the airplanes twisted and climbed and plunged "like wild things".

"In the rain and mist," recalled Göring, "the danger of midair collision was added to all the other hazards. Other planes would suddenly appear like phantoms. An adversary would emerge as a shadow for a fraction of a second, then vanish into the black clouds. There was something uncanny, sinister, about this flying in rain and storm, cloud and mist."

The pilots, German and British alike, were "half-dead, exhausted and worn to tatters by the inhuman strain and the nerve shattering tumult". It was eerie and unearthly, like some "frantic witch's sabbath in the air". That was how Göring remembered it. But in that one reminiscence he conveyed to me, of how *he* had seen it, George Lush remembered only Göring.

I struggled to envisage Göring as George saw him, lean and well-favoured, if not actually handsome, imbued with the spirit of chivalry that still infected those early knights of the clouds, no matter how appalling the cost they might pay for their mistakes. But the later image, of the puffed-out toad he became as Hitler's henchman, kept getting in the way. For a man quoted as saying "Guns will make us powerful; butter will only make us fat", Göring must have eaten a lot of butter.

Nevertheless I could hardly contain myself. I had flown with the man who had pitted his skills against Hermann Wilhelm Göring! I dashed home on my bicycle, forgetting all about my resolution *not* to tell about my adventures in the Klemm monoplane, and blurted out the news to my parents. My father weighed the implications. "You flew with the man who fought Göring in World War One? What exactly were you flying in? Some kind of biplane?"

"A monoplane actually. A Klemm monoplane."

"What's that?"

"Well, you know…It's that plane with the very long wingspan that flies over occasionally."

"The one that sounds as if it's flying with a motorcycle engine so under-powered that it's about to stall and crash?"

"Well yes, that one."

My mother was aghast. "Oh my God, and you never told us! How long has this been going on?"

"A few weeks."

"A few *weeks*! And every time we thought it was going to crash at any moment. Little did we know that you were *in* it."

"It's perfectly safe. It's probably the safest plane in the air."

Dad interjected "It might well have been the *first* plane in the air. It looks old enough. Have you taken leave of your senses?"

That was the last occasion on which I ever flew with George Lush.

Memento of the Great Australian Air Race

Deprived of further adventures in the Klemm, I languished on my bed, staring up at the dangling scale models of mainly World War Two aircraft suspended from the ceiling, with just the odd Spad, Albatross, Fokker Triplane or Sopwith Camel looking incongruously out of place in their midst. I had never been any good at making my own models. I either shaved off too much balsa, or didn't file enough from the earlier wooden kits on the market, and when the plastic ones arrived I couldn't get the two halves of the fuselage to combine without leaving ridges of superfluous cement that got stuck all over my fingers.

Furthermore, while I might be a reasonably talented artist on paper, with watercolours and acrylics, I wasn't much good with the silly little bottles of paint supplied with the model parts. The effects were never smooth, and the transfers of aircraft markings were seldom in exactly the right places. One couldn't look at one of my finished models and see it as a perfect miniature of the real thing. So most of my models came readymade, from a war surplus junk store in Hastings Old Town. Uniformly painted black, they had been used for aircraft recognition practice to train antiaircraft crews to shoot at hostiles and not at friendlies.

Among them was a battered wreck of the beloved Beaufighter I remembered from Kanchrapara days, its pugnacious little twin radial engines thrust forward, ready to take on anything it encountered. It seemed so long ago and far away; almost as removed as that younger George Lush, sitting in the cockpit of his SE5a, defiantly hurling his empty Lewis drum. The world wasn't ever going to be like that any more. I had arrived in it too late.

In my pocket, carried with me everywhere like a sacred talisman, was a piece of silver fabric from the fuselage of a plane that never made it past my birthplace of Allahabad in the great London to Melbourne air race of October 1934. I had been given this by my father on my twelfth birthday, when I was deemed "old enough to appreciate its significance". Both my parents had been at the Allahabad airstrip to watch the competitors coming through. My mother at that time was one month pregnant with me, so in a sense I was there too.

Allahabad had proved something of a hurdle for quite a few of the contestants. Roscoe Turner and his navigator Nichols, in their Boeing, had trouble getting there through storms which drove them some two hundred miles south of the city. They were in the middle of a line of thunderheads, and Nichols couldn't distinguish Allahabad's revolving beacon from the lightning. In the dark, Turner circled for ninety minutes while Nichols tried to contact the tower. Their fuel was very low when he finally succeeded. Turner asked that the airport searchlights be blinked. When the tower responded to this request, he made his approach but, uncertain in which direction to approach, he landed downwind. The airport officials expected a crash, but Turner brought his ship to a stop with consummate skill.

Jim and Amy Mollison were flying *Black Magic*, one of three De Havilland Comets entered in the race. Taking off from Allahabad, they did not get very far before being forced down at Jubblepore for refuelling. As this was not an approved landing place, Jim found there was no aviation fuel available. He chose to have a local bus company fuel his craft with sufficient ordinary gasoline to enable their return to Allahabad. By the time the Mollisons reached Allahabad, a piston had seized on one engine, rupturing an oil line. With no hope of repairing the engine in time to continue, they withdrew from the race. This was a particular blow for them because Jim had followed this route to Australia for his record flight of 1931.

Less fortunate than either the Boeing or the Comet was the Dutch Panderjaeger, whose crew had been compelled to carry out extensive repairs at Allahabad. When they were finally ready for take-off, it had become dark again, and field officials ordered their two searchlights to illuminate the strip. The Dutch pilot requested they be turned off, as he felt they would only distract him. There must have been some missed communication, because the searchlight operator, thinking the pilot was *not* going to take-off, hooked one searchlight wagon to an ambulance and began towing it back to the hangars across the field. The Pander pilot began his run and crashed into the ambulance in mid-field. At least some luck was with the crew, all of whom escaped alive. But the wooden Pander was destroyed by fire. My father was among the souvenir hunters who salvaged his strip of fabric before flames consumed the rest.

Fingering that piece of fabric, it suddenly occurred to me that even my era had its vestiges of romance. There was still the Bristol Brabazon, due to make its debut at the Farnborough Air Show. In return for promising never again to fly in the Klemm monoplane, I would exact a promise from my parents, enabling me to attend that aerial jamboree.

Bristol Brabazon

The Farnborough air show was only a year old when I attended it in 1949. Previous shows of the Society of British Aerospace Companies had been held at Hendon, Hatfield and Radlett. But Farnborough had a much earlier and more lasting association with aviation. Colonel William S.F. Cody, who toured the States and Britain with his "Wild West" shows, had flown there on 16 October 1908. In fact his many man-lifting kite experiments had contributed to the establishment of Farnborough as a seat of this new science of aeronautics, and eventually to Cody's place in history as the first man in the UK to make a sustained powered flight.

I couldn't guess then how fleeting would be that brief display of Brabazon braggadocio. In its day the largest airliner ever built, it seemed the consummation of everything the industry had striven to achieve. It had become airborne in a mere four hundred yards on its maiden flight just days earlier, on 4th September that year. When it made its appearance at Farnborough, flying slowly, languidly and very low overhead, it gave all of us a breathtaking look at its eight Bristol Centaur engines and its seventy metre wingspan.

There was much else to see at Farnborough that year; our first jet-propelled bomber, the English Electric Canberra, which had also made its test flight earlier that year, even beautifully restored and still airworthy survivors of World War One, including a Sopwith Camel and Sopwith Pup, but I couldn't get enough of the Brabazon.

Uncle Trevor and Aunt Ursie were living at Bristol, not far from Uncle Denzil and Aunt Dora. The Brabazon's home base at Filton airfield was a mere bus ride away. I decided to accept their long-standing invitation to visit. Bristol was a revelation to me; an English port that somehow conveyed a sense of being not quite house-trained enough to *behave* as if it were wholly English. Instead it looked as if it yearned to cast anchor and put out to sea. It reeked of its long, and sometimes disreputable association with maritime trade in all manner of shady commerce, including of course slaves.

Bristol's historical mistake had been its failure, at the start of the nineteenth century, to foresee the ruin of the sugar industry which would occur over the next fifty years. Ignoring the stirrings of the campaign against slavery, its merchants continued to concentrate on trade with the West Indies, where many of Bristol's most important citizens held large capital investments. Its fortunes hopelessly bound up with the Caribbean, Bristol's prosperity declined along with the islands themselves. But despite all that, and quite unlike Hastings, it had weathered the years well, wearing its intriguingly tarnished reputation lightly.

The expansive acres of Clifton Downs, at the top of Whiteladies Road, reminded me of the Calcutta *maidan*. And Whiteladies Road itself had a distinct whiff of the Raj about it. With a name like that, how could it not? I *almost* felt as if I were back in familiar surroundings. Isambard Kingdom Brunel's elegant suspension bridge, heroically vaulting the Avon deeps from the Clifton heights, did nothing to dispel that impression. Wasn't it but a precursor of the manner in which Howrah had spanned the Hooghly?

And what of Isambard himself? What could possibly have been English about *him* (except perhaps for his mother)? Judging from the famous portrait of him standing by the chains of his steamship *The Great Eastern*, he didn't even *look* or *dress* like an Englishman, leave alone *sound* like one. I was enchanted with Isambard. I was enchanted with his life, and I wasn't even interested in engineering! I wished that the money for that spectacular bridge had stretched to the inclusion of the Egyptian sphinxes he had intended to place there. It would have given the project that extra Isambard touch.

But I was getting diverted from my purpose. I was in Bristol to see a much more recent marvel of engineering, hopefully at closer quarters than I had managed to achieve at Farnborough.

Disconcerted WRAF

The bus deposited me on the far side of the field from the giant hangar, outside which reposed the completed Brabazon with, in the shodowed background, a second Brabazon in course of construction. I hadn't realised that production was so far advanced. The trouble was, never having owned a telephoto lens in my life, I possessed only a simple box camera with which to photograph these marvels, and I was too far away to do them justice. Between us stretched a high, barbed-wire topped chain-link fence, and the width of the considerable boundary enclosing Filton's newly extended runway. I had to get closer.

I can't recall how I overcame the difficulty of getting *in*. But since I had succeeded that far, I did not anticipate any insurmountable problem getting *out* again. Clearly it would be unwise for me to make a beeline for my target by simply marching boldly across the intervening space. Better I should outflank it by working my way around the perimeter, to approach it from the other side. I walked and walked, conscious that I had left it rather late, that the winter afternoon was drawing in and it would soon be dark.

By the time dusk had fallen, I was actually *further* away from Brabazons One And Two than I had been at the outset, and getting somewhat weary of struggling through unkempt gorse fringes in order to avoid detection by whoever might be on the lookout for adolescent aeronautical enthusiasts armed with box cameras. Furthermore I had strayed into a built-up area, laid out with streets and street lamps and filled with neatly suburban prefabricated housing. Had I somehow blundered *outside* the wire fence? The only certainty was that I had lost all sense of direction. Abandoning my by now quite hopeless mission, I wanted simply to get home.

There was a light on behind the curtains of the nearest bungalow-styled dwelling. I decided to seek directions. Knocking at the door, I heard a breezy female voice coo with barely suppressed excitement "Coming!". The door opened to reveal an attractive young brunette displaying more of her charms than I had expected to see. Standing there in very brief black knickers and bra, she simply said "Oh", in a flat, disappointed voice.

I told her I was lost; a conclusion she must already have reached from the somewhat frayed condition of my raincoat, bearing the tears inflicted by spiteful tangles of briar, from the pathetic camera dangling at my wrist and from the anxious, overheated appearance of my face. "Come in," she said, opening the door a little wider and leaning forward to give a quick glance up and down the deserted street.

I sat on her sofa while she fetched a dressing gown to wrap around her well-proportioned figure. Taking out a cigarette, she offered me the pack. "Do you smoke?"

I shook my head. I didn't at the time.

"Look Love," she continued, lighting her cigarette and drawing in a deep lungful of smoke. "I wasn't *expecting* you. I mean I wasn't expecting *you*. But now you're here, I suppose I'll have to do something about it, which is easier said than done." She paused to examine me at slightly closer range. "How old are you?"

"Fourteen."

"Tall for your age, but I won't argue with that. How did you get here? And why?"

I answered both questions.

"Christa'mighty, you break into a closed area to get pictures with *that* thing?"

I nodded disconsolately. "How do I get out?"

"When did you last eat?"

"Several hours ago," I admitted.

She made me a sardine and tomato sandwich, which she placed beside a cup of tea. "Tell me about yourself."

I gave her a brief summary of my life to that point, through which she sat silently, almost disbelievingly. Then she reciprocated with an even briefer and much more concisely edited version of hers, while I wolfed her sandwich and washed it down with tea. She was from somewhere up north and a sergeant in the Women's Royal Air Force. This was her staff quarter; in the middle of a supposedly secure RAF camp. I repeated my question. How could I get out?

She looked at her watch. Whoever she *had* expected was either very late or wasn't coming. "Give me a moment."

When she reappeared from her bedroom she was wearing a WRAF greatcoat, and presumably something under it other than her bra and knickers. She donned a cap, and a pair of shoes over her stockinged feet and said "Right then, let's get going before it gets too dark to see in front of our noses."

We zigzagged at tangents across roadways to avoid the fullest glare of street lamps, presumably so she would be spared the obligation, if accosted by an acquaintance, of explaining who I was. I looked perhaps a trifle too young for the sort of person she *might* have preferred to be seen with. When the housing and the street lamps began to thin out, we found ourselves alongside a row of back yards, beyond which stretched a strip of no-man's-land separating us from the identical fencing I had surmounted with such unexpected ease on my way in. And looming just this side of it was the wrecked fuselage of a Bristol Blenheim bomber, its cockpit and turrets gone and much of its metal twisted out of true.

"Look, this isn't Stalag 17 or anything, but it *is* patrolled by guard dogs," she cautioned. "There should be one along any minute now. When it's gone, climb as high as you can on top of that thing and you'll find the barbed wire is a little slack there. It's the regular route for those of us who get caught out too late without a pass." She squeezed my arm. "I'll say goodnight then. Been nice knowing you."

I shook her hand, and mumbled something about my immense gratitude for her understanding of my predicament. With a wave, she was gone.

I waited in the shadows for the guard dog; an Alsatian on a lead, held by a uniformed man with an armband. The dog never looked up, sniffing its way along the perimeter by the fence. Neither did its escort. When they were well clear, I made a run for it and scrambled over with ease.

Consorting with an Arsonist

But the aviation fixation had not done with me yet. The following summer, shortly after my fifteenth birthday, I commenced what was supposed to be a vacation job as an apprentice journalist with the *Bexhill-on-Sea Observer*. And I used every moment of my weekends to travel to aerodromes within reach of my monthly rail pass.

At Shoreham aerodrome, just the other side of Brighton, I encountered a fellow enthusiast, also armed with a notebook to jot down particulars and registration numbers of the privately owned aircraft we happened to spot there. He was at least ten years older than me; almost too old to be quite so preoccupied with boyish enthusiasms. But what the hell, I figured; maybe I would never outgrow mine either. We exchanged experiences, and it turned out he had travelled more extensively, and acquired a far more formidable list than I had. However he had never been to Pebsham, so he proposed that we swop addresses and keep in touch. He would let me know about his further aircraft spotting expeditions if I informed him of everything that passed through Pebsham. This struck me as a good idea; we were forming the kernel of a club—something of a precedent in my anti-social lifestyle.

I left Shoreham in a Miles Messenger, hitching a ride with a kindly pilot who had just launched an enterprise in Redhill, moulding aircraft parts in fibreglass. From Redhill I caught a train back to Hastings, returning not so late as to cause my mother acute distress.

After a few weeks, the first of his letters arrived; breezy chronicles of where he'd been and what he'd seen, with lists of aircraft registration numbers. I responded with whatever comparatively brief notes I could supply on the somewhat scarcer movements through Pebsham, where I continued to help George Lush assemble his Klemm monoplane, though I conscientiously declined his invitations to renew our mutual flights.

Several months went by, in the course of which I was still working at the *Bexhill-on-Sea Observer*, having by then decided to abandon all further education in order to get to grips with what I had decided was going to be my career. And then one night there were two plainclothes policemen at the door, asking if they might have a word with me. My parents invited them in, tense with anxiety, and were allowed to sit with us in the living room as our visitors posed their questions. They had a whole list of dates to bring to my attention. Could I recall where I was on those dates? I struggled hard. It wasn't easy to recall where I was *last* weekend, leave alone weekends stretching back all the way to summer.

But mercifully it was easy to recall that on none of those weekends had I travelled outside the periphery of Hastings, St. Leonards or Bexhill-on-Sea, all of which were aligned in immediate east-west succession along the East Sussex coast this side of Eastbourne. How about Shoreham? Not since that day in August. How about Redhill, or a number of other aerodromes dotted around the wider orbit of the southern counties? Redhill yes, on the same day as Shoreham, but others definitely not, and my parents could vouch for that.

Had I met this man? They showed me his mug shot. Yes, I recalled meeting him, and how we had exchanged addresses, and how we had occasionally written each other. Did I have any of his letters in my possession? I went upstairs to my bedroom to recover and hand them over. They went carefully through the lists of registration numbers, nodding as they went, ticking off the ones they were looking for. Could they keep the letters? By all means. Already I was beginning to figure out where this was leading.

Then they explained their reasons for having enlisted my cooperation (as they diplomatically phrased it). They had apprehended the man after the most recent of several incidents of arson, scattered among different aerodromes and always involving one or other of the aircraft listed in the notes he had sent me. In each case the incident had occurred within days of the corresponding letter being mailed.

Why had he done it? we asked. While he had willingly admitted each offence, he could not *explain* why, other than the fact that it gave him pleasure to watch them burn. He had also freely admitted his correspondence with me. Hence the constabulary visit, just to see if—by the remotest chance—I might be similarly inclined; an accomplice in *everything* he did. Thanks to my frank answers, supported by my parents' evidence on my behalf, they had now dismissed that possibility.

When they had gone, my father turned to me. "Your flying days are over, young man. From now on you can consider yourself grounded."

I felt I effectively had been. For a long time.

Premature End to my Education

It was Dad who had suggested I start looking for a job. He pointed out that I had a year to run before I completed my last term at Hastings Grammar, and I still hadn't the faintest idea what I wanted to do with the rest of my life. I was fifteen years old; the age at which he had commenced his apprenticeship with the Indian Railways. I couldn't afford the luxury of waiting for something to occur to me, because he couldn't afford to maintain me in further education once my years of grammar school scholarship were up.

"Work doesn't come looking for you," he said. "You have to take whatever comes. It's a fallacy to suppose you're going to find yourself some congenial career. A career is just a fancy name for work, and work is not something to be enjoyed. It's something that has to be done in order to survive." They were the saddest words I ever heard him utter.

I scanned the small ads at the back of the *Hastings and St. Leonards Observer*. What the hell *was* there to do in a fishing port that doubled as a permanently off-season seaside resort? Should I settle for shop assistant, garage attendant, restaurant waiter or butcher's boy? I couldn't see myself putting out to sea, even if they'd let me, in one of those oversized dories hauled up on the beach at Rockanore, still dependent on masts and sails.

Then I looked more closely at the newspaper itself. I rang them up. Did they have any need of a young reporter, willing to learn on the job? They didn't, so I got hold of the number for the *Bexhill-on-Sea Observer* and tried that instead. I found myself speaking to the editor, Mr. Samuels, who was noticeably slow of speech, as if weighing the context of every sentence he heard, and how it might have been better expressed. I assured him English had always been my best—indeed my *only* school subject worthy of mention—and I could produce numerous essays that had scored high marks to prove it. I could tell from his silence that I had aroused his curiosity.

He suggested I present myself the following Monday, and come prepared for a further written test. In those days there was no such thing as a course one might take in journalism, and certainly no academic qualification that would have any direct bearing on the subject. Providence was being kind to me. It was letting me through the last crack in a fast closing window of opportunity, when it was still possible to become a reporter simply by getting on with the job of reporting.

My test assignment was an obituary. And for that I was in luck, because the deceased had bequeathed me a story to tell. For many years he had served in the Egyptian Police Force, attaining a number of senior positions before eventually retiring to live out the rest of his years in Bexhill-on-Sea. He had come to the right place. Bexhill was more a sanatorium than a town; a mortician's windfall, its calendar set permanently to autumn and the dead dropping like leaves from the trees. It was a last resting place for those grand old elephants of empire who recognised their end was nigh. Migrating south from all over the British Isles, they eased their weary, sometimes battle-scarred hides through the orchards of Kent and Sussex to await the moment when their bones would settle in some likely burial plot, preferably facing out to that sea they would never cross again.

In the years of postwar withdrawal, the whole map of Britain had altered. No longer the hub of global dominions, it had become an archipelago unto itself. And when the social structures were shaken and stirred, the dregs of empire settled to the bottom, all the way from Kent to Cornwall. With a wary eye on prevailing trends, the elephants chose places like Bexhill and Cooden for their last-ditch stand against the inevitable. Here they could protect what little they had salvaged, of all they had known, holding at bay an environment ever less familiar, ever more hostile. The new, alien world in which they found themselves had crept up on them and caught them unprepared; a world that had already forgotten the empire, not recognizing its survivors, or even why they had ever existed.

I could see something of that in the eyes of the widow before me, clearly concerned that one so young had been chosen to encapsulate a life so long and rich in incident. I told her something of myself, and how well I understood what she must be feeling. She took my hand and led me to the sofa, where she passed me a cup of tea, sat beside me and opened up to me. What a life her husband had led! And she with him.

When I finally left her, it was getting late. Even though the *Observer* was a weekly newspaper, published every Friday, Samuels had stressed he wanted obituaries, as far as possible, in the early pages. The actual funerals could follow, a week later if need be. This was my first day at work, and I hadn't even sat at my desk. I hurried back, renewing acquaintance with colleagues to whom I had been briefly introduced earlier in the day. There were three of them, all seated around the same enormous rectangular table in the middle of the editorial room. At the centre of the table were stacked shelves of stationery, old newspaper files, coffee cups and the metal spikes on which discarded sheets of amended copy, stale press releases and unwelcome reader's letters had been speared like the gory trophies of butcherbirds, arrayed in a thorn bush.

Smiling with what might have been taken as a gesture of friendship, but looked to me more like ruthless anticipation, Mike Green, aged about twenty and newly emerged from National Service, nodded to indicate the enormously elderly typewriter I had been allocated. The only typewriter I had ever used before was a small portable belonging to Nicholas Thomas Nicholas Carter. The keyboard of this one might have served to awaken a cathedral organ. Beside it was a stack of blank copy. Mike explained to me that the sheets, about half the height of an A4 folio, must be typed in double spacing, landscape format.

I got to work, everyone else in the room busying themselves as though oblivious to my efforts. Paragraph after paragraph, sheet after sheet slipped by, some torn up, some started again. I was aware of watches being examined, of hours slipping by. The retired RAF squadron leader from the far side of the table was the first to leave. He stood and superfluously announced it was time to go home. He was the deputy editor, and it was Samuels who would be checking my copy. In due course Mike, and his neighbour, an older man dreaming of becoming a farmer, also cleared whatever they were working on and bid me goodnight. I hardly noticed their exit. I had the whole story in my head, and it was nearing its conclusion.

I can't remember now how many sheets I typed. Perhaps thirty, perhaps enough to fill two columns of newsprint. I tapped on Samuels' door and pushed it open when I heard his gruff response. He was clearly not there because he was waiting for me. He still had work to do, and it didn't much matter to him what time of day it was. Without looking up, he extended a hand, into which I surrendered what might be the passport to the rest of my life. Then I tiptoed out and closed the door behind me.

One word had eluded me, compelling me to leave a blank space in the narrative, to which I returned once the *mot juste* sprang into my head. Thinking back on it again, now that it was too late for changes, it suddenly occurred to me how wrong, how hasty, how foolish I had been. I sank my head on my arms, anticipating that this one mistake had ruined a career.

It came, minutes later, the roar of disapproval I had expected to hear. I returned to Samuels' desk, where he chewed on a pencil, holding out the offending sheet with the tips of his fingers. He was a small, thick-set man, quite Churchillian in appearance and every bit as daunting. "Anti-*neurotics* division?" he barked.

"Anti-narcotics, Sir," I countered. "I knew it as soon as I left your desk."

He glared at me over his glasses, returning the sheet to its proper place in the sheaf. "The piece is too long, of course."

"I expect so."

"But difficult to know what to leave out, isn't it, when there's so much to say?"

"Exactly, Sir."

"Well that's my job." And from the red pencil marks on my virgin copy I knew he had commenced it. "You can go now. Be here at nine tomorrow. I hope they're treating you right in there."

"I'm sure they will, Sir. Good night."

On the other side of the door I would have danced, had it been possible to do so without the sound of it making it obvious that I did.

Case of the Missing Bicycle

Memory is eventually reduced to episodes. The long barren in-betweens recede into a vague background blur. One such episode further threatened an end to my budding career at its outset, more effectively than the inadvertent use of "neurotics" could ever have done. It was the case of the missing bicycle.

I had by now settled into a tedious routine of weddings, flower shows and school sports. The latter category was as far as I was permitted to go, once it was discovered that my enthusiastic report of a home win for the local soccer team was the exact reverse of the outcome, because I had mistaken their colours for those of the opposing side. Denial of a potential future on the "sports desk" came as a huge relief.

Among this less promising grist to my mill, obituaries stood out like strawberries in a cereal bowl. I used to haunt the local undertakers, yearning to discover that somebody reasonably eminent had quit our mortal coil, so that I could compress a lifetime of distinguished service into a pertinent column or two. Besotted by empire, and still nostalgic for *Boys Own Paper* tales of derring-do, I hankered for lives less ordinary, lived for the most part far away from these shores. I prided myself on my graveside manner, my ability to talk widows—and sometimes widowers—into surrendering reams of reminiscence. In that sense, I fulfilled to the letter the unflattering description of reporters as ghouls and vultures.

Always the less attractive sequel was the funeral itself, which required me to stand, notebook in hand and black band around my arm, at the door of the church, chapel, synagogue or whatever, taking down the names of mourners and being extremely careful to spell them correctly and not miss any. Old Samuels was an encyclopaedia of local knowledge, carrying in his brain the entire contents of the local telephone directory. How could Miss Rosaline Allston *not* have been there? She was well known as an old flame of the deceased, who had gone into virtual seclusion on learning of his marriage. Had I looked inside, in case she had slipped through from the annexe?

The timing of my arrival, in order to record the wording of the more prominent wreaths, might sometimes prove a shade premature. On one occasion I was directed to the house of the all too recently deceased, where a pre-funeral gathering of relatives and friends was barely under way. There I was left alone with the open coffin in the parlour, stooping over floral arrangements to try and read often indecipherable handwriting. Caught off balance, in my effort to avoid stepping on a wreath that was barring my progress, I dropped my notebook and leaned out to steady myself against the coffin, which swayed ominously on its trestle supports before shaking itself violently back into place with a disconcerting crash. Casting an anxious look inside, in case the corpse had become noticeably disarrayed, I was aware of a highly pregnant pause next door, before the conversation nervously resumed.

On the day the office bicycle went missing, it was drizzling. The residence of the lately departed lay on the seafront, not far from Bexhill's De La Warr Pavilion. Inaugurated the year I was born, and reputedly the first example of Bauhaus-inspired architecture in Britain, the pavilion was named after the eighth Earl De La Warr, who in May 1902 persuaded the Automobile Club of Great Britain and Ireland, subsequently the Royal Automobile Club, to make Bexhill the "Birth Place of British Motor Racing".

On that occasion thousands had lined the seafront for the novelty of witnessing snorting, panting behemoths of steam and gasoline pitted against each other for the first automobile races ever conducted on British soil. Among two hundred or so entrants were Lord Northcliffe, founder of the *Daily Mail,* in his Mercedes, and Monsieur Leon Serpollet, clocking the fastest speed of fifty four miles per hour in his steam-driven "Easter Egg". The success of the meeting encouraged De

La Warr to pursue more ambitious endeavours that would have enshrined Bexhill's pole position as motoring centre for British racing drivers of the day. By 1906 plans had been drawn up for a circuit extending almost to Beachy Head, with garages, restaurants and hotel accommodations. These were abruptly shelved the following year, when the motoring set moved to the new Brooklands circuit.

The lustre of pioneering automotive achievement had faded over the half century before my assignment on the Bexhill promenade that rainy September day in 1950. The wide Edwardian elegance of the Marina and De La Warr Parade spread wet and empty alongside the even duller expanse of beach and sea. Given those conditions, I had decided to expedite the expedition by helping myself to the office bicycle, found leaning against the wall of the garage immediately below the editorial office in Western Road. What I did *not* notice was the ragged "logbook" and pencil, dangling from a hook above, along with the bicycle clips. Nor was I aware that we were required to record in this logbook the times at which the bicycle was removed and returned, together with the signatures of the persons responsible.

I parked the expropriated bicycle against a lamppost outside my destination, conducted my interview and emerged half an hour later into brilliant sunlight. The unexpected contrast was so uplifting in its affirmation of renewal and continuity, following the termination of yet another life destined to find its brief record in our news columns, that I walked back to the office lost in contemplation of the endless recycling of existence.

A week went by, during which several more stories passed over my desk, before I became aware anything was amiss. I was surrounded by an escalating air of bewilderment as to what had become of the office bicycle. Most of my colleagues had long outlived its usefulness, graduating to their own modes of transportation, so that the bicycle had by now become the near exclusive preserve of Mr. Samuels. Its unaccountable absence had caused him considerable inconvenience, for it remained his sole mode of conveyance.

The bicycle clips were still on the hook, and his was the last name recorded in the logbook. The only conclusion to be drawn was that the velocipede had been stolen. I was delegated to report the theft to the local police station, and ascertain if they had recovered any vehicle matching its description.

The duty constable affirmed that such a bicycle was indeed in their possession. It had been surrendered to the station the previous week, by someone who found it leaning against a lamppost on the Marina. It was in good condition, showing no sign of damage. The shock of recognition was such that I could not conceal from him an explanation of how it came to be there. I even obliged him by entering a brief note of the circumstances in his register. Hence there was no point feigning ignorance on my return to the office.

My mind reeling with the implications of my inescapable admission, it never occurred to me to *ride* the bicycle back to its normal place of repose. I *walked* it back, reflecting on all I might have accomplished had I been permitted to continue earning twenty five shillings a week at the *Bexhill-on-Sea Observer*.

Samuels heard me out in complete silence, which persisted as I remained standing before him. Eventually he allowed himself a "Dear, dear, dear!", shook his head in disbelief, and dismissed me.

Our ex-RAF assistant editor voiced a reaction a shade more expressive. He said "Tch, tch, tch", as he might if he were back in the cockpit of his Hawker Hurricane, made suddenly aware of a Messerschmitt Bf-109 on his tail. The others were silent, but Mike Green rolled his eyes expressively towards the ceiling. I felt I should begin clearing out my drawer, not that there was much in it. Evidence of my brief occupation was scant in the extreme.

Samuels' voice summoned my return to his office. He regarded me gravely, informing me he had weighed my case very carefully and had reached the conclusion that I deserved a second chance, if only because I had been so honest in confessing my incomprehensible absence of mind. I would be denied use of the office bicycle for the next fortnight, following which I would only be permitted to loan it in strict conformity with the rules, logging each instance in the approved manner.

Experiments with Television

Granddad and Nana Moss had moved from Barnstaple to take up residence in Bexhill Old Town. Once a week I was invited to take lunch with them, and would steel myself for more of William George Moss's predictable reminiscences. I wish now that I had taken the initiative of asking for further information on other aspects of his career. He had been caught, I knew, in a mustard gas attack in the trenches during the First War, but he didn't appear willing to talk about his wartime experiences at all.

I shouldn't have been, but nevertheless *was* surprised to learn he was a Freemason, and this was only because I raised the subject of Freemasonry as one that bewildered me because of its dependence on secret rituals, which I felt signified an appeal to immature minds. He did not take kindly to that interpretation.

Once again he was in competition with my father, busy constructing a slightly larger television set from war surplus radar parts than Dad had managed to do from the sources available to him. But it pleased me to know Dad had assembled his the year before, between bouts of electrocution in his tiny boot cupboard of a workroom beneath the stairs. Granddad had more room in which to move.

Hastings had been the birthplace of television. It was here, in his attic, that the pioneer of television broadcasting, John Logie Baird, began his experiments with the medium back in 1923. "An old tea chest formed a base to carry the motor, which rotated a circular cardboard disk. The disc was cut out of an old hat box, and a darning needle served as a spindle. An empty biscuit box housed the projection lamp. The necessary bull's eye lenses were bought from a bicycle shop at a cost of fourpence each."

Dad had obtained most of his parts from the same war surplus outlet that had supplied my aircraft recognition models, but his cathode-ray tube was only six inches across, and coloured a bright green. Nevertheless it was a marvel to us gathered before it, waiting for the traffic around Piccadilly Circus to be dramatically freeze-framed by an announcer declaring "Stop!" in order to introduce *In Town Tonight*.

The catchy signature music to *In Town Tonight* was Eric Coates' *Knightsbridge March*. Years later in Hong Kong, I would meet the composer's son, the writer Austin Coates, who told me how his father was summoned from his darkroom in his Baker Street flat one evening when *In Town Tonight* was launched. Austin's mother recognised the music and said "Eric, they're playing something of yours on the radio; I can't think what it is."

Eric emerged from the darkroom, where he was developing a batch of film, listened a moment and said "No, neither can I." and went back again. "Half an hour later," recalled Austin, "my mother called him again and said they were repeating his music, which sounded as if it were being used as a signature tune. Dad called out 'Well I don't suppose it will do it any harm!'." It didn't. Twenty thousand letters descended on the BBC mail box, requesting the title of the piece and the composer's name.

Early black-and white (or in our case green-and-white) television shows engendered a fierce loyalty among us viewers; *Billy Cotton and his Bandstand*, *The Grove Family* and their naïvely simplistic soapbox affairs, *Panorama* with Richard Dimbleby, Arthur Askey, Dickie Henderson and Diana Decker in *Before Your Very Eyes*, Philip Harben teaching us how to cook, the thriller serials entitled *Francis Durbridge Presents*, Eamonn Andrews' *This is Your Life* and, in our collective view best of all, *What's My Line?* with David Nixon, Lady Isobelle Barnet,

Barbara Kelly and the irascible Gilbert Harding. We would take bets as to how long it would take Gilbert to reach boiling point.

Critics have accused television of disrupting family life, but we saw it as a gathering point around which family life revolved. That it never took over our lives was perhaps due to the fact that broadcasting hours were so limited as to provide only a brief interlude in the midst of the day's routine, and we never had to argue over what to watch because there was only the one channel.

Final Solution to the Pigeon Problem

At the end of the summer vacation, when it was time for me to commence my last term at Hastings Grammar, I had a heart-to-heart with Samuels. He felt I had the potential to further improve my journalistic skills, and if that was what I wanted there really wasn't much point in going back to school. He recommended, and I decided, that I might as well continue my apprenticeship. I had my father's and grandfather's examples to serve as precedents, and I could certainly count on their support. My scholastic record had been good but not brilliant, and best in precisely the area I wished to develop. I opted to stay on at the *Bexhill-on-Sea Observer*.

To reward me for that decision, Samuels offered me better assignments, trusting me with court reporting and the proceedings of the Bexhill Town Council. One court case that sticks in my mind concerned the unlawful use of a privately registered motor vehicle for the conduct of business transactions, in that it was employed to convey and deliver boxes of eggs.

"Good heavens, we can't have that!" spluttered the officiating magistrate, in his sensible brogues and country tweeds. He turned to his two fellow Justices of the Peace, seated beside him on the bench. "What an utterly ridiculous law. If that were to be strictly applied, I'm guilty of breaking it myself, every time I take my tomatoes to the local market." His fellow magistrates nodded in vigorous agreement. The court clerk cleared his throat and asked to approach the bench, where he crouched in a deferential stoop, lowering his voice and compelling all three to lean forward like gargoyles overhanging a hunchback. On learning what he had to say, the trio exchanged astonished glances and the one in tweeds addressed the defendant, informing him that, given the extenuating circumstances, his case was dismissed.

Municipal affairs were enlivened by a discussion of what to do about the pigeons that were taking over Egerton Park, making it impossible to sit on benches covered in their droppings. Various proposals were put forward, including noise-making machines and food additives that would curb population growth. Through all of this, one member of the municipal staff, whose name and office now escapes me, sat silently listening, contemplating a more radical solution.

The following day, little old ladies braving the chill air with their newspapers, which they spread cautiously over benches before endeavouring to seat themselves, were treated to the spectacle of a man in a raincoat tossing crumbs on the grass from a brown paper bag. Given the prevailing mood of opposition to the whole idea of consorting with pigeons, they thought it kindly of at least one citizen to display such consideration. Smiling with approval, they watched flocks of birds settle about this benefactor, pushing each other aside to feast greedily. When sufficient had gathered about him, the man abandoned his bag and produced from his raincoat a double-barrel shotgun, with which he let fly at close range. Scores of bloodied pigeons lay threshing feebly at his feet while elderly spectators swooned in horror.

But Bexhill was that kind of place; disarmingly ingenuous on the surface, but concealing hidden and sometimes alarming passions. Remaining unresolved through all the time I was there was the mystery of the elderly Tarzan of Cooden Beach, described as fit and wiry despite his years, who would descend naked from the branches of wayside trees, gibber at passing female pedestrians and vanish into the vegetation without a trace other than a faint scent of aftershave.

This was, after all, the quiet seaside resort that inspired the Goons' classic radio skit on the *Dreaded Batter Pudding Hurler of Bexhill-on-Sea*. Said Seagoon: "I turned to see the speaker. He was a tall man wearing sensible feet, and a head to match. He was dressed in the full white outfit of a Savoy chef. Around his waist were tied several thousand cooking instruments. And behind him he pulled a portable gas stove from which issued forth the smell of Batter Pudding. I watched the strange man as he pulled his gas stove away into the darkness. But I couldn't waste time watching him. My job was to find the Dreaded Batter Pudding Hurler".

"More Things in Heaven and Earth, Petruccio"

To get to work, I used to commute on the train from Ore Station, lying at the foot of the ravine below Mount Pleasant and our home in adjoining St. George's Road. It was a short, steep walk, but its monotonous repetition, as autumn stretched into winter and the day narrowed into a brief slab of grey between two cliffs of darkness, settled like an early tombstone laid across my soul. I remembered what my father had said, about work being something that had to be done in order to survive, and I felt doomed to drudgery for the rest of my life.

J.D. Salinger's *Catcher in the Rye* wasn't published until the following year, and I wouldn't get to read it until much later. But when I did, I identified immediately with the adolescent tribulations of Holden Caulfield. When I was the same age, I too felt that the world around me had not catered for my needs, but was bent on following its own wilful course in another direction entirely. I was aching with a hunger I could not comprehend.

I would sit by the window of an otherwise invariably empty railway compartment, staring past the legend *"gnikoms on"*, inscribed into the glass to be read from the other side. Rattling through the tunnel between Hastings and St. Leonards, I wondered if the face reflected there would age, and wrinkle and grow grey through the years that lay ahead, in exactly that setting, in exactly this endlessly repeated cycle. And I remembered the blinkered ox, ceaselessly toiling to water the parched fields of Alighar.

Arrived at Bexhill station, I would glance across the tracks at the other platform and see the same young man standing there, as he did every day, waiting for the train in the opposite direction, trapped in a reversed mirror image of my life. I would muse upon the subtle difference that dictated I should come here and he should go there, to whence I came. What chance fate had determined that reversal? And did he rebel against it as much as I?

Big, heavy-set, and clear-headed, with feet planted firmly on the ground, Mike Green seemed to have emerged unscathed from his own trouble-free pubescence, picking up a rich repertoire of rugger songs and dirty stories en route. He was the last person in whom I could confide the problems of my own agitated adolescence. Yet even though he couldn't have guessed what was going on inside me, I was grateful to him for his efforts to let some light into my gloom.

He had a way of convincing me, with enormous solemnity and patience, that I had completely missed the point with so many conclusions I had reached in my brief, uninformed life. Deliberately garbling his Shakespeare, he would say "There are more things in heaven and earth, Petruccio, than are dreamt of in your philosophy". And he would find in me the perfect gullible victim for every practical joke in the book. He knew them all, and I knew none. He would send me to the stationers to ask for a "long weight", which he assured me was a very necessary piece of office equipment designed to hold miscellaneous objects in place on one's desk. The stationer, tipped off in advance, would take note of my request and keep me waiting until the penny sank.

On another occasion he rubbed his elbows, claiming they were sore from too much typing. Thrusting a ten shilling note into my hands, he urged me to hurry across to the chemist and buy him some elbow grease. I scorned the suggestion that any such product existed, since even *I* knew it was just a expression to signify hard work or mental effort. Turning to our colleagues, Mike gestured helplessly as if to inquire what was to be done with one naïve and misinformed enough to believe that elbow grease was a mere figure of speech. Preoccupied with work, both cast in my direction a look of infinite sympathy before burying themselves in their typewriters once more. So of course I ended up crossing the street to Boots, asking for elbow grease and suffering the humiliation of incredulous giggles from the girls behind the counter.

Such diversions probed but fleeting rays into my gathering melancholy. Outside of my work, all my attention, my reading matter, my focus, my aspirations lay beyond my narrow confines, indeed geographically far removed from this still unloved land to which I felt so unjustly condemned. I would invent spurious assignments to get away from the office, cycling along the empty Bexhill promenade, where twilight already trespassed into afternoon, wishing that George Lush, in his Klemm monoplane, would swoop down from the sky and bear me off across the channel to the wide world stretching far down south, into sun and warmth and colour and life.

Occasionally I would pass a solitary car, parked by the road with its bonnet aligned like some reversed compass needle on our polar opposite, and a huddled figure, alone or accompanied by a companion, in the front seat, gazing out to sea. Was he—were they—sunk in the same nostalgia for the adventurous exploits of the Great British people? Did they feel impelled to stare outwards, across an ocean once commanded by Great British fleets, rather than inwards at the sunken shadow of the spirit that had fired such enthusiasms?

Now that their people had withdrawn from the global stage, flying distress signals, expansionist vistas were out of fashion, something to be viewed privately, guiltily, from a parked car on a near-deserted promenade. Even the supposedly still English Channel was reduced to the flimsiest of barriers, incapable of defending them against the geopolitics of a Europe looming much more palpably than in the days of Napoleon or Hitler.

Lost in such thoughts, I would risk running into other stationary vehicles, so that it would come as no great surprise to learn, a few years later, that my brother Paul had done precisely that, at almost precisely that point. Following me into the *Bexhill-on-Sea Observer*, when I departed to serve my obligatory National Service, he too would cycle along the promenade, lost in thought. And one evening he cycled straight into the back of a car, parked without lights. The impact was of such force that it ripped all the tendons in his muscular left thigh, causing damage that would require surgery, leave a scar from groin to knee and prevent his participation in sports for months to come.

Dreams of Tank Turrets and Guardsman's Uniforms

Two years of National Service was still a compulsory requirement for all young men reaching the age of eighteen, unless they could produce sound reasons for deferring that obligation in order to complete a university education. Denied any academic pretext, I could only envisage sound reasons for advancing it, impatient for a posting overseas, to some exotic locale where the sun shone and the colours were more vibrant. I would go to sleep seeing myself in the uniform of the Horse Guards or the Grenadiers; preferably with my head sticking out from the turret of a tank. Oddly enough, despite my enthusiasm for aviation, I could not picture myself in the contemporary Royal Air Force, with its increasing dependence upon jet fighters and bombers, and technical aids to navigation. There was no longer any romance in the air. Everything was performed at near supersonic speed, before one even had time to think, leave alone consider the view.

Looking across the desk in the editorial office of the *Bexhill-on-Sea Observer*, at a recently retired squadron leader turned journalist, I reflected on the demise of that sporting camaraderie that had existed in earlier generations of flyers; of the kind briefly established between George Lush and his adversary Hermann Wilhelm Göring. Nowadays you didn't even get to see your opponent's *face*, so you couldn't tell *who* he might be, leave alone whether you stood a sporting chance with him if you happened to run short of ammunition.

In the army it was probably no better. Military men were hardly renowned for their sportsmanship. But I felt there were at least better prospects of an overseas posting; perhaps to Malaya, where the communist-inspired Emergency was still at its height, rather than Korea, where the war was already in its final stages (the Armistice that ended it was declared on 27 July 1953; a month before I commenced my military service). Newsreel coverage of winter conditions in Korea was not reassuring.

Malaya looked tropical, and infinitely more enticing. Having seen Jack Hawkins and Claudette Colbert in *The Planter's Wife*, and having already been smitten by Claudette in *Three Came Home*, both films taking the Malaysian Archipelago as their setting, I fancied the thought of fending off communist insurgents attacking the barbed wire perimeter of some remote jungle plantation. I might just get my tank there in time to save the place from being overrun, and rescue Claudette, or someone like her.

My papers duly arrived, instructing me to report for a medical examination at Brighton, where I joined a line-up waiting to be pinched and prodded, to drop our pants and cough on demand. None of the others looked overjoyed to be there, so I curbed my own enthusiasm for fear of seeming indecently eager. I was found to be A1 and—I hoped—excellent material for active duty. Filling in the form which invited my preference, I asked to be posted to any of the Guards regiments currently serving overseas. Then I returned to work and impatiently bided my time to learn my fate.

I opened the long-awaited letter to discover I have been assigned to the Royal Army Pay Corps, and that there was no possibility of appealing this decision. Only later did I find out that the army invariably directed you to the exact opposite of your stated choice, on the basis that your choice had nothing to do with your competence. In my case they could not have been more mistaken. Any occupation involving accounting procedures, or merely calculating numbers and figures, was quite beyond my capacity.

Left to our own Devizes

The objective of the Royal Army Pay Corps training camp at Devizes, in Wiltshire, was to bludgeon body and mind into such a state of insensibility that mere survival became one's sole preoccupation. In that, it differed in no marked degree from training facilities for any other corps or regiment, except that Devizes did it better. Enduring this hell on earth, and moving on to the rest of one's life, became the goal of every recruit unfortunate enough to be posted there.

I had earlier fallen in love with Wiltshire, from holidays spent with my Uncle Len and Aunt Zena. They had returned with their children from a posting in Germany and, after brief sojourns in other parts of England, settled into Bulford Army Camp on the Salisbury Plain, within walking distance of Stonehenge. Len was at that time still with the Royal Signals, holding the rank of Major. Together with my cousins Jacqui and Gordon, I would roam the Wiltshire Downs, relishing their stark, almost treeless contours, affording vistas wider than I had encountered elsewhere in England.

Larger in area, but smaller in population, than the average English county, Wiltshire is composed chiefly of chalk hills, the highest of which are in the north, where an escarpment overlooks the Vale of the White Horse. To me it was a landscape steeped in antiquity. The stone circles at Avebury were ancient long before Stonehenge was constructed, and most experts believed Avebury remained more important than Stonehenge when both were at their early bronze age peak of importance. As for the labour that went into its construction, Silbury Hill, the highest ancient construction in Europe, also surpassed Stonehenge. The creation of that hill, over one hundred and thirty feet high and covering an area of five and a half acres, is estimated to have demanded about four million man hours.

The nearby megalithic Long Barrow of West Kennet, entombing important inhabitants of the settlement at Windmill Hill, was constructed more than five thousand years ago, becoming a sealed and disused ancient monument before the laying of even the first stone of Stonehenge. Yet Stonehenge, of course, received—and is still accorded—the lion's share of attention.

The area surrounding Bulford Camp fell within the portion of Salisbury Plain given over to army manoeuvres. It was perfect tank country, which accounted in part for my fascination with the armoured regiments. But the martial nature of the terrain had a genuinely historical basis, for Wiltshire was the scene of important battles between the Celts and Saxons, and later between the Saxons and Danes, culminating in Alfred's final victory at Edington in 878 AD. The county also saw much fighting in the battle for supremacy between Stephen and Matilda, and again during the Civil War, especially at the major Battle of Roundway Down, near Devizes. Conflict sputtered on well into the 19th century, when Wiltshire became embroiled in the Swing Riots, during which agricultural workers pitted themselves against the Industrial Age, smashing machinery they saw as threatening their employment.

In those early fifties, when I first roamed Salisbury Plain, I would come across the corpses of rabbits that had died agonising deaths from myxomatosis, the man-engineered viral disease that had just been introduced into Britain from Australia. Their pathetic, wasted bodies looked like the remains of unacceptable sacrifices offered to the gods of ancient Druids. Within two years myxomatosis had reduced Australia's rabbit population from some six hundred million to fewer than a hundred million animals.

At Devizes my perception of Wiltshire quickly shrank to a wire-enclosed encampment composed of barrack huts, a parade ground, mess halls, an assault course and little else. Issued with a uniform, bedding, mess kit and a serial number in place of a name, it struck me that most penitentiaries would seem more glamorous than this. The serial number 22905648 remains branded on my brain. More than fifty years later, it still takes precedence over the innumerable telephone addresses, car registration plates, bank accounts and passport numbers issued to me since.

The dehumanisation of our National Service intake (we all rated seniority by the intake to which we belonged) began the moment we arrived. My platoon was unfortunate enough to become the responsibility of Sergeant Wrattan. If he had a first name, it would have been pointless for us to know it, because familiarity would neither have been desired not encouraged. "Rotten Wrattan" we called him, and if he were aware of it I'm sure he would have thoroughly approved. The parade ground was invariably full of platoons being drilled simultaneously by their respective sergeants, most of whom kept pace with their charges to observe their form at close hand. But not Wrattan. He prided himself on his ability to remain stationary, at a point approximately in the centre of the drilling fields, and bark instructions in a voice of such distinctive harshness, volume and penetration that it would carry above all else.

Mostly this was the case, and we would dutifully thread a course through infinite permutations of other platoons, sometimes narrowly averting collision with some last-minute left or about-turn, until we once more arrived before him to be thoroughly abased within raucous earshot of the entire parade ground. But there was one occasion when, at an extreme distance from where he stood, his order reached us in conjunction with another from a sergeant closer at hand, so that both became unintelligible. The result was utter confusion. One half of the platoon turned right while the other half turned left, both sections shambling to a stop as we realised what had happened.

Wrattan ran towards us, removed his beret, flung it to the concrete and jumped on it, shrieking hysterically. It was an awesome spectacle, calculated of course to render us incontinent with terror. But I couldn't take it seriously. I even wondered if he was committing a breach of regulations by damaging army property. His beret, by this time, was developing holes from his repeated trampling. I half hoped that a team of white-clad men would arrive with a stretcher to forcibly remove this gibbering lunatic, but the army seldom fulfils such wishes. Whether it was play-acting was really beside the point. The result was that we were marched and marched and marched, well past twilight and suppertime.

Infinite Rottenness of Wrattan

Wrattan had other foibles equally odious. He loved gasmask training. After running us around its perimeter until we were gasping for air, he would fill a small, crowded cabin with tear gas and herd us into it at the point of a bayonet. Locking the door behind us, he would leave us gagging until the order to don gasmasks, aside from being too late, would exacerbate our predicament by further reducing our oxygen intake.

For our initial circuit of the assault course, he graded us according to height, the tallest being the first off the mark. I realised Wrattan had long chosen, as his particular victim, a thin, lanky youth about an inch taller than my six foot one and three-quarters. This unfortunate had the limb coordination one associates with gangling harlequin puppets, and was the frequent target of Wrattan's sadism. On this occasion, carrying his rifle with bayonet to the fore, ready to engage the sandbags we knew lay somewhere in wait for us, the victim set off at a lolloping gait, leapt a couple of ditches, crawled under the netting stretched across another, surmounted a hillock and disappeared.

We waited and waited. The minutes went by, but there was no sign of the soldier's return. Wrattan glanced at his watch and ordered me to follow in his wake. On the other side of the hillock I found the youth sprawled unconscious in a ditch. His helmet had rolled away from his head, which had caught the edge of a low, corrugated iron retaining wall. There was a jagged gash above one eyebrow which brought on a spasm of my blood phobia. I fought this off and reversed direction, calling back, from the top of the hillock, to report a serious accident.

Wrattan   screamed   at   me.   "Who   told   you   to   stop? Who—told—you—to—STOP? KEEP RUNNING!"

I continued, followed by "NEXT!" and "NEXT!" and "NEXT!" as others were dispatched after me. Only when we were all back where we started did Wrattan walk the course to the spot where the accident had occurred. Mercifully the victim recovered without serious ill effects, but from what I had glimpsed of him he could well have been dying.

We discussed what to do about Wrattan. Surely the man was psychotic? This was way beyond the normal bounds of sadism practised in most army training establishments. We could endure being made to clean the yellowed walls of urinals with nothing but our finger nails. We could even accept having to cut the grass on hands and knees with razor blades. This was all part of the cumulative, ongoing chronicle of the army's inhumanity to its raw recruits. But being secured for prolonged periods in close confinement, down the inspection well of the sewage outlet, with the lid screwed down on top of us—wasn't that evidence of a seriously unhinged mind?

And what about the time when, on a blazing hot, late summer's day, he had made us wear greatcoats and full pack and run on the spot, with rifles elevated at arms' length over our heads, in a laundry drying room with the temperature notched to the highest point on the dial? What about those of us whose efforts to keep our thighs parallel to the ground had finally faltered until, one by one, we passed out? Were these the actions of a sane man?

The Pay Corps may not have been every national serviceman's dream posting, but it wasn't *that* notorious. Founded in 1878, as the Army Pay Department, it had acquired a reputation for fairness and dependability, as implied by its motto *"Fide et Fiducia"*. The regimental quick march *Imperial Echoes*, composed by Arnold Safroni, and adopted by the corps only a year before our intake was called up, even had a certain appealing resonance to one such as myself. How could such a basically honourable institution permit the likes of our sergeant to besmirch its good name? Was there someone in the War Office to whom we could write about Wrattan?

Life seldom seems less fair than when one is at the bottom of the pecking order in an establishment where pecking is the very basis of existence. We could only accept Wrattan as the crocodile in our slough of despond. He was the demon of the deep we had to cross in order to get to the wicket gate at the far end of our purgatory in boot camp.

Telltale Sketchbook

Although I lacked a diary, I still had with me a sketchbook in which I could depict our tribulations as a bolster against insanity. For this purpose at least, Wrattan proved a godsend. His face was a caricaturist's dream, dominated by a large, hooked nose over fleshy, superciliously cruel lips, set above a receding chin. But his most prominent feature were his ears, which doubtless contributed to his keenness of hearing on the parade ground, so that every slightest misstep, a mere hundredth of a second out of synchronisation with the rest of the platoon, would bring him tearing down on us like an African bull elephant in heat. They were ears that flapped in the breeze, sensing its drifts and currents.

I loved drawing him. I could hardly wait for those brief moments before lights out, when we had completed our seemingly unending chores and could snatch some respite for conversation, for a cigarette, even for a letter home. I used them to draw Wrattan, in all his permutations of brutality, mindless oppression and uncontrollable rage; Wrattan stamping on his beret, Wrattan tearing at his hair, Wrattan bayoneting our behinds into the gas-filled chamber of horrors.

Those with whom I shared my barrack room were familiar with my work, and in the habit of passing my sketchbook around, so all could enjoy the satisfaction of seeing Wrattan reduced to a comic book cartoon. I therefore thought nothing of leaving the book lying on my bed, opened to reveal its latest additions, when I headed with my towel to my evening ablutions. I had not counted on Wrattan making a snap inspection during my absence.

The room was long and narrow, with collapsible iron spring beds on both sides, painstakingly and uniformly made up to display layer-cake stacks of neatly folded blankets and sheets. At the foot of each bed was a locker, containing the current tenant's kit in scrupulously arranged symmetry, ready for just such scrutiny as Wrattan was bent on conducting that particular evening. I returned from my shower and shave, whistling the Toreodor's song from *Carmen*, to note, even before entering to room, that an unaccountable silence had settled upon it.

I stood in the doorway, frozen in my tracks. On both sides of the room, my platoon were standing stiffly to attention by their beds. Those that had not as yet undressed had their thumb knuckles aligned with the seams of their trousers. All, no matter what their state of deshabille, looked like pillars of salt that had collectively looked upon Sodom and Gomorrah and were petrified by what they saw.

Sprawled on his back upon my bed, his boots on my blankets, was Wrattan, leafing through the pages of my book. I caught the cautious, sidelong glances of my friends, conveying their accusations for landing them in the proverbial four letters. I was too paralyzed to consider anything except my impending death, and the manner of its execution.

In the dead silence, I became aware of a low, almost subterranean rumbling, which increased in volume and intensity until I detected it was unmistakably issuing from Wrattan. He was chuckling. Turning again to the front of the book, he embarked on a second perusal, a slow smile of enjoyment spreading across his latex-upholstered lips. The chuckle turned to laughter; one of the most terrifying sounds I could ever dread to hear.

Finally he demanded to know on whose bed he was lying. Since there was no point delaying the inevitable, I stepped forward and admitted responsibility, both for the bed and the book. He stood up and examined me, head to toe, as I stood shivering with nothing but my towel around my waist and my toiletries in my hand.

He nodded slowly. "Not bad. Not bad. But I'd like to sit for a proper portrait. And I think some of my friends would like you to do the same for them." He handed back the book. "Let's say every Wednesday evening, in the sergeant's mess. You'll be excused whatever else you may have on your time table."

"Yes, Sergeant," I managed to find the vocal cords to utter.

Still chuckling, he left, his snap inspection abandoned only halfway through.

I couldn't say anything further. The silence continued until, very slowly, we began to relax, looking at each other in amazement. Then the chorus of recriminations began. "You stupid bastard, you could have had us all *killed*!", "Don't think he means it for a moment. He's only playing some vicious *game*.", "We'll all be up on a charge, so fast our feet won't touch the ground.", "He's surely going to have our guts for garters *this* time! How could you be so careless?"

How indeed? The possibility that he might actually have meant what he said seemed almost more appalling than the likelihood that it was indeed some vicious game. To be seduced into the enemy stronghold, on the pretext of sketching portraits of the lions already circling for the kill! But the order had been given, and the next Wednesday was less than a week away. I decided I was desperately in need of reassurance. I requested, and was granted, a 24-hour pass for the weekend, so I could visit my uncle and aunt in Bulford and appeal for Len's advice.

Ever Capricious Jacqueline

Len and Zena couldn't get over how well I looked. I was leaner, fitter, darker—although Zena wasn't too pleased on *that* point—and obviously bursting with vitality. Much as she might applaud my general state of health, my aunt would have preferred me looking quite a bit less tanned, and thus in danger of giving the game away. She was always wary of the ease with which I began to "show colour" the moment I was subjected to the sun. It was all too revealing a family trait to make a welcome appearance in the life of a respectable army officer's wife; almost as bad as my habit of shaking my legs under the table "in typical Bengali fashion" whenever we had company for dinner.

Nevertheless, both she and Len agreed that my spell of National Service was clearly doing me good. I hadn't stopped to think about it, so preoccupied was I with the objective of simply staying alive. But they were right. I was feeling better than I had felt in years. Forced out of solitary seclusion, into a mix of young men my age from all walks of life and all corners of the British Isles, I was at last learning the social skills necessary for acceptance into the basic tribal unit. I had even acquired friends, who stood up for me against my accusers over the episode of the telltale sketchbook.

Jacqueline, now nearing her sixteenth birthday, looked stunningly self-composed and vivacious, with the slightest hint of a smile playing about her lips at the sight of her cousin in the uniform of a mere private from some minor branch of the armed forces that kept the army marching on its proverbial stomach. It was doubly amusing to her that I, of all people, should be both a soldier and—as she saw it—a trainee accountant dealing with Dickensian ledgers and columns of figures. None of the young men already beginning to chase after her were lower than the rank of subaltern, and all belonged to corps and regiments a great deal more distinguished than the RAPC.

I had pursued a love-hate relationship with Jacqui for years. She could be a delightful companion on long country walks, musing with me on the origins of Stonehenge, the devastation caused by myxomatosis, or the possibility that man might one day set foot on the moon. Alternatively, without warning and exactly like her mother, she might suddenly take offence at some ill-considered remark that would place her beyond my unworthy reach for days. She was always intensely passionate about some new cause, credulous to the point of gullibility, vulnerable to charlatans espousing every faddist conceit that human cunning might devise—until, much later in life, she was destined to go to the opposite extreme, withdrawing into a faith that would concede no explanations but those contained in the Bible.

She was also one of the few truly psychic people I have ever met; a trait she shared with her younger brother Gordon. When he was little more than ten years old, staying with her parents in a rented house in Germany, during Len's protracted tour of postwar duty in that newly divided country, Gordon had found it impossible to sleep at night. He would repeatedly wake from the same nightmare in which he would be lying in bed, staring up at a pair of feet dangling through a trapdoor in the ceiling of his attic bedroom.

Finally his parents moved him to another room where his sleep was less disturbed. But their curiosity aroused, they inquired into the history of the house and discovered that an earlier occupant had hanged himself through the attic trapdoor.

I asked Jacqui what I should do about Wrattan's instruction to play commissioned artist in dangerously non-commissioned company. She said I had no alternative but to accept. She believed I would come to no harm. The weekend sped by, to the point where the last connecting bus had already left on the Sunday evening, and there seemed no way I could get back to camp before my pass expired. Len borrowed his dispatch rider's motorcycle and rode it himself, still in his Major's apparel, with me in my private's uniform on the pillion behind him. I wondered how he might explain this had he been stopped by the military police, but he got me back to Devizes undetected and unharmed.

More Bullring than Lions' Den

The "lions' den" proved a lot less terrifying than I had supposed it would. This particular sergeant's mess looked disarmingly ordinary, with about half its members in uniform and half not, all of them behaving as one would expect if they were in a regular public saloon bar. I had anticipated that the conversation would comprise titillating accounts of how this one or that one had got his squad to really shit their pants at the firing range, or cut their fingers enough to bleed during weapons instruction. I had expected descriptions of how many recruits had passed out in the line-up for inoculations, and how many had fled the cinema to throw up after compulsory screening of the educational film on sexually transmitted diseases, with its close focus on genitalia in the last stages of syphilis.

But I was proved wrong. They had left their parade ground manner at the door, Like our own, their conversation largely concerned plans for the next weekend pass, or how many days they still had to serve before their discharge. There were the usual ribald stories, of course, but more in demand were anecdotes of where they were and what they were doing before the Army caught up with them.

When the discussion turned to their charges, us "squaddies" under their command, the tone was more of sorrow than of anger. But a sorrow flavoured with bitterness. "Mummy's Boys" we were. All of us "sproggies" were "Mummy's Boys". As soon as our basic training was over, we'd slip back into our mamby-pamby ways, forget how to dismantle a sten gun, perform the sloppiest of salutes—and then only under extreme provocation—and think of nothing except the next pay day. Now was the only time in our lives when our betters were presented with the opportunity to make real men of us, or if not, at least ensure we got our balls knotted in the attempt.

I began to see what was happening here. Not all sergeants were enlisted men, but even those who weren't had become contaminated by the prevailing disdain for us conscripts, who were only in the army for two years because we *had* to be. This was an opportunity for payback time in the perpetual class struggle that had risen increasingly to the fore in postwar Britain. It was absurd, of course, to think national servicemen were from the upper or middle classes. More likely the majority of us were not. And I, with my St. George's Road background, was most definitely among the latter, no matter how misleading my manners and accent might appear. But the trouble was that the piss-elegant among us—and there were a few of those—stood out a mile, seeming so conspicuous as to constitute the norm. To our sergeants, we "sproggies" were collectively "them". So the many would pay for the imagined sins of the few.

All this went through my head as I endeavoured to fulfil my obligations amid the enemy, without being entirely sure how I was expected to set about this task. Did they want my portraits to flatter them? Judging by the exaggeratedly fierce expressions most of them adopted, as soon as they sat down to model for me, I supposed not. This supposition was quickly reinforced by the spectators clustered behind me. "Make his nose more prominent.", "Get his nostrils flaring, more like a bull in the ring.", "Emphasize his frown to make him more scary.", "My God, you've made him look like a cuddly *bear*! We can't have that."

Yes indeed, it was, when they willed it to be so, a world of distended nostrils and blazing braggadocio. One could almost smell the testosterone in the air. How far would it have flared had they only sensed the susceptibility of he who had unwillingly been corralled into their bullring, the quite genuine "Mummy's boy" who was struggling so hard not to appear the least bit piss-elegant?

It was difficult—for more reasons than they could imagine—to work under these conditions, but I found myself unexpectedly responding to the challenge. I readily let myself be guided by the majority vote. If they wanted exaggerated nastiness and macho mayhem, they would have it. I enjoyed lampooning them at their personal request. It was my own form of sanctioned payback, for all the humiliations we suffered at their hands. I threw myself into the task with mounting relish, using my own editorial red crayon to show blood dripping from slavering jaws and fingers, sometimes the dismembered limbs of hapless victims clenched in hairy fists, occasionally a string of skulls threaded in a necklace around a cannibal neck. The more I laid it on, the more they loved it.

And yet, once or twice, in the midst of all that guffawing, back-slapping, androgenically overdosed tribalism, I would find, in a quiet moment, a more reflective soul, happy to let me portray him as he was, perhaps with a dreamy, far-away look in his eyes, or just the faintest air of puzzlement as to how he came to find himself in those surroundings. Sensing a humanity I had too seldom discovered elsewhere in that room, I would yearn to have that sergeant in charge of my platoon. I could imagine, from his soft-spoken manner of speech, that he would achieve results far better than those obtained by the baying and bawling headbangers. With a few sane, intelligent instructions, clearly and concisely articulated, he could have me eating out of his hand.

Such a man would become the object of my fantasies as I lay sleepless at night, in a barrack room haunted by the snores of dog-tired comrades in arms. Yet oddly enough never to the point where I sought release for my pent-up sexuality. It must have been true that they put bromide in the tea to lower our libido.

Under Very Afflicting Circumstances

When we finally passed out of the wretched life of Devizes boot camp, I and a few others from my intake found ourselves posted to Woolwich Barracks, which cannot have changed one whit in appearance since an account of the "Dreadful Event at Woolwich Barracks" was published—exactly one hundred and twenty three years earlier to the day—in *Bell's Weekly Messenger* of Sunday, October 17, 1830. This read:

"Considerable excitement has for the last few days prevailed at Woolwich, by a rumour that Lieutenant Edward John Jones, of the Royal Horse Artillery, had been killed in a duel by a fellow brother-officer, and that it was the intention of his relatives to bury him without any investigation of the circumstances. This report, however, proved to be incorrect, although the deceased met his death from the effect of a pistol-shot under very afflicting circumstances.

"An inquest was held on Tuesday at the King's Arms Tavern, Woolwich, before Mr. Charles Junior. From the evidence it appeared, that on Tuesday night (the 6th instant) the deceased, who lived in his quarters at Woolwich Barracks, went to his bedroom in apparently good health and spirits. The next morning, about seven o'clock, William Sinclair, his groom, went into the room, as was his usual custom, and was astonished on finding two candles burning in the sockets of the candlesticks, and his master not in bed, nor, from the undisturbed state of the clothes, had he been in bed.

"Upon looking behind the screen which divided the room, he discovered the deceased, quite dead, sitting on the sofa, with his head reclining over the side, weltering in blood, which appeared to have come from his mouth, although his lips were closed. An alarm was immediately made, and the attendance of surgeons procured, who declared him to have been dead for some hours. The deceased was undressed, with the exception of his drawers and stockings, about which a pistol was found hanging, which appeared to have been recently discharged.

"Upon opening the lips of the deceased, the upper jaw was found to be completely shattered, and the ball lodged in the back part of the head. The deceased had, a short time before he entered the bed-room, been spending his evening with a party composed, in a great measure, of his brother officers, where he appeared in high spirits. Several present there were examined at the Inquest, and all gave it as their opinion that the deceased, who is highly connected, had never meditated suicide, and that the discharge of the pistol must have been caused by some accident whilst he was inspecting it. Verdict accordingly—Accidentally shot. The inquest was attended by numerous friends and brother officers of the deceased, and it excited considerable interest."

I could well have been assigned the very room where this sad event took place. It certainly looked in character; the miserable fireplace much as it would have been then, incapable of adequately heating a space so large. And here was I, one hundred and twenty three years later, sharing it with six of my fellow national servicemen who fervently hoped, as I did, that we would no longer be referred to as "sproggies".

Also in evidence was a screen, no doubt of the kind that had initially concealed the recently deceased Lieutenant Edward John Jones from his groom. As then, it still partially divided the room, from the far side of which issued an eerie, indescribable sound. Peering around this barrier, we saw, naked and whistling in a small aluminium tub set before the sputtering fire, the one enlisted man who would be our co-tenant. He was an elderly Lance Corporal of the one-step-forward-two-steps-back variety; the kind that never make it much further up the ranks because they keep going on charges and being demoted for their transgressions.

He was a chatty individual, solemnly addressing us from his bathtub on the rigours he had endured in the last Korean winter. "Glad to be out of that one, *I* can tell you. So fucking cold it would freeze the balls off a brass monkey. So fucking cold it actually froze my fucking *arse* off." He paused theatrically to let this information sink into us, without making a move to offer evidence of this claim. We were too polite to demand proof, so he continued. "No fucking shite house where we were holed up. We had to do it over the fucking parapet. So there I was, squatting and straining, in air so cold it froze the shit right out of me, when all of a sudden my boots slip and I ends up sitting on the fucking freezing cold ground." (Not to mention the recently released excreta, I thought to myself.)

"No fucking kidding, I froze there. With the skin of my arse actually stuck to the *ground*. I thought, Christ, I'm going to be sitting here all fucking night, till the rest of me freezes as well. What should I do? Call out for help and risk my mates having fits of fucking hysterics to see me in this position? Not that they'd be any help either. No fucking way. I hauls myself up with all the strength in my body, and of course I leave a substantial chunk of my fucking arse behind. Not that I could feel it straight away mind you, I was so fucking frozen."

By now we were consumed with impatience to view the ruins of his posterior, but he was in no hurry, gently lathering himself as he relapsed into his nerve-rackingly tuneless whistle. When he did finally rise from the tub, very considerately presenting us with our long awaited proof, it turned out to be somewhat disappointing. Just one livid scar across both buttocks, rather than the implicit crater we had hoped to see, left by the missing "substantial chunk". Better a slice off the bum than a bullet lodged in the back part of Lieutenant Jones' head.

Tramp of Boots and a Military Drum

Constructed in 1776, the Royal Artillery Barracks, Woolwich, boasted one of the longest continuous Georgian frontages in the United Kingdom. Our room overlooked a wide parade ground. From our large and draughty windows, one of our number, the eccentric Morland Clinton, was disposed to drop water-laden condom bombs on those female camp followers in the habit of congregating below. Beyond the parade ground, once resounding to the tramp of boots bound for the battles of Waterloo, the Crimea and the Boer War, were ancient cannons, their muzzles pointed towards Woolwich Common, which stretched southward into the smog-laden distance. It was a handsome façade, extending over a thousand feet, behind which was a warren of decrepit buildings providing accommodation for some four thousand men, most of whom were in the Royal Artillery.

We were quartered in the midst of the soldiers whose pay rolls it would be our responsibility to calculate and reconcile! It was a frightening thought. In the event of some rumoured discrepancy in the accounts, we would be hopelessly outnumbered.

John Bell's Crimean War Memorial stood opposite the main entrance, and not far away was the Rotunda, an intriguing tent-like structure built by John Nash for a celebration in St James's Park in 1814. The mock-Tudor Royal Military Academy, on the south-east side of Woolwich Common, was known to the British Army as "The Shop". Set up to train officers for both the Royal Artillery and the Royal Engineers, "The Shop" continued to do so until 1948, when it closed down, following amalgamation of its establishment with Sandhurst. It too had enjoyed a considerable history, having been founded in 1805. Its pupils included Lord Kitchener of Khartoum and General Gordon; the latter more famously connected with that desert outpost than the former.

I could not but reflect that my grandfather, William George Moss, had spent time in Woolwich during his days as a young gunner. I felt closer to him there than I had ever felt, and it made me realise how little I really knew him. I had judged him as would a castaway judge the continent of Asia, simply from the mangrove swamp on which he was shipwrecked. The news of his death would not reach me until I was in Malaya, some four years later, when I would keenly regret not having made a greater effort to learn more of his life. He left so little of his passing, other than an impressive array of medals.

Back in 1953, nearly two centuries after the place was built, I could only speculate that my grandfather—had he visited me then—would find Woolwich entirely unchanged. I made inquiries, and discovered that earlier in the twentieth century the barracks had in fact been condemned as unfit for further habitation. Learning of its ancient provenance, the producers of the film *Beau Brummel*, in which Stewart Grainger was cast as Brummel, and Peter Ustinov as the Prince Regent, obtained permission, while we were in residence there, to shoot some key footage within the barracks, because of its perfectly preserved Georgian ambience. Observing, in the course of this production, the gorgeous costumes of Regency dandies cast as extras, we were stunned at the thought that the barracks had survived unchanged across that enormous span of time. No wonder that, on winter mornings, we had to break the icicles off the taps before we could coax enough water for our outdoor ablutions.

Woolwich was curiously linked with the inception of that highest award for British bravery, the Victoria Cross. The first proof was not to Queen Victoria's taste. "The Cross looks very well in form," she admitted, "but the metal is ugly; it is copper and not bronze and will look very heavy on a red coat". Someone suggested it would be fitting to extract the bronze for the new medals from Russian guns captured in the Crimea. Accordingly, an engineer was dispatched to Woolwich Barracks, where two 18-pounders were placed at his disposal. Despite the fact that these cannon were clearly of antique design, and inscribed with very un-Russian characters, nobody pointed out, until years later, that the "VC guns" were not Russian but Chinese, and may not have been anywhere near the Crimea.

The Chinese gunmetal proved so hard that the dies began to crack up, so it was decided to *cast* the medals instead. This proved a lucky chance, resulting in higher relief and more depth in the moulding than would have been possible with a die-stamped medal.

Short-Changed

Although quartered in Woolwich, we had a considerable journey to make each day to the pay offices where we worked. These were located in a former factory building at Foots Cray, a small and undistinguished suburban town in Kent. We travelled there on a red London double-decker omnibus, to a world far removed from the sufferings of Devizes, a world in which we could walk abroad, unchallenged, without berets, and with hands in our pockets if we felt like it, a world in which kindly officers looked on us with sympathy, as if commiserating with the ordeal from which we had so newly emerged. All told, it was a slightly incredible species of national servicemen's heaven.

And yet I still felt short-changed, robbed of that overseas posting I had yearned for in Malaya, or Cyprus or *anywhere* beyond the English Channel. Nevertheless I reluctantly conceded that if I *had* to be in England, at the onset of another dreary English winter, there were worse places to be caught in than Foots Cray. The entire office was on one level, a wide expanse of open floor plan, partitioned into sections by head-high removable screens. The roof was one of those typical, unevenly zigzagged structures that looked, in profile, like the graph of an exceptionally regular heartbeat. It let in abundant light and—from goodness knows where—thousands of sparrows.

The whole place was one enormous sparrow incubator; an indoor bird sanctuary heaven-sent for any student of the life cycle, mating rituals and breeding habits of London's inexplicably beloved exemplar of Cockney cheekiness. From being initially entranced, I soon learned to hate sparrows with a passion. Short of working under tarpaulins, it was impossible to seek protection from the steady rain of sparrow droppings. One quickly learned never to leave a coffee mug uncovered.

I pined for the well-intentioned but misunderstood minor official of the Bexhill Municipal Council, who had taken matters into his own hands with his shotgun approach. Nobody seemed to be doing *anything* about the Foots Cray sparrows. It was as if we had collectively tuned them out of our consciousness, as something to be borne, along with the Great British weather. It didn't personally matter to *me* that some unseen artilleryman's pay record might be rendered illegible, by a spreading blob resembling the rancid contents of a broken egg, but what about the accuracy of the final accounting? What about the consequences of trying to read between the imprints of avian excrement?

My conscience was salved. I was posted to that graveyard of old soldiers' long forgotten roll calls, the terminated accounts section. I was in my element; a sort of accounting equivalent of a funeral undertaker, extracting and replacing dead files in their mortuary pigeonholes. No sparrow spoilage could any longer blemish the lives and fortunes of those columns of departed gunners marched off to their posthumous repose. They somehow put me in mind of the poems of Wilfred Owen and Siegfried Sassoon. "Yet no blood reached there from the upper ground, and no guns thumped, or down the flues made moan. 'Strange friend,' I said, 'here is no cause to mourn'."

I would try to envisage the nature and appearance of the sleepers lying undisturbed in that documentary archive, constructing images of their military careers from dates and distributions of their postings, the ups and downs of their regimental rankings. Equipped with an automatic enumerating counter, which imprinted numbers in sequence on the identification cards to be stored in the alphabetically organised filing cabinets, I would *bonk, bonk, bonk* my way through an entirely satisfying, rhythmically soporific afternoon. Lost in thought, I would stare fixedly into space, far, far past sparrows, partitions, cabinets, desks, office walls, Foots Cray and beyond.

One afternoon the intensity of my gaze caught the eye of a passing officer, who got it into his head that I was looking at *him*. He made his way, nearer and nearer, desk by desk through my section, where all work had come to a standstill, awaiting the outcome of this unexpected disturbance to the day's routine, and *still* I stared through him, locked eye to eye, *bonking, bonking, bonking.* Completing his journey, the officer stood in front of my desk, mesmerised by my apparent insolence. He turned to my colleagues, seeking an explanation. They shrugged their shoulders to indicate this was, to them, nothing out of the ordinary, but merely how I habitually behaved.

He snapped his fingers under my nose, and I returned to reality as rapidly as if smelling salts had been applied to my nostrils. Leaping to my feet, I stood at attention. It wasn't possible to salute, because I didn't have my beret on.

"You were daydreaming," he said quietly.

"I was Sir."

"Of your demobilisation?"

"Too far to go for that, Sir."

He nodded. "Mustn't let it interfere with your work. Carry on."

He continued on his way and I almost wept with relief, remembering Sergeant Wrattan and how jubilant he would have been at such an opportunity as the one I had presented.

We later learnt that Sergeant Wrattan had been court-martialled and discharged for wanton cruelty to recruits. Apparently he had been observed by an officer through the windows of the drying room, putting some other unfortunate platoon through precisely the ordeal he had inflicted on us, by making them run on the spot with full kit and greatcoats, weapons extended at arms length above their heads until, one by one, they lost consciousness.

Seldom, but at least just often enough to keep our hopes alive, we discover that there *is* justice, even in a military world.

Inimitable Morland Clinton

Morland Clinton was an updated version of Nicholas Thomas Nicholas Carter, but with the added bonus of an extremely *noir* sense of humour. He would respond to his anxious mother's last despairing appeal for word of him by writing a letter filled with gobbledygook, carefully devised and scanned so that none of it could conceivably make any sense, even if interpreted as code. He assured me it was an extremely painstaking process to perfect pure nonsense, because too often what we *thought* was nonsense was influenced by subconscious thought processes to the point where it made partial sense, no matter how obscure.

He didn't mind his mother spending hours trying to read between the lines, so long as she couldn't glean anything of value from that perusal. Occasionally, after having laboured at length to produce two closely typed sheets of utter incomprehensibility, he would follow them, under separate cover, with a brief one-word postscript such as "sknchssftxx!". In doing so, he hoped that his mother would then employ the postscript as a Rosetta stone that provided the rubric to the preceding text, so that her quest would commence all over again.

I suggested he must hate his mother as passionately as I hated the sparrows, but he dismissed that possibility. He was merely teaching her that he was not prepared to conform, in any way, to her values and expectations. Morland consistently failed to conform, in any way, to *our* values and expectations, so that we quickly learned not to entertain any where *he* was concerned. He invited us to accompany him for a night on the town, at his expense, and then proceeded to lead us through the seediest dives in Soho, on a conducted tour of every conceivable vice and iniquity that the fifties had perfected. We huddled after him, like a group of maiden aunt tourists en route to the land of milk and honey, unexpectedly diverted through Sodom and Gomorrah.

I remember a fleeting image that, for me, veered too painfully close to home; a tableau of bored old men in drag, breathing stale cigarette smoke over each other's lipstick, sequins and false eyelashes, their arms halfheartedly entwined around each other while elevated eyebrows permitted sidelong glances at every other transvestite in the room. They stopped whatever they were doing, in exaggerated freeze frame, as we innocents flitted furtively by, trying to avoid their incredulous glances. There but for the grace of God, thought I.

Afterwards I wondered if these were Morland's familiar haunts, and then decided that he was as much a stranger there as we were. He had simply taken pains to prepare an itinerary that exposed us to the maximum shock value. But Morland also had his practical side, and self-sufficiency was one of his objectives.

He was the man to go to if you wanted to know where to find work that would supplement your miserable army pay. Half of my meagre income seemed forever disappearing on obligatory fortnightly haircuts and the other half on packets of Wills Woodbine cigarettes, for which I had developed a guilty craving.

"Nippy" Waitresses of Lyons Corner House

Thanks to Morland's help, I landed a part-time evening job at the oldest Lyons Corner House in London. Located at Piccadilly Circus, it was launched in 1909. With their uniformed "Nippy" waitresses, so called because they were trained to "nip" speedily between tables, Lyons Corner Houses were an early example of the chain diner in Britain, and had done very well at it for many years. Lyons had, even earlier, made its name from coffee. The original founders, J. Lyons & Co, had prominent sites in and around Central London, and were at the forefront of coffee retailing at the dawn of the twentieth century.

Changing into "civvies" after completing my daytime chores at Foots Cray, I would make my way up to Central London by the regular suburban commuter train, or else by bus direct from Woolwich. The "Nippies" were beginning to look a lot less so when I joined the kitchen staff. They moved more slowly, and with considerably lower levels of enthusiasm than were presumably displayed by their predecessors. Recalling the opening sequence of that popular television show *In Town Tonight*, with its whirl of traffic suddenly arrested around Piccadilly Circus, I longed for the announcer's invitation, at the end of the programme, to "Carry on London", so that the tempo could pick up again.

To me, in the early fifties, London seemed caught in a permanent postwar depression. We were still surrounded by the scars of the Blitz. The 1951 Festival of Britain, with its Skylon, Dome of Discovery and Rowland Emett's "Far Tottering & Oystercreek Railway", had been designed as a tonic to uplift British spirits. But its effects were ephemeral, leaving only the Royal Festival Hall on the South Bank as permanent reminder of its fleeting presence there. Herbert Morrison had described the Festival as "A national display, illustrating the British contributions to civilisation, past, present and future, in the arts, in science and technology, and in industrial design". By largely glossing over all evidence that there had ever been an empire, it struck me as reinforcing emphasis on Britain's increasingly go-it-alone-and-to-hell-with-the-Commonwealth mentality.

The last vaguely imperial pageantry on public view in London was the Coronation of Queen Elizabeth II on 2nd June 1953, when the massively genial Queen Salote of Tonga, accompanied by a diminutive Malay sultan, had refused his request to erect the canopy on their landau carriage. Millions watching under umbrellas, or glued to their televisions, lost their hearts to her as she continued waving cheerfully through the rain. Asked who the soaked and dejected looking sultan was, Noël Coward replied, "Her lunch."

My job at Lyons was to clear the tables and help with the washing up. I soon learnt, without glancing at my cheap Timex wristwatch, what time it was simply by the change of clientele. You always knew when the prostitutes were taking a breather for a fag, or when their pimps were checking up on them to see how many tricks they'd turned. You knew when the theatres were letting out and the last cinema show was about the start. You could tell from the snippets of conversation how good or bad the show was, or how much or little expectation was entertained for the one about to commence.

When I didn't need the money, and just wanted a night on the town on my own, I queued up for free tickets available to servicemen for West End matinees. I saw Valerie Hobson make her final stage appearance, partnering Herbert Lom in Rodgers and Hammerstein's *The King and I*, Rex Harrison and Lilli Palmer in John Van Druten's *Bell Book and Candle*, Cole Porter's *Can Can*, Terence Rattigan's *Separate Tables*, from which I recall the line "You can be in the Horse Guards and still be common, dear", and many others that escape my memory.

Hitchhiking Adventures

Most weekends I would head for home, catching a bus over to Bromley, standing by the side of the A21 in my uniform and hitching a ride within minutes. If I chose not to wear uniform, the wait would be longer. Picking up a hitchhiker in those days was not the dubious game of chance it is now. Most motorists were glad of the company. A ride usually meant sharing the back seat with the kids or the family dog, occasional trays of seedling plants, the morning's shopping or a stack of books headed for a garden fete. On one journey, a massive and newly reframed painting took up the whole width of the backrest, requiring me to crouch forward with my elbows rigidly locked on my knees to avoid being flung back in counter-momentum from any sudden stop at traffic lights. There were no fitted seat belts to bother with either.

I too enjoyed the company provided by these journeys. Farmers, vicars, retired army officers; you never knew who you might meet or what you might end up talking about. One former Desert Rat, serving under General Montgomery at Alamein, had contracted complications from a stomach disorder that prevented his digestive tract from manufacturing hydrochloric acid. The result was that his system could absorb no nourishment, and became clogged with undigested waste. He was sinking rapidly, until an Indian army doctor correctly diagnosed his condition and started administering diluted hydrochloric acid, establishing the right strength to produce the desired result without toxic side effects. The cured patient had thrived ever since, preparing the correct dosage himself to accompany every meal.

One driver, pulling over to pick me up in a spanking new Sunbeam Alpine open-topped two-seat tourer, recognised me immediately, in the same heart-stopping moment that I recognised him. He was the salesman who, earlier that week, at the Earls Court Motor Show, had tried to sell me a tomato red model of the same marque. I had gone up for the show in my flannels, cravat and blazer, with my hand stitched, gold-thread *Noli Me Tangere* touch-me-not pocket badge, putting on the airs, graces and accent of an officer in the Horse Guards.

Because the Sunbeam Alpine was the dream car of my secret fantasies, I had spent an inordinately long time in the seat, asking supposedly informed questions—without ever having driven, leave alone owned a car—about torque, miles per gallon and revolutions per minute. And now here I was, in the uniform of a private in the Pay Corps, rather than an officer in the Horse Guards. Horse droppings, he must have thought. Perhaps he had even seen Rattigan's play and remembered the line. I owned up immediately, and we had a good laugh about it. He claimed he hadn't really been fooled, but he was so proud of the car he'd have spent time demonstrating it even if I were an eighty-year-old, wheelchair-bound invalid.

For my return journey to Woolwich Barracks, late on a Sunday night, I would catch a train to Waterloo and then change to the local line. Staring at my reflection in the carriage window, past the same *gnikoms on* sign engraved into the glass, I was gratified to see a new, improved model of me staring back. Life had changed dramatically for me in the course of a few months, thanks to an enforced spell of National Service that had done me such a power of good.

From a secretive recluse I had been transformed into a young man who, despite his secret, was no longer finding it necessary to be quite so reclusive. I was acquiring social skills, making friends and developing a healthy curiosity about the real lives around me, rather than those I read of in the virtual realms of literature. My world had become a fuller, richer, more satisfying place than I had known since my childhood in India, but it was still contained within this brief span of countryside, traversed in less than two hours on the London to Hastings line. I clung to my resolve that, the moment the opportunity presented itself, I would quit these shores and head for the wider spaces beyond.

Holidays on the Broads

For Dad too, things were looking better. The years slipped into reverse when he acquired a secondhand motor-cycle sidecar combination, which he tarted up to look like new. He was back in the days of his giddy, feckless youth, except that this time he had to provide conveyance for as many of our family as he could accommodate.

His father could no longer compete, because the years were sliding out of his grasp. Long troubled by the lingering effects of the poison gas that had entered his lungs in the trenches of World War Two, William George Moss would soon go to his repose, leaving his widow, my sole surviving grandparent, to move to Devon, where she lived alternately with her eldest daughter, Alice, and her second daughter, Susan. Her youngest, Vera, having married a teacher, Ken Rogers, had by then moved to Australia with her husband and their two children Sally and Paul.

Possessed of a nervously hearty voice and manner, Alice was married to retired postman Reg Bond and retreating ever further and deeper into Devonian backwaters, choosing obscure villages not even visible on the map, as if defying relatives to beat a path to her door. Susan, married to a tall, handsome Scotsman whom she had nursed through his war injuries, was securely established in Exeter, from which she had no desire to stray, holding it to be the very exemplar of a model country town. There her husband, Andrew McDonald-Bell, practised as a chiropodist and gave lessons on the bagpipes. We saw a lot of Susan and Andrew, who developed a great fondness for my mother in particular and were always extremely hospitable to us on our return visits to Devon. Both were intensely interested in the First World War, and particularly in the history of the Scottish regiments deployed along its blood-drenched battlefronts. They spent repeated holidays touring the former war zones of France and Belgium, returning with souvenirs in the form of shell fragments, cartridge cases and belt buckles they had unearthed from ploughed fields and hedgerows.

Dad took a two-week summer lease on a bungalow on the Norfolk Broads. The plan was that, while I made my way from Woolwich by train, he, Mum, Paul and Robert would travel to our rendezvous aboard the "combo". In view of accompanying luggage, requisite household effects and food supplies, the logistics of the expedition called for careful experimentation. Final disposition of the full complement set Dad in the saddle, Paul on the pillion, Mum in the sidecar and Robert in an extremely tiny dickey seat behind her, with all sundry articles and effects distributed in shoulder packs and side panniers or on laps.

It was a long trip from Hastings to the bungalow on the River Yare, in the vicinity of Brundall, and it rained several times en route, requiring elaborate evacuations and airings of drenched passengers and equipment under the nearest available shelter. So it made for a slow journey, related to me at great length when we finally gathered around the fire to dry out.

The bungalow placed at our disposal a small sailing dinghy with an outboard motor, tethered to a rickety jetty at the foot of the garden, and came ready equipped with a nosey next-door neighbour, whose pleasure on learning that I was in the army (her late husband had been colonel of an infantry regiment) abated as soon as she discovered I was a private in the Pay Corps, so that she never bothered us again.

We filled the tiny tank of the outboard motor with gasoline and set off up the River Yare for Norwich; an excursion that took all day and nearly entailed the loss of our overburdened vessel in the wash of a large, fast-moving launch, headed down river. The holiday was nevertheless voted a great success overall, prompting Paul and I to resolve we would return to the Broads the following summer.

By that time Paul had followed my footsteps into my vacated chair at the *Bexhill-on-Sea Observer,* and I was in my last year of National Service. The two of us rented a dual-berth cabin cruiser and set off down the Yare to the mouth of Breydon Water, where we tied up late in the evening, not realising we were in a tidal estuary. During the night, we were awakened by the crash of crockery falling from the shelves, to discover the tide had receded, leaving our cruiser suspended from its mooring ropes on the river bank There was nothing to do but hope that the ropes would hold until the tide came back again.

Working our way in a leisurely manner up the River Bure, we turned into the River Ant, traversed Barton Broad and ended up, some days later, in the vicinity of Stalham. The river began to narrow and we needed to tie up again for the night. Unfortunately the leeward bank was fully occupied by vessels that had arrived before us, so that the windward bank was the only expanse available for mooring. Paul was at the wheel, nursing us alongside the reed covered shore at a cautious speed, while I stood in the prow, rope coiled in my hand, ready for action. As he cut the engine, and I leapt for the land, two things happened simultaneously: a) a sudden offshore gust pushed us well back into the stream and b) I found I hadn't let out enough rope.

The result was that I crashed back into the side of the launch, hanging on to the rope as we drifted further and further across the river. By this time the initial gales of laughter from delighted spectators had turned to cries of alarm as we were observed to be bearing down upon them. Not being able to see over the side, and not receiving any response to my calls for Paul's assistance, I deduced something was seriously wrong. Hauling myself back aboard, I found the stern cockpit deserted, and assumed my brother must himself have fallen overboard.

Grabbing the wheel, I restarted the engine and achieved just enough momentum to narrowly miss the vessels with which we were about to collide, whose crews rallied to fend us off, hurling unsolicited advice as to where we might go in order to learn how to handle a boat. Casting an anxious look inside the cabin, I saw Paul seated there, hunched into a quite unmistakable sulk. I proceeded further upstream, to a position sufficiently deserted and sheltered to allow me to moor single-handedly. Then I joined him in the cabin to seek an explanation of his conduct.

Paul had long got it into his head that I enjoyed playing the role of buffoon. He claimed I had chosen that most inopportune of moments to stage the kind of clown act typical of me.

"You think I did that on *purpose?*" I gasped.

"How else would you get yourself into such a mess?"

"You mean I *chose* to throw myself into the water, just in order to entertain those people at the prospect that we were about to crash into their midst?"

"You'll do anything to get attention. It's the only way you can be accepted into conventional society."

"This is too much. How could you suppose *I* have a hankering to be accepted into *conventional* society, when it consists of the kind of jerks *you* associate with?"

Ah for those days of sibling rivalry! Ah for the hot flush of youth and its misunderstandings! Now that my brother is beyond recall, how I yearn to have them back again!

Something out of the Ordinary

One day our notice board at Foots Cray displayed something out of the ordinary. Alongside postings and general orders was a sheet of paper inviting volunteers for an experimental programme to be conducted at Porton Down in Wiltshire. Successful applicants, to fill the relatively small complement of "research subjects" required, would be those found to be in first-class physical condition. In return for their services, they would be afforded special benefits, including a long period of paid leave once their spell at Porton Down was complete. Although the notice did not emphasize this point, Porton Down was operated by the Ministry of Defence as a top-secret chemical and biological warfare centre.

The invitation provoked much wistful speculation and light-hearted banter. Somebody had heard that volunteers responding to a similar appeal, in connection with studies into the nature and behaviour of the virus responsible for the common cold, had enjoyed conditions not far removed from a Butlin's holiday camp. We decided that, just for a lark, we would all apply. Not everyone subscribed to this proposal, but enough of us did that we felt the laws of football pools might govern the odds. Surely at least one or two of us would be chosen, even though the same invitation was being extended to every military unit in the British Isles. Besides, just by turning up for the obligatory medical examination, we would be taking time off from our normal chores.

In the event one of us *was* chosen from Foots Cray, and that particular volunteer happened to be me. At first I thought there must be some mistake. By no stretch of the imagination could I be accounted one of the fittest physical specimens in the British Army. I had never taken my health or physique seriously enough. But the evidence was there, and surely the medical report could not be disputed? I was roundly congratulated by my friends, and enviously regarded by others who were even more dubious of my selection than I was myself. Nevertheless, I did feel that a great honour had been bestowed upon me, and I believed that my parents would be equally gratified when I divulged this information to them the following weekend. I could not have been more mistaken.

Their reaction caught me quite unprepared, for my father, immediately suspecting cynical motives in opportunities of this sort, did a little investigating that uncovered the nature of Porton Down and what it was up to. He simply checked with Uncle Len, who knew enough about the programmes conducted there to—as Dad expressed it—"put the wind up Aunt Zena". My aunt and my mother jointly insisted I withdraw my application. I couldn't do that, I protested. I would never live it down. I might never live to survive Porton Down, Zena pointed out. God knows what kind of monstrous chemical and biological brews they were concocting there to try out on inadequately briefed victims like myself.

Zena took matters into her own hands. She directed Len to take the issue to the highest levels at the War Office, if need be, in order to have my name removed from the list. Len, as usual, did as he was told and my greatly relieved parents were informed the following week that I could disregard my orders to report at Porton Down on the due date. I was of course mortified, but at the same time inwardly relieved, for by now I was suffering a relapse of hypochondria on a scale I had not experienced in years, my sleep disturbed by visions of my skin peeling off, my hair falling out and my teeth rattling in my gums.

Years later, Porton Down would be placed at the centre of a scandal exposed by the *Observer*. In December 1996, reporters Paul Lashmar and Tom McCarthy described how, in 1952, the year before I entered National Service, simulated biological warfare tests were carried out in secret at Salisbury. The Ministry of Defence claimed the substance released on the city was "smoke", but parallel experiments carried out in the United States cast doubt on this claim. The *Observer* further revealed that the Ministry was suppressing a file on a biological warfare accident that same year, when the crew of a fishing trawler off the Scottish coast was doused with plague bacteria.

The report also disclosed that Britain secretly carried out a series of biological warfare tests off Caribbean islands in the late 1940s and 1950s, placing their populations at risk of contact with deadly bacteria and other toxic agents. The experiments were at the time concealed from people living close to the Antigua and Bahamas test sites. Military chiefs of staff looked to the prospect of developing a biological bomb as a novel weapon of great potency. Weight for weight, they hoped it would prove as effective against unprotected human beings as atomic bombs had already shown themselves to be.

The official position was that biological warfare at Porton Down was studied to *defend* Britain against biological attack. However, a Chiefs of Staff memo, dated March 1952, argued that it could be used *offensively after* a nuclear strike. "The possibility of employing biological agents immediately following an atomic attack should not be overlooked," the memo claimed, going on to point out that biological warfare attacks on a highly disorganised population, of greatly lowered morale and diminished physical resistance, could be devastating.

Toxic Shock

I was unexpectedly and surprisingly affected by my last days of National Service. Having impatiently ticked off the days on my calendar, I now found them running out too fast, and wished I could somehow hold them back. My barrack room mates decided to get me thoroughly "plastered" to prepare me for my return to the rough-and-tumble of the real world. They took me on a crawl of just about every pub in Woolwich, at the end of which I was assured I had consumed ten pints of beer. Then they propped me under my arms and virtually carried me home, pausing to lean me against darkened doorways whenever they spotted a military police patrol.

The following day I developed a raging temperature and came out in a violent mauve rash all over my body, with the merciful exception of my face and hands.

Never before having absorbed more than the odd half pint of ale, my system had gone into toxic shock. Even Porton Down could hardly have produced more visibly spectacular results. There was no way I could report on sick parade, because the army deems it a grievous offence to knowingly cause oneself bodily harm. Having completed virtually my entire twenty-four months of military service with a clean record, I did not want to blot it by going up on a charge in my last few days. I carried on working as usual, suffering in silence and resolving never, never again to get into that condition.

Another rite of passage occurred when I confessed to having considered the acquisition of a small tattoo as a souvenir of my army days. My companions could hardly wait to rush this casual whim to full-blooded fulfilment, and full-blooded it proved to be. They found a hole-in-the-wall tattoo parlour, located up a steep, dark staircase, where they sat with me through an album displaying the patterns available. These were not of any notable artistic merit, but among the least offensive was a skull-and-crossbones design, immersed in a glass of red wine. For some bizarre reason this appealed to me, and the tattooist rolled up both his sleeves and mine, and set to work. The implement he used was clearly homemade, consisting of a tiny hypodermic syringe attached to a small electric motor that transformed it into a miniature pile driver.

The employment of this device proved surprisingly painful, and I rapidly recovered from the state of semi-anaesthesia to which my prior alcohol consumption was supposed to have rendered me. Before the ornamentalist had completed half a crossbone, I passed out. When I came to again he was reluctant to carry on because he didn't want to take responsibility for any medical condition I might have failed to report to him. I insisted he persevere, on the grounds that the existence of half a crossbone would be more difficult to explain than the full regalia.

Progress was slow, repeatedly interrupted by my having to be revived from another fainting spell. Finally, after completing the skull-and-crossbones, the "artist" declined to continue, pointing out that, at this rate, completion of the wine glass, not to mention the ruby red wine in which the piratical emblem was supposedly immersed, would keep us there all night. Slapping a couple of sheets from a roll-your-own-cigarette pack on my bloodied arm, he quoted his fee and showed us the way down a by now extremely darkened and even less inviting staircase.

The skull-and-crossbones remains with me yet, slowly fading on my right arm, its skeletal mouth open in a rictus of recrimination for my failure to plunge it into full-bodied burgundy. It helped to complete the description of my physical appearance in the paybook that provided closure to my military service. This read

"22905648—Complexion: spotty. Distinguishing marks and features: Poorly executed tattoo, upper right arm".

Nothing Like it Since the Greeks

Looking back now, I see that the tattoo was a desperate but misplaced—and in the end wholly unsuccessful—attempt to assert my masculinity. And it was provoked by an incident that began on the top deck of a double-decker bus, returning to Woolwich Barracks from an early evening shift at Lyons Corner House.

For some reason I can't recall, I was in uniform, which was not my customary practice when going up to London. An elderly gentleman found a seat beside me, introduced himself and struck up a conversation, admitting a susceptibility to young men in uniform. He delivered this admission with such disarming frankness that he took me off-guard. My initial impression was that he was just a sociable, perhaps slightly lonely old man who also happened to be a well travelled and engaging raconteur. Furthermore he was entirely sympathetic towards my professed intention of leaving England at the earliest opportunity in order to see something of the world.

When the time came for him to disembark, on the outskirts of Woolwich, he invited me to share a pot of coffee, pointing out that he might be able to help me choose an itinerary for my travels. Curiosity, combined with my resolution to make up for years of withdrawal from human company, by being as sociable as possible to everyone I met, drove me to accept.

His home was in the basement of a terrace house typical of that area, where he left me on the sofa, to adjust to my unexceptional surroundings, while he prepared the coffee. Nothing in the furnishings or décor was remarkable enough to provide any clue to his character or interests, other than a framed lithograph of a lissome Arab youth holding a large earthen jar. I took this as confirmation that he was well travelled.

He returned with the coffee and a heavy photograph album, which he placed on my knees. This, he said, was a record of his travels.

The travel experiences illustrated therein were not of the kind I had anticipated. In every photograph the participants—all male—were either partly or fully unclothed and engaging in the wild extremities of conduct that had figured in my most salaciously erotic fantasies. I turned page after page in mounting incredulity. The closest I had come to seeing such activities portrayed elsewhere was on the sides of Grecian urns illustrated in the pages of *Encyclopaedia Britannica*. Could I possibly have been mistaken in assuming that such practices had died out with the Hellenic civilisation, and that I was some rare, freakish throwback to that earlier age?

My host began fingering my uniform and its contents. Since nothing repels so much as the guilty desire one secretly craves, I abruptly set the album aside, stood up and apologised for the fact that I had to leave. He was very understanding and decent about it, showing me to the door and bidding me goodnight with just the faintest wisp of a sadly resigned smile about his lips. I hurried up the basement steps as if evacuating the onset of an earthquake.

All that repressed torrent of sexuality came flooding back, in danger of sweeping me away. But where to? The only destinations I could discern for such indulgence were the sad little drag-queen bar to which Morland Clinton had taken us, or a vision of myself, years from now, finding a seat on an omnibus alongside some uniformed young man and practising precisely the approach that had brought me to this pass. Oh Oscar, I thought, your Wildeness and its fatal aftermath are not for me.

Yet where could I go, in whom could I trust and confide, to redress this anomaly in my nature? None of my perusals in the Brassey Institute reading room had unearthed anything more helpful than Lord Baden-Powell's advice in such *Guides for Young Manhood* as *Rovering to Success* and *Paddle Your Own Canoe*. Founder of the Boy Scout movement, which had exerted for me much the same wholesome appeal as *Kellogg's Corn Flakes,* Lord Baden-Powell had warned me that if masturbation becomes a habit, "it quickly destroys both health and spirits". He who practised such "beastliness" would become "feeble in body and mind and often end in a lunatic asylum".

The prospect was chilling. Neither did I much fancy his remedy of plunging into a cold shower whenever assailed by unclean thoughts. So clearly desperate measures were called for. I had to train myself to become heterosexual, to develop a healthy interest in girls. I started subscribing to *Titbits* and other big tits magazines, which I left lying around on my barrack room bed to assure my room mates that any suspicions they might have entertained concerning my sexual orientation were entirely misplaced. Most of these publications rapidly disappeared, or were cannibalised for other people's locker doors.

But who was I kidding? Certainly not the girls in whose company I allowed myself to be landed when my mates took me out on the town. One hint of sneaking away with them upstairs, or round the corner, or behind the curtains at the back of the shop, and I'd start sweating, hyperventilating and mouthing excuses faster than hand-towels unrolling from runaway dispensers.

A tattoo might not be the answer. But it was a beginning; a sort of brand mark to identify a hopefully familiar looking product.

Key to the Door

When I emerged from National Service, Paul, who had sought deferment to complete his education, was due to be called up himself, ironically to the Royal Artillery, whose accounts my unit had managed at Foots Cray. The fact that I had been employed on them, in no matter how minor a capacity, made him justifiably suspicious as to their reliability. We decided we would rededicate our fraternal bonds with a coming-of-age tour of the local night spots, commencing with an investigation as to whether Hastings still possessed anything that might pass as such. I was in my twenty-first year, Paul was approaching his twentieth. We felt entitled to regard ourselves as men about town.

Since this was a Saturday night, we checked out Hastings Pier to see if the old dance band was still in residence there. It was, and we lingered awhile for nostalgia's sake. It had never been a regular haunt for either of us. Then we started on the pubs, working our way through a few, not drinking much. It was about half past midnight when we decided to call it quits, walking home through a clear, mild autumn night. We rang the doorbell at 95, St. George's, and waited, and waited. Eventually we heard Dad on the other side, informing us that because we were so late, we could consider ourselves locked out. We also heard Mum in the background, remonstrating with him, but he wouldn't budge. We inquired, "May we ask why, since it is not yet one o'clock?"

He replied that neither of us had as yet earned the key to the door.

Paul and I looked at each other. The *key* to the *door?* Could he possibly mean that archaic institution whereby a young man was not officially recognised as an adult until he reached his twenty-first birthday? We posed this question through the letter box, and he confirmed we had assumed correctly. Paul and I exchanged further glances. Neither of us were in the mood for prolonging this ridiculous argument. By unspoken mutual consent we turned on our heels and left.

Although it could not be properly described as a cold night, it had certainly chilled enough, by early morning, to make us wish we had brought our overcoats. Our unyielding benches, in the elaborately decorated but largely exposed Victorian promenade shelter we had chosen for our repose, had grown increasingly uncomfortable as the night progressed. And even before dawn broke over a leaden sea, the cacophonous seagulls were in full shriek, noisier than a whole compound full of the chickens we had suffered in our Indian boyhood.

But it was worth it, for the point we made. We were never to be locked out again.

That night on Hastings esplanade also healed the last vestige of a scar left by our row on the Norfolk Broads. We mutually agreed that we were remarkably empathetic, more like identical twins than brothers born over a year apart, We understood each other, thought the same thoughts at more or less the same time and frequently found ourselves simultaneously raising the same subject in conversation, quite out of the blue. And although we avoided mentioning *that* particular subject, the only point on which we differed—quite extremely—was in regard to our sexual orientation.

Paul had ever been a ladies' man, sought after as much as seeking their company, and though he never once posed a question regarding my own preferences, I knew that he knew, and that he knew I knew that he knew. It just didn't bother him, and I don't suppose it occurred to him that it might bother me.

Knickerbockered Horace Beddington

While Paul's own apprenticeship in journalism had been interrupted by National Service, I still had mine to complete, not on the *Bexhill-on-Sea Observer*, as it transpired, but in its sister newspaper the *Hastings and St. Leonards Observer*. I didn't object to this because it meant saving the money I had previously spent on train fares. I could walk to the office from St. George's.

Serving a wider catchment area with a larger readership, the Hastings paper employed a bigger staff than I had worked with in Bexhill. But of all of them, the fellow journalist I remember best was Horace Beddington, who looked a human incarnation of Toad of Toad Hall. He even dressed like that memorable character from Kenneth Grahame's *Wind in the Willows*, in country tweeds and knickerbockers, with the kind of strange little cap worn by riders to hounds. I could picture him turning to Ratty and declaring "There's real life for you...The open road, the dusty highway, the heath, the common, the hedgerows, the rolling downs!"

Short and bunched-up, with a face that seemed wider than it was tall, Horace grinned amiably and produced wonderful doodles in the margins of his notebook, which confirmed the impish sense of humour one suspected from his appearance. I was told that, until recently, he had covered his "beat", in the rural outskirts of Hastings, on horseback. I pictured him, having chanced upon some hot "scoop" in remote Sussex byways, spurring his trusty steed and racing down the A21, mane flying, yelling "Stop the presses!" In this role he fitted the imagery inspired by Browning's *"How They Brought the Good News from Ghent to Aix"*:

> "'Good speed!' cried the watch as the gate-bolts undrew;
> 'Speed' echoed the wall to us galloping through.
> Behind shut the postern, the lights sank to rest,
> And into the midnight we galloped abreast.

In Hastings the news was seldom conspicuously good, but even less likely to be bad. Mostly it was bland, to the point where a bowls tournament on the greens above the White Rock Pavilion might be accounted an event worthy of front page headlines.

One treasured edition found the captions for two photographs, of identical size, mixed up to inject a mood of totally unexpected suspense. Depicted on the front page was a trio of heavy-set ladies in white bowling outfits, looking very much as if they sprang from a painting by Beryl Cook, bearing down with their bowling balls upon a larger group of spectators slouched in deck chairs. Beneath this, the legend ran: *"Spellbound with horror, the crew of the lonely polar station shrink from the approach of the things from outer space."*

On the entertainment page, one found the picture that should have accompanied that caption, a cowering, terrified trio, backs to the wall, across whom is cast the shadow of an invisible presence. In this case the substituted legend read *"Spectators at the bowls tournament applaud the appearance of the winning team"* One suspected that those with the most cause to be upset by this unfortunate muddle were the things from outer space.

"Winkle Up!"

My greatest coup at the *Hastings & St. Leonards Observer* was when I obtained the help of Field Marshal Bernard Law Montgomery in persuading Sir Winston Churchill to part with the only copy of his celebrated Winkle Club speech. My darkest hour followed almost immediately afterwards, when I lost it.

The Hastings Winkle Club was a long established institution in the Hastings Old Town, founded at a pub called the Fisherman's Arms. Its badge was the replica of a winkle shell, and members were required to shell out a fine—that went to charitable causes—if they failed to produce their winkle at the command, "Winkle Up!". Montgomery of Alamein, an honorary member himself, must have persuaded Winston to accept an invitation to join. Sir Winston, in his eighty-first year, had just retired from office, a much honoured man. Perhaps he had changed since Labour M.P. Joseph Clynes, in his *Memoirs* (1937) recorded:

> "He cannot visualize Britain without an Empire, or the Empire without wars of acquisition and defence. A hundred years ago he might profoundly have affected the shaping of our country's history. Now, the impulses of peace and internationalism, and the education and equality of the working classes, leave him unmoved."

Changed on not, Churchill was in the mood for lighter things in the late evening of his life, and the Winkle Club fitted that bill precisely. On 7th September 1955, "Winnie" drove down to Hastings with "Monty" in the latter's open-topped Humber Staff car of Desert Rats fame. Their destination was the White Rock Pavilion, focus of Hastings' cultural pretensions and the scene of the annual Hastings Grammar School prize-giving ceremonies, at which I had once received a trophy for an English essay.

My English seemed to have deserted me on that September day in 1955. I had barely emerged from National Service a month earlier, my shorthand rusty with neglect. Our *Observer* team was so hard pressed that day, trying to cover all the bases in Churchill's itinerary, that the speech was assigned to me by simple luck of the draw, and I faced the appalling prospect of letting them all down. Seated around me in the White Rock auditorium were seasoned hacks from Fleet Street, scribbling at a leisurely pace in their notebooks, easily keeping up with Churchill's deliberately slow, purposefully pregnant manner of delivery. All I could get down were unintelligible syllables knitted together by lacework scrawls of the more common Pitman symbols.

Hovering in the lobby, when the ceremonials were over, I watched Churchill chatting with the mayor and local dignitaries while Montgomery stood beside him, casting a roving eye around the room. I caught that eye, and held on to it for dear life. Emboldened by the fact that Montgomery must have detected something amiss in my panic-stricken face, I advanced towards him. "Sir," I whispered hoarsely, deciding to gamble on a military pretext that might be dear to Monty's heart. "I've just completed my National Service to rejoin the local newspaper. I'm afraid I've rather neglected my shorthand in the service of Queen and country. Do you suppose Sir Winston might be persuaded to part with his speech?"

Monty took this in and nodded. Turning to Winston, and interrupting his pleasantries with an alderman's wife, he said "Young man here needs your speech. You don't want it any more, I'm sure." With hardly a glance in my direction, or a pause in his conversation, Churchill reached into his inside coat pocket, removed the folded sheets and handed them to Montgomery, who passed them on to me with a wink.

Thanking him profusely, I ignored the stupefied glances of fellow journalists, who must have ranked this among the most brazen examples of cheek they had ever witnessed. Triumphantly I bore the precious, horizontally-formatted demifoolscap from the White Rock Pavilion and hurried back to the office. Idiotically I informed my editor that this was the actual speech, with Sir Winston's actual corrections on the double-line spacing. And look, *look* how he broke his sentences up into short phrases, with rows of dots to represent the pregnant pauses. The old trouper, having been a journalist himself, knew how to achieve maximum effect with those sentence breaks. As in "Never have so many…owed so much…to so few."

That was the last I ever saw of Sir Winston' speech.

Paddling my own Scooter

Sister paper to the *Hastings & St. Leonards Observer*, in the F.J. Parsons newspaper group, was the *East Sussex Express and County Herald*. My elevation to the position of district reporter for the latter weekly was accompanied by the offer of a free Vespa motor scooter and fuel expenses. Which meant that I would have to acquire a motorcycle licence. Dad considerately tutored me in the necessary skills, and I duly passed the test. But there is a world of difference between a motorcycle and a scooter. Two tiny wheels, a relatively low top speed and an awkward cornering angle, combined with a sit-up-and-beg riding posture, do not collectively constitute a motorcycling experience. The thrill of the road was going to be relatively subdued and circumspect. And since I was both negligent in my responsibility to properly maintain this vehicle, and sufficiently absent-minded not to keep the fuel tank topped up, I was frequently compelled to "paddle my own scooter", in a derivation of the immortal Baden-Powel phrase, along some rustic byway in search of the nearest petrol station.

My "beat" was the Rye district. This formed a misshapen triangle, at whose eastern point was Rye itself, aimed like an arrow into the flank of the adjoining county of Kent. At the northern apex was Northiam, reached from Rye via Peasmarsh, and at the southern point was Guestling, on the Rye to Hastings road. The distance of some fifteen kilometres from Rye to Hastings was deemed too far for me to commute from home, so I was provided with sufficient allowance for rented accommodation in Rye itself, which was to be the fulcrum of my territorial coverage.

Rye was another in that confederacy—or should one say conspiracy?—of *Cinque* ports virtually licensed by Royal Charter to engage in freebooting of every species, so long as it made its ships available to the Crown in the event of some declaration of war against those of malevolent intent on the other side of the channel. Unlike Hastings, however, Rye had conspicuously failed to sink. Instead it had been left high and dry, above a large expanse of marshland, by a retreating sea that, many centuries earlier, had islanded it by encircling its base.

Approached from either east or west, Rye loomed like some primitively forti-fied hilltop bastion, ready to fend off both hell and high water. In fact through a large part of history it had alternatively survived, or succumbed to, one assault after another. Prior to the Norman invasion of 1066, Rye in its insular manifesta-tion was granted, in 1027, to the Abbey of Fecamp in Normandy, only to be reclaimed for Britain by Henry III in 1247, in exchange for other lands. But the French never knew when to let go. Rye survived their frequent subsequent attacks, and a few stone buildings still bear witness today to the burning and sack-ing of 1377. The sixteenth century saw Rye reach the zenith if her power. Every kind of cargo was handled at Strand Quay, and records show that up to two hun-dred ships could anchor near the Strand Gate.

However, by that century's end, the fortified town with its embattled mental-ity embarked on a long decline, as the harbour slowly silted up. The Civil War lent a brief return to prominence, as a staunch Puritan stronghold, and in 1773 John Wesley called there to find the population "willing to hear the good word," but refusing to part with "the accursed thing, smuggling." They wanted to have their celestial cake while still enjoying their terrestrial cookies. Indeed the "accursed thing" never left them. By the eighteenth century, Rye's prosperity depended as much on smuggling as on any legitimate trade.

The effects of all this patchwork of miscellaneous, cumulative circumstance had left a historical hodgepodge, a museum piece accidentally accreted rather than artificially arranged. I found it a very daunting place from which to glean the fleeting frailties of contemporary news. What, from all the paltry chronicles of twentieth century incident, could possibly be of consequence when measured against that earlier and immeasurably greater ebb and flow of tide and fortune? As well might the prizewinning results of the latest Women's Institute crochet con-test be appended to the Bayeaux tapestry.

Stretching to the east of Rye, on the other side of the Kentish border, were the Romney Marshes, home of the fictitious *Doctor Syn*, vicar by day and smuggler by night; a much more titillating contrast of good and evil than was ever achieved by R.L. Stevenson in *Dr. Jekyll and Mr. Hyde*. This morally challenged character was reportedly conceived when Arthur Russell Thorndike stayed up late one night to provide company for his sister, later to become the renowned actress Dame Sybil Thorndike. Both had earlier that day seen the body of a shooting victim in the street outside the London theatre where they had rehearsed *The Tempest*. Sybil felt the corpse was staring up at her bedroom, preventing her from sleeping. From her discussion with her brother, of that macabre image, was born the unsavoury character of *Doctor Syn, Scarecrow of the Romney Marshes*. His one redeeming feature was that he "never attacked a British ship".

Redoubtable Mrs. Bannister

In my view much more formidable than Doctor Syn, with a substantial and tangible girth and presence that would put any scarecrow to flight, was my landlady, Mrs. Bannister, owner of a three-floor terrace house in Winchelsea Road. She made that important point of ownership plain to all guests who might otherwise have assumed it was her good-for-nothing husband who held the title deeds.

Mrs. Bannister was a self-made woman, she was, long before all that rubbish about female emancipation or whatever you might call it. She had been in service, she had, in the days of all them grand houses when servants was put in their place and expected to serve the tea on silver trays without talking back. She had survived all of that parlour maid stuff, all of that curtseying and carrying on. She had saved her pennies till they became shillings and pounds, enough to put away for a house of her own, where *she* would be mistress and tell other people what to do.

I was one of those who would now be on the receiving end of being told what to do, without talking back. I was one of her paying lodgers, with a room of my own, breakfast and dinner included (no lunch; she never did lunches, she didn't!)

Mrs. Bannister had a creased, deep-set mouth, because she made it a point never to wear her false teeth indoors ("They're enough trouble in the street, they are."). Below this curiously sunken, slightly concertina effect, her jaw stuck out like a miniature battering ram, ready to thrust its way through any argument and push aside anything that smacked even faintly of "talkback". In her house, you spoke when you were spoken to, otherwise you'd go straight upstairs to your room.

She looked askance at my appearance, and even more dubiously at the paraphernalia of my profession. She was used to having navvies in her rooms, who were all right as long as they behaved themselves, didn't drink on the premises, and left their shovels and things out in the yard. She wasn't used to her guests bringing strange machinery into the house.

"What's that then?" she inquired of my portable typewriter.

I opened the lid to demonstrate its function.

"I don't care if it types right or wrong, I'm not having them keys flinging their ink all over my lilac wallpaper."

I assured her they wouldn't, and nervously demonstrated my point. I even offered to type her letters for her.

"Well make sure it don't keep me awake at night."

"I shall be extremely quiet, Mrs. Bannister. You won't be aware of my presence."

"That won't suit me. It gets me worried when I don't know what my guests are up to in their rooms."

"I shall cough occasionally. Discreetly of course."

She regarded me with narrowed eyes over the tops of her half spectacles. Was I having her on?

Mrs. Bannister's cooking left much to be, not so much desired, as yearned for. Boiled potatoes with everything, spare ribs on which scant flesh clung tenaciously to the bone, stews composed largely of boiled gristle and glutinous gravy with the half-cooked peas floating on the surface. And for afters there was her speciality, well pudding, so named because the unwary might plunge a fork through the crust and receive an eyeful of hot treacle. The recipe was simple enough; take a lump of lard, thoroughly blended with brown sugar, encase it in a mould of flour mixed with suet, bake it in the oven until the inside melts to form its concealed well, and then serve.

My fellow guests and I would feign astonished delight. "Well, well, well, look what we have for dessert!"

Breakfast was a one-woman production line. Toast after toast was submitted for incineration in the oven, while eggs were smashed together for the accompanying omelette; all to be washed down with thick mugs of tea. In the midst of this, her good-for-nothing husband, in pyjamas and threadbare cardigan, would materialize, chamber pot and contents either borne triumphantly to their disposal in the outdoor loo or else—just for a laugh—balanced on his head as he sashayed his way through the combination kitchen-dining room.

"You stop that this minute, Bill Bannister," she would decree. "Now go wash your hands and make yourself presentable. Can't you see we have guests for company?"

With his drooping walrus moustache, Old Bill, had he been born some forty year earlier, could have been the model for that other "Old Bill", the much loved cartoon figure of World War One created by Bruce Bairnsfather. Except that our

Old Bill was too perennially cheerful to develop his famous namesake's cynical character.

The Kikuyu Bishop Who Won her Heart

By 1956, British troops were gaining the upper hand in bringing Kenya's Mau Mau rebellion under control. They were undertaking a massive programme to relocate the Kikuyu tribe and drive the rebels into the hills. A Kikuyu bishop, on a tour of Anglican churches throughout England, preached at one of our local churches in Rye. He followed this with an absorbing account of conditions in Kenya and the problems of being a Kikuyu during those troubled times, when his tribe had supplied most of the Mau Mau conscripts.

At the close of the talk, he was so immersed in admirers wanting to learn more that it was impossible for him to grant me an interview in those surroundings. He proposed we get together later in the day, and I could think of nowhere better to suggest than my digs in Winchelsea Road. He expressed interest when I cautioned that I had a strange and slightly unpredictable landlady. When I explained to Mrs. Bannister who he was, and asked if she would mind offering him some tea when he arrived, she was at first horrified and then indignant. "I'm not having a black man in *my* house," she declared flatly. "I never even *seen* one except on TV."

"He's an Anglican bishop, Mrs. Bannister."

"He can be an Anglican *pope* for all I care. He's *black* is all I need to know."

I was in a quandary. If I pursued the subject I would be committing the cardinal sin of talking back to her. I could see the jaw thrusting pugnaciously forward like a turtle head from its armour plating, ready to repel all boarders. There was no time to telephone the bishop and suggest an alternative. He was already on his way by taxi. I waited on the sidewalk to intercept his arrival. At the top of the steps behind me, standing in the doorway with arms akimbo, was Mrs. Bannister, ready to physically bar his presence if need be.

The taxi pulled up and the bishop dismounted, looking straight past me and smiling instantly at the sight of the redoubtable Mrs. B. Lunging by me, and taking the steps two at a time, arm extended in greeting, he said, "You must be Mrs. Bannister. I've heard *so* many good things about you that your ears must be tingling. Allow me to say what a pleasure it is to meet you at least."

Mrs. Banister melted faster, and infinitely more gracefully, than any of her famous well puddings. She not only took his arm, but led him off to her *parlour*; a concession unheard of in all the months I had lived there. Her parlour was her shrine, her tabernacle, the exaltation of all she had striven for, not to be used by mere guests. It was to be a good while, measured out in numerous cups of tea served in her best china, before she surrendered the bishop to my care.

She would have regretted, I know, not having had a chance to instal her false teeth, for they, like her parlour, were reserved for exhibition on such special occasions. Their normal place of repose was a tiny shelf below the face mirror on her ornamental hat-stand in the hallway, where they sat on a lace doily in the manner of a blessed sacrament upon the altar. They served a pivotal role in the ritual of going out, which seldom varied in its order of ceremonial. First to be donned was the overcoat, followed by the scarf. Next came the hat, usually a round pill-box affair with a hatpin to hold it in place, then the teeth, wiggled around until they fell into the least uncomfortable position, and finally the gloves, plus umbrella if need be.

When all was in place, she would lean forward towards the mirror, as if challenging it to talk back to her by revealing who was the fairest in the land. Her lips would curl in a half smile-half snarl which helped calm her anxiety regarding the possibility of the dentures falling out halfway down the street. Then she would be off, hoping not to meet any acquaintance who might detain her in conversation and—heaven forbid—force her to respond by speaking through her teeth while simultaneously preventing them from leaving her gums.

Upon her return, the order of ceremonial was reversed, the gloves positively torn off in her impatience to remove the teeth, at which point she would pause, smacking her gums loudly as if consoling them for having suffered in silence.

"I met that Carter woman," she would announce to the mirror. "Oh she was a right pain, carrying on about her liver. I ask you, *her* liver! Which isn't a patch on mine, I can tell you. Why I've had at least five times more operations than she has. But could I tell her that? Not with these teeth. It would have taken all day. She *knew* she had me at a disadvantage, the old bat. So what did I do? I just nods and nods and nods, as if I agreed with everything what she was saying. Oh the cow!" Catching my reflection in the glass, she would turn and ask, "Feel like a cup of tea? My poor old gums could do with a cup of tea, they could."

Urgency of Buttered Kippers

There were special treats for me when Mrs. Bannister's other boarders—mostly itinerant navvies with the occasional travelling salesman—had gone their separate ways. I was her only regular, so I deserved indulgence now and then. Mostly it would be buttered kippers for supper and—if I was really in luck—*new* potatoes.

These special treats were not to be taken lightly. If one was on the way I was informed of it well in advance, in a "you be sure and be here now" tone of voice.

One special treat day I had to report to the police station again to reclaim my missing wallet. This would be the fourth or fifth time I'd left it in the same telephone booth, near the bottom of Mermaid Street. I would assemble my stories for the week and then spend anything up to an hour reading them over the phone to a copy stenographer in Lewes, where the *East Sussex Express and County Herald* had its headquarters. My wallet would be lying open on the shelf where the telephone directories were stored, enabling me to continue feeding change into the slot to keep the line open. Too often I would leave the wallet there and not remember it until I needed change again.

By that time it would have found its way intact, via one or other thoughtful, kindly soul, to the police station, whose occupants were by now thoroughly familiar with it and would know straight away whose it was. Sometimes a constable whose beat took him past my lodgings in Winchelsea Road would remember to drop by and inform Mrs. Bannister I'd done it again.

My absent-mindedness was by now unmistakably established as a chronic condition, its recurrence especially marked in the vicinity of telephone booths. One such lay at the other end of St. George's Road, some two hundred yards from our home at number 95. I might ride there on my scooter, put through my call and then walk back home. Later I would find my scooter missing from the front of the house and leap to the conclusion it had been stolen. My father, busy tending his motorcycle by the kerb, would look down the road and point out that whoever stole it had inexplicably left it outside the telephone booth.

He had special cause to suspect that my still formative mind was losing the struggle to make adequate sense of the world. Perhaps the failure lay in my optic nerve; in its inability to convert what I saw into what I thought. On one occasion, threading my characteristically rapid course through pedestrians on Queen's Road, I had collided with him, apologized, and sped on, unconscious of who he was, despite brief eye-to-eye contact. He was so incensed, he ran after me to upbraid me for my inconceivable rudeness.

On the occasion of the promised kippers, the constable on duty at Rye police station leaned over the desk and waggled the wallet at me. "Some day you're going to lose this, young man. Or else you won't have all your money in it by the time you get it back."

Strolling back to digs, I decided I would drop by my favourite bookshop in Rye, located in Market Street near that pinnacle of Rye's pyramidal perfection, St. Mary's Church. It was near closing time, but leaving me enough latitude to see what might be new. Unfortunately the owner wasn't there, but his daughter Delia was. A girl more ample than appealing, Delia was the sort you'd expect to see captaining the hockey team in Ronald Searle's "*St. Trinian's*". She had cast predatory eyes upon me before, but her father's presence had served to safeguard me.

On this occasion she made her intentions clear by locking the door, turning the hanging sign from "Open" to "Closed" and advancing upon me in the back shelves. Rolling on the floor, somewhere between early volumes of *Encyclopaedia Britannica* and Gibbon's *Decline and Fall of the Roman Empire*, I ventured to protest that Mrs. Bannister's kippers would be getting cold if I didn't hurry back to my lodgings. The thought of hot kippers seemed merely to inflame her ardour, so that I began to reconcile myself to the fact that, if I did have to lose my virginity, at least it would be in literary surroundings in a secondhand bookstore.

At this point the phone rang. Initially ignoring this intrusion, she must eventually have decided it was her father calling, for she petulantly relieved me of her weight and went to answer it. I made my escape. Coping with Delia's anger was a prospect less daunting than facing up to my landlady's.

That night I dreamt I was standing at the altar rails, before a waiting priest, who was looking past me towards the door. The church was filled with swelling organ tones of the bridal march from *Lohengrin,* and I was conscious that a woman in white had materialised beside me. Turning, I saw Delia, a smug smile of satisfaction on her face. I had dreamed of this situation before, but always hitherto the woman had been a complete stranger. Now that she had acquired a face, the nightmare seemed more palpable. I resolved that there were quite enough secondhand bookshops in East Sussex without requiring me to return to the one in Market Street.

Seeking the Undercurrents

My Vespa scooter got a fair bit of use. At least once a week I had to make a circuit of all the villages in my district; Rye Harbour, Winchelsea, Icklesham, Guestling, Udimore, Brede, Broad Oak, Beckley, Northiam and Peasmarsh. I chose different days for different sectors. Regular ports of call would include the vicarage, the undertaker and the social secretary of the local community hall.

Always I would hope for some hint of scandal, some breath of the morally tainted or even downright reprehensible; any spice to enliven the catalogue of weddings, funerals, whist drive results and jumble sales. I would pose cautiously phrased questions, designed to draw admissions of other miscellaneous doings, perhaps of a less "routine" nature. It seemed at times that the respective verger, vicar, mortician or district nurse was about to divulge the inadmissible, only to be reined back from the brink by contemplating the consequences of such indiscretion. Was there a general assumption that the columns of the *East Sussex Express and County Herald* must not be sullied by that secret other life, running like a dark river below these rustic acres? Were they saving it up for the *News of the World?* I fervently hoped so, for their sakes, because the alternative would mean they were little better than lobotomised patients, languishing in a sanatorium.

How could all of those people be leading entirely circumspect lives? If Rye had been such a haunt of writers—including Henry James and E.F. Benson—where had they done their haunting? What could possibly have inspired them among this insipid and unsullied populace? Henry James, of course had turned back to his American homeland for subject matter. Only Benson populated Rye (renaming it *Tilling*) with the characters of his *Mapp* and *Lucia* books. But those brittle satires were set in the 1920s. In my day I found no one to compare with Lucia, dominatrix of the teacup, and Miss Mapp, her unwilling stooge.

Both authors had lived, successively, at Lamb House, five minutes walk from my digs in Winchelsea Road. In 1950, six years before I arrived in Rye, Lamb House was presented to the National Trust by Mrs. Henry James Jr, wife of Henry James's nephew. The white-panelled Henry James Room displayed some of the writer's furniture and part of his library. On rare days when I was entertained to tea there, I envied James and his successors their quiet seclusion at the top end of West Street, just around the corner from historic Mermaid Street. It *felt* like a writer's house. In James's day, his guests had included Hugh Walpole, H.G. Wells, Ford Maddox Ford, Rudyard Kipling, Max Beerbohm and Edith Wharton.

The Benson brothers, E.F. and A.C., took over Lamb House after James's death in 1916. A later tenant was Rumer Godden, for whom I felt a particular affinity because of her own Indian childhood and her wonderful books with Indian settings, such as *Black Narcissus* and *The River*. Her obituary in *The Times* records her moving, with her second husband, James Haynes Dixon, to Rye where:

> "One dramatic night their house burnt down, though one of Godden's daughters managed to salvage the manuscript of her next novel. They moved, then, into Lamb House, previously the home of Henry James and then of the 'uncontrollably prolific' writer E. F. Benson."

Three Wheels and a Prayer

My dreams of escape from rusticity—to my mind synonymous with rust corrosion and retrogression—took tangible if misguided form when I invested fifteen pounds towards the purchase of a BSA three-wheeler. This at last presented me with the means of returning to India.

The initiator of this enterprise, and my proposed partner in its execution, was Mike Townson, who was also my newspaper rival from the opposition rag, the *Kentish Gazette*. Mike, who later in life went on to produce documentary television programmes for the BBC, working with the likes of Alan Whicker, Trevor Philpott, Julian Pettifer, Fyfe Robertson and Cliff Michelmore on that pioneering example of investigative journalism, the *Tonight* show, was adept at pulling surprises out of hats. His father had been a talented magician, and Mike had acquired many of his skills. He had found this dilapidated vehicle of 1935 vintage on offer for a mere thirty quid, which he persuaded me we could afford if we split the cost. Mike had a driver's licence, but mine was valid only for motorcycles, so he began to provide me with driving lessons in this highly irregular mode of conveyance.

B. S. A. Cycles Ltd. had launched their three-wheeler in 1929. Designed by F. W. Hulse, it was powered by a 1021 cc vee-twin engine, which drove the two front wheels, independently sprung by transverse springs. The third wheel trailed at the stern, where the coachwork tapered like the back end of a cockroach. Driver and passenger were seated side by side in an open cab, fitted with a folding roof in the event of rain. From its inception until production ceased in 1936, some 5,200 two-cylinder models and 1,700 four-cylinder models of this three-wheeler were sold.

It quickly became apparent that our particular two-cylinder BSA lacked power. But this, we felt, was nothing that a good garage couldn't sort out. We began to get together every evening, poring over large-scale maps of Europe and Asia, plotting the course of a cross-continental odyssey that would take us out to Burma and beyond. I wrote off to BSA's parent body, declaring our intentions and seeking their sponsorship for a project that would "revive the enduring spirit of the three-wheeler as a flagship for BSA workmanship and design". Mike came up with the draft of a press release, together with photographs, that we proposed to issue when the time came to set forth on our historic journey. He also produced a presentation kit to market to prospective clients, showing where their products and services could be advertised on the bodywork.

We calculated what luggage and equipment we would require, and how much could be stored in the limited space available. A spade, we thought, was indispensable for digging our wheels out of any bogs or deserts we encountered. We also debated when we should inform our respective newspapers of our intended resignations. Mike's mother was very supportive and sympathetic, in the way that mothers are when they encourage their children to believe in and write to Santa Claus. She was in no real danger of losing her son, since she must have seen that our wild ambitions couldn't possibly be realised. She ran Fletcher House, the teashop just below the clock tower of Rye's crowning achievement, St. Mary's Church.

Most of the original 12th century church had been destroyed by the French in 1377, but was replaced during the following century. On the outside of the north transept was the elaborate face of the 16th century clock. There two gilded cherubs struck bells at quarter past and quarter to the hour. The eighteen-foot pendulum inside was believed to be the oldest in England still working with its original mechanism, dating from 1561-62.

The spectacle of the cherubic chimes drew patient onlookers to cluster in the street outside the teashop, and then adjourn within when their curiosity was satisfied. Fletcher House was thus assured a constant supply of patrons for its cream teas, consisting of four cucumber and cream cheese sandwiches and a large scone, served together with whipped cream and jam, plus tea. When not running around competing with each other for stories—for one must never confuse friendship with business—Mike and I would frequently be found at a back table, bent over empty plates and cups, plotting our BSA strategies.

Fletcher House was so named because John Fletcher, dramatist and contemporary of William Shakespeare, was born there in 1579. Fletcher is chiefly remembered for his collaboration with Francis Beaumont. His earliest independent play was the pastoral *The Faithful Shepherdess* (1608/09). Before then little is known of his life. Fletcher also probably collaborated with Shakespeare on *The Two Noble Kinsmen*. He is reported to have died of the plague. His father, the Rev. Richard Fletcher, had resided in Rye for some years, and was aggrieved at not being appointed vicar. He was denied that opportunity because of the refusal of the Rev. Richard Connope to resign, despite the latter's continued absence from office. Leaving the town when his son John was only two years old, Fletcher senior was eventually installed as Bishop of London.

The house remained a private residence for many hundreds of years, but in 1932 it became a restaurant. As with the majority of buildings in Rye, few alterations were allowed. Even the original front door, with York and Tudor Roses carved on its lintel, had been retained. And in a manner entirely suitable to Rye, with its abundance of ghost stories, Fletcher House had quite recently exhibited evidence of paranormal manifestation.

At four o'clock one afternoon in 1951, Mrs. Betty Howard, one of the owners of the restaurant, was walking upstairs when she heard a noise. Turning around, she saw on the landing a few feet below a youngish man in dark lounge suit. Thinking him a customer, she reversed course to speak to him, at which point he dematerialized. He was described as six feet tall, and in his early thirties. The figure had not been seen since, but I was informed that sounds of footsteps on the stairs were still audible from time to time.

As surely and rapidly as that apparition had vanished, so evaporated our grand delusions when Mike drove with me to 95 St. George's Road, to acquaint my parents with our intentions. My father took one look under the bonnet of the BSA and declared that one of its two cylinders had jammed solid, and was beyond recovery. He did not give much for our chances of spanning half the circumference of the world on the remaining one.

Winter of My Discontent

That disappointment marked the onset of the true winter of my discontent. I felt I would never escape from provincialism, from the suffocating restraints of a life with which everyone other than me appeared to be perfectly, even infuriatingly satisfied. In earlier generations, malcontents like myself had the option of running away to sea, but the Suez Crisis earlier that year had closed the door to that particular escape route. On July 26, 1956, Egyptian President Gamal Abdel Nasser had defied the West by nationalizing the Suez Canal. He did so in retaliation against a joint American-British decision not to finance Egypt's promised construction of the Aswan High Dam, which in turn was their response to Egypt's growing ties with communist Czechoslovakia and the Soviet Union. This act eventually led to an Israeli-British-French attack on the canal zone, led by the Israelis on October 29,1956.

The timing of the invasion could not have been worse from the American perspective. With their presidential election only a week away, and the Soviets already beginning a brutal crackdown on a short-lived revolution against their authority in Hungary, the US were faced with the seemingly impossible choice of standing on principle or abandoning their allies. They chose the latter course and denounced the invasion as a belated and blatant example of long unfashionable gunboat diplomacy. The only one to emerge victorious from the whole regrettable episode was Nasser himself, seen as a hero in the cause of Arab and Egyptian nationalism. Meanwhile, the canal lay hopelessly blocked with ships deliberately scuppered to make it unusable. Many years would pass before its restoration to service.

If I couldn't afford my own passage east, on a sea voyage suddenly made considerably longer and more costly by the necessity to circumnavigate the Cape of Good Hope, I decided I would apply for an assisted passage of the kind still offered for potential settlers of Australia. The novels of Nevil Shute, particularly his *Town Like Alice, Far Country, In the Wet* and *Beyond the Black Stump,* had awakened in me a hitherto unsuspected hankering to become a sheep farmer in the vast antipodean outback.

At the time I saw no contradiction in the fact that I was surrounded by sheep farmers of Rye and the Romney Marshes. Their association's recent annual dinner, with its insufferably boring conversation on sheep diseases and the current wool market, had driven me to quit the table and drive my scooter down to Rye Harbour. There, under a suitably moon-shy sky, I roamed the strand, disconsolately kicking the hull of every beached vessel I thought might belong to a sheep farmer. I felt driven to such desperation that I was beginning to lose my last vestiges of reason.

I wrote, with the enthusiasm of a volunteer eager for antipodean endeavours, to Australia House in London, suggesting I would make a small but hopefully valuable contribution to the population of Australia's less developed interior. They wrote back to say they had no need of settlers lacking any experience other than journalism. I next turned to Canada House. Theirs was a sub-continent that lay in the wrong direction, but offered an abundance of outback, far enough removed from Great British shores to permit a fresh start in life.

This application received more sympathetic consideration, and I was invited to London for an interview. Passing both my medical examination, and whatever other criteria applied to the selection of would-be Canadians, I was accepted for an assisted passage to my future home, towards which all I would have to pay was a contribution of ten pounds sterling. I was also given a fairly generous time limit in which to settle my affairs and book my berth.

Trying to decide where to make my new start in life, I studied the map, most of which—like Australia's—looked promisingly empty in the middle. While coloured illustrations in *National Geographic* suggested it might be full of Baden-Powell enthusiasts paddling their own canoes, I knew little of Canada, other than the fact that a fellow Hastings Grammar School graduate had gone there long before me, to become Indian mystic and nature lover Grey Owl. I closed my eyes and stabbed a pin into London, Ontario, which lay sufficiently far south to be farthest away from the snow. Since the northern hemisphere was heading into the middle of winter, I decided to defer my departure until the following spring. This would allow me sufficient time for a Christmas holiday with Zena and Len in Bulford.

Accelerated Expectations

The intended Christmas holiday became a leave-taking, because events moved faster than I had planned, precipitated by the cancellation of my already approved vacation. I was informed by the *East Sussex Express and Country Herald* that their trusted equine reporter Horace Beddington would not be available to cover the Boxing Day hunt at Battle, which they were therefore assigning to me. I was furious. Battle wasn't even within my district. I hated horses, never having forgotten my distasteful experiences with the ponies of Darjeeling, and I especially loathed bloodsports. The more I contemplated the prospect of interviewing the master of the hunt, mounted in his saddle and raising a stirrup cup to his fox-slavering lips in the steaming, early morning air, the more I rebelled.

My life was coalescing into a single crucial decision. It was one of those make-or-break moments that would determine my future destiny. I lifted the phone, asked for the editor and informed him of my resignation with immediate effect. He could keep the salary due to me for all I cared. I booked my passage on a ship due to sail for Canada in January. I would be arriving in London, Ontario at the worst time of year, with no plans laid but with boundless zeal and optimism, looking for whatever work was available, which might prove as far removed from journalism as the Horse Guards from the Pay Corps.

Len and Zena were first on the list for my round of family farewells. Next would come Roley and Barbara, who lived at Amesbury, within walking distance of Bulford Camp, followed by other aunts and uncles more widely dispersed across the British Isles. It was a rare and curious juxtaposition of postings that had brought, into such close proximity; those two particular and highly individual aunts, with their very different conceptions of what it meant to be an officer's wife. To Zena the role came naturally. If she couldn't be an opera diva she would be star of the cantonment. This was her chance to play the *Burra Memsahib*, regal in bearing, commanding in manner, exemplary in conduct; the sort of major's wife than even a general's wife could look up to. Her husband might be midway up the ladder, but there was no rank higher than hers when it came to consorts.

To Barbara, the whole idea of playing officer's wife was anathema. It mattered not that her lieutenant-colonel husband was the British Army's most eminent authority on sexually transmitted diseases. She did not feel obliged to play *doyenne*, lording it over her fellow officers' wives. She would rather die than be trapped in their company for a single moment longer than the more unavoidable ceremonial occasions demanded of her, and she would sit through *those* with a barely concealed grimace of distaste on her lips.

Zena had managed to escape ever having to learn to cook, because such menial occupations were beneath the dignity of an officer's wife. However she did make an exception for curry, because nobody else could cook a curry as hot as her palate demanded. I had seen her in a cook-off duel with Ursie, whose tastes were similarly combustible, both of them lost in a kitchen swirling with clouds of acrid vapour, cigarettes hanging from their lips, eyes streaming in anticipation of the feast in store. *From the food that is about to consume us, may the Lord deliver us, amen.*

Barbara was no dab hand in the kitchen, but she wouldn't expect anyone else to cook for her. When the sheer size of her family—five children of her own, plus four adopted—made it necessary to engage domestic help, she would roll up her sleeves alongside the hired hands, enjoying their company and absorbing them into the extended family circle. Zena would invite fellow officers' wives to elevenses, in a house spotlessly maintained, where a large proportion of the furnishings were meant entirely for display and not for use. Formalities would be akin to paying respects at court. If in doubt, it was safe to assume that hats and gloves were required. She was constantly having to point out which chairs one could sit in and which ashtrays one might employ.

When Barbara entertained, her guests would be the wives of privates or non-commissioned officers, very much come-as-you-please-and-bring-the-pram. The air would be completely relaxed, in a house showing conspicuous signs of substantial occupation by both humans and animals. The noise would be considerable but the level of enjoyment palpably greater. And no one would be *permitted* to, leave alone *expected* to put on airs and graces.

A lover of classic British cars, Len always owned either a Jaguar, a Humber, a Rover or an Armstrong–Siddeley, in which Zena would require to be driven, even if it was just to the corner shop to place an order with the grocer. And no matter how short the distance, or mundane the objective, she would spend at least half an hour before the mirror, preparing for her public appearance. Barbara would throw on the most comfortable of thrift shop clothing, surmounted by her favourite but by now rather tired overcoat, and wheel out the battered perambu-

lator no longer needed for her children. With this she would head off for the corner store on foot, ignoring the discreetly parted curtains she left in her wake. But
then her preference would be to live as far away from officers' quarters as it would
be possible for Roley to arrange.

Yet in their later years of widowhood, when by the luck of the Watsons they
would once more find each other located within visiting distance, in the outer
suburbs of Sydney, Australia, Zena would be drawn closer to Barbara than to
anyone else. She would grumble at being surrounded by birds, dogs and cats, and
at Barbara's propensity for cluttering her small bungalow with life-sized plaster
saints rescued from oblivion, when the local Roman Catholic church went unpar-
donably "modern". But since Barbara wasn't prepared to make compromises, it
was Zena's turn to do so, even though in appearance she remained tall and stiff as
a ramrod, with a voice the match of Brunnehilde's.

I commiserated with Zena over the inconvenience of living with that beati-
tude of saints. It took me a while, when I was staying in that bungalow, to stop
apologising to St. Joseph whenever I stubbed my toe on him in the dark, outside
the bathroom door.

Abrupt Change of Plan

It needed just one evening for Zena and Len to talk me out of Canada. I was
mad, they said, to choose a country that spent half its life buried in snow and the
other half thawing out. The fact that I had applied to go to Australia, and was
now planning to emigrate to another of the old imperial dominions, indicated
that I was still pathetically fixated on the outmoded concept of empire. In just
two weeks' time they were sailing for Malaya, where Len was taking up a posting
with the Royal Corps of Signals in Seremban. Malaya was still—if not for much
longer—a part of that frayed old imperial tapestry. Furthermore it was hot, tropical, abundantly Asiatic; everything I had missed. Why not make my new life in
Malaya instead? I could live with them to start with, and then see how things
developed from there.

I pointed out that, whereas I need only spend ten pounds towards the subsi-
dized sea passage to Canada, I didn't have the money to sail to Malaya, especially
now that the Suez Canal was closed (Len and family would be sailing there via
the Cape). That should be no problem, said Len. It would just mean working a
few months longer than I had anticipated, until I saved up enough for the difference in fare.

But I had lost my job. I couldn't go back to the newspaper with my notebook penitently in hand, ready to record the indignities of horse trials and fox hunts. I'd have to find something *else* to do, and I hadn't been *trained* to do anything else.

What had I planned to do in Canada?

They had me there.

Len said I was in luck. The army was civilizing many services that were not required to be carried out by military personnel, such as communications for example. In Bulford Camp itself his Signals regiment were already in the process of that transition. He would see to it that I was employed in the capacity of a teleprinter operator.

But I knew nothing about operating a teleprinter.

I could type, couldn't I?

With two fingers maybe, but not fast enough for that kind of traffic.

I'd soon pick it up, he assured me. He'd see about fitting me in, first thing in the morning.

Where would I stay?

With Roley and Barbara, of course. They lived just over the hill in Amesbury.

And so, in those few minutes, that evening in December 1956, my whole future changed. I would be heading not West, but East, beyond India even, to the farthest ends of Asia.

Jacqui, seated side-saddle on the back of her father's armchair, regarded me with wry amusement, trying to picture me in the life of Bulford Army Camp. She hadn't really seen me at ease in my two-year spell of National Service, and didn't expect me to be so now that I was returning to that ambience, albeit at one remove, as a civilian in a military establishment. The schizophrenia of it appealed to her sense of humour.

Looking beyond, if I *did* make it to Malaya, to join them in the military life they would be leading there, what did I expect to find? How could I hope to adapt?

Zena and the Zulu

I went down to Southampton to see them off. I can't remember now what ship it was, but there were the usual streamers, the dockside band, the lingering good-byes. It didn't seem possible I would be seeing them again, before the year was out, on the other side of the planet. Too many things were changing too fast. Standing beside me was Jacqui's latest beau, another young subaltern of course, for those were the circles in which she moved. No doubt he too was soon destined to join the growing list of discards bobbing in her wake.

Barbara welcomed me with her customary warmth. By then Roley had left for Libya, where he had taken up his next posting and was looking for a place to stay before summoning the family. In addition to India-born Robin and Kim, the children now numbered Arleen, Deirdre and Philip. We were all living in a rented farmhouse at Amesbury, in comfortable walking distance of Bulford Camp. There I reported to the telecommunications centre at which, thanks to Len's initiative, I was to be attached for an indeterminate length of time. I was the only man in mufti, in a still military outfit whose establishment looked forward to a change of scene once all their posts were civilianized. Accepting me as one recently discharged from the army myself, they proved a decent, comfortable mob to work with, showing me how to bluff my way through the telecommunications business with a minimum of effort.

I soon learned that life was easiest on the night shift, despite its longer hours, because after about eight o'clock in the evening teleprinter traffic dwindled to a trickle that sometimes dried up altogether. Most of it, inward bound, was low priority stuff that required a simple acknowledgment before being consigned to the in-tray, where it would wait to be dealt with by the morning shift.

Only once did I have to cope with a snap inspection by a duty officer, surprised to find me lying by the teleprinter in my collapsible camp bed. Mercifully I had a book in my hands, when I might otherwise have been fast asleep. I got to my feet in my underwear and he looked around the room for my uniform, presumably hoping to discover what rank I was. He was clearly weighing whether or not he should put me on a charge, but his hopes were dashed when he learned I was a civilian. I pointed out that even if I did happen to be asleep if a message came through, the clatter of the teleprinter would instantly waken me. I demonstrated the point by persuading the quick brown fox to jump over the lazy keys a couple of times.

Mostly it was monotonous if undemanding routine. I would set off across Salisbury Plain in the darkness of a winter evening, torch in hand, sandwiches, thermos, a paperback and the latest copy of *Mad* magazine in my shoulder bag, bemused at the sight of the odd rabbit lolloping across my path, already resistant to the receding plague of myxomatosis. En route I would calculate, on my meagre weekly pay packet, how long it would take to save enough money for a passage to India, leave alone Malaya. Too long, I thought. I needed a daytime job to supplement my income.

Lying on my cot, I would lose interest in whatever I was reading and return to the pressing question of what else might contribute to my earnings. Even if I cut back on cigarettes, gave up cinemas, magazines and all other diversions, it would be well over a year before I would get to see the far face of the world. What on earth could I find to do other than what I was doing already? Amesbury was not a very large village, but it had windows. And it lacked, as far as I had been able to determine, a window cleaner. There was my answer! Better than being an over-grown chimney sweep that had outlived the pages of Kingsley's *Water Babies*. I could borrow a bicycle—which would also come in handy for cycling to work—a ladder, a bucket, a sponge and some liquid detergent and off to work I'd go.

Barbara helped organise the wherewithal to get me started. She also got me a soft chammy leather to polish the panes after I'd washed them. I mastered the art of pedalling a bicycle with a ladder over my shoulder and the bucket balanced on the rear carrier. I went from door to door, introducing myself, quoting a fee of five shillings for ground floor windows and another five for upstairs. I couldn't reach higher than that and avoided the houses where I might be expected to; but there were few of those in Amesbury.

House by house, shilling by shilling, the piggy bank began to fill. Sometimes the woman of the house would follow me out on to the lawn for a chat, sometimes she would ply me with biscuits and tea; occasionally she might stand in the doorway, weighing me up, calculating if I might be good for something other than cleaning her windows. Fortunately I was never called upon to disprove that supposition. But then I guess Amesbury was so small a place that a ladder and bicycle, parked any length of time by the front door, would be certain to attract both attention and speculation.

The first of a series of encouraging letters arrived from Aunt Zena, containing photographs of the voyage out. At Durban the family had gone ashore to savour the customary tourist sights. One snapshot was of a Zulu warrior, his massive midriff girded by a leopard skin, menacing Zena with a spear. Undaunted, she was portrayed raising herself to her fullest extent on high heels, ready to retaliate with her handbag.

Subsequent letters enclosed vignettes of the new lifestyle as the family settled into their military quarters in Kuala Lumpur, with Zena queening it on the verandah, attended by a tray-bearing Chinese houseboy, Len in tropical uniform, standing by his Armstrong-Siddeley with one foot on the running board, Jacqui and Gordon disporting themselves in the officers' club swimming pool.

Over an early supper, before I was due to report for night shift, I would ask Barbara if I could play again her 78 rpm record of *Moon Over Malaya*, with its haunting evocation of singsong girls, eastern stars and native bazaars. Running around my head like an *idee fixe*, the tune became my talisman.

Overland Option

Long-distance flights were prohibitively costly then, and sea voyages still by far the cheaper alternative. But flying was the way to go if you were a serviceman's wife. When Barbara and her children left for Libya, aboard a prop-jet military transport that would take forever and a day, I moved into digs with a neighbouring farmer and his family. The cost of room and board was going to add to my outgoings and slow down my savings. Already I had exhausted the possibilities of both Amesbury and Bulford where window cleaning was concerned. There is a limit to how often you can turn up at the door, asking to clean the same windows.

I decided to invest in a train ride to Southampton, to see if there were any opportunities in the merchant marine. Maybe I could work my passage to Singapore and jump ship there. But the queue outside the recruiting office, even before it opened, was so long, and so stocked with hardened sailors whose experience would count in their favour, that I didn't hang around to learn the inevitable. With fewer ships now sailing the longer route via the Cape, there was little likelihood of vacancies for complete novices like me.

My landlord kindly offered to reduce the burden of my rent. He suggested I defray some of the cost through helping with odd chores around the farm. I assisted in herding his cattle and learned to drive his tractor. I spent glorious spring days ploughing his fields, craning my neck to ensure I followed a more or less straight furrow. I got so nut brown I wondered if my aunt Zena would acknowledge me as her nephew.

Entrusting me with the farm, and all their possessions, the family set off for a motoring holiday in Dorset. The wife was particularly anxious that I should take good care of a litter of pure-bred Siamese kittens her prizewinning cat had just produced. It was very important that I should not let too much light into the small back room where they were kept, because excessive sunlight could ruin the blue of their eyes. I dutifully prepared their formula food and—being careful to close the door behind me—conveyed it into semi-darkness, to be spat on and slashed at by the most wicked, vicious and ungrateful kittens I have ever encountered in my life. I could cheerfully have drowned the lot of them.

One day I saw an article in the *Daily Express* on the introduction of the first commercially operated overland bus service from London to Calcutta. The report was accompanied by a photograph of the bus, down the side of which was depicted the route of the journey, which embraced such cities as Paris, Milan, Venice, Trieste, Istanbul, Ankara, Kerman, Teheran, Amritsar and New Delhi. The pioneer expedition was set for the Easter of 1957, with a second to follow in the autumn.

It seemed too good to be true. I wrote to the address given and received a reply from the secretary of the director, Mr. Paddy Garrow-Fisher. Mr. Garrow-Fisher, I was told, was away, personally leading the party that had signed up for the first trip. He hoped to return in late July or early August.

Could I put my name down for the next trip?

Yes I could, for a small deposit. The total fare would be eighty-five pounds, one way.

I calculated I could save enough for a seat on the bus, but that was all I would get for my money. Living expenses en route would be met by the passengers. I would have to work extra hard to cover those expenses.

India Bound

Some two weeks before departure, we met in London for a briefing and getting-to-know-you session, There were sixteen of us on the manifest; eight men and eight women of varying age, from early twenties to late sixties. We included two Canadian architects, who had never met before, two Australian nurses and a Pakistani, also of that profession, who would be joining us later, en route. The rest of us were British (although I privately regarded myself as not falling quite so conveniently into that category).

We were shown slides from the first journey; unbroken vistas of desert, dust-caked faces smiling wearily through the flaps of pup tents, groups squatting around primus stoves, preparing their meals. It all looked very rugged and alfresco. We were reminded we should, by now, have obtained a whole slew of visas, together with jabs for every known disease we might conceivably encounter en route. We would also require lots of Enteroviaform and insect repellant. Whatever clothes we took with us would not long survive the conditions we would encounter, because no matter how tightly our luggage might be sealed, dust would get in and slowly, relentlessly grind the fabric threadbare.

We were left to wonder, was our journey really necessary? Oh yes it was, for some more than others perhaps, but none of us were prepared to back down. I packed in my job at the teleprinter office in Bulford, said goodbye to my kindly farmer and his family and headed home to Hastings to make my farewells.

Mum was disconsolate. She felt I was leaving England because, in some way she couldn't quite understand, she had failed me as a mother. Why else would I be so discontent with life in a country that she had learned to accept, and even love? My decision had nothing to do with her, I assured her. I just couldn't bear to think that the country she had learned to accept, and even love, was all that life held for *me*.

Dad told me in no uncertain terms that he thought me stark, raving mad. In addition to the eighty-five pounds I had expended on my fare, my total allowance for all additional expenditure would be forty-five pounds. From this I must not only find the means to survive a journey across two continents, but save enough to make a fresh start in life at the other end. God, I naïvely assured him, would provide. If only *He* could make allowance for the fact that so far I had evidenced very little faith in my ability to attract his attention or engage his concern. What I really meant to say, as Dad accurately judged, was that my optimism was so supreme, my self-confidence so overweening, that I simply hadn't allowed for the possibility of failure.

Mother couldn't bring herself to see me off on the train to London, so it was left to Dad to accompany me to the station. On the platform, as the train was about to pull out, he suddenly clutched my hand and wept. It was so shatteringly unexpected that it left me speechless. I could only grip his fingers in response and then let go as the train pulled us apart. I sank back into the seat of my otherwise empty compartment and gazed, as ever, at my reflection when we entered the tunnel. What was I doing? What had I *done?*

There really is no room for such questions once a course has been set. You can only press on and see it through. I was twenty-two years old. I was leaving on a train without a return ticket. I would not be seeing my face in that haunted mirror any more, or asking those same questions of myself ever again. Though admittedly still a virgin, and possibly forever doomed to remain so, I was finally breaking through the cocoon that had so tenaciously wrapped itself around my life.

I stared defiantly back at the glass.

Gnikoms on, the windows mocked. *Gnikoms on.*

Destination Bombay

It is perhaps true of any journey that the longer it lasts, the more it palls. If so, it is especially true of journeys undertaken in the company of fellow travellers in whose selection you played no part. We began with the highest of spirits and best of intentions, that day at the close of August 1957, that day when Malaya was declaring an independence whose inauguration I would arrive too late to observe. We assembled in the crowded bus lanes of Victoria station, where coaches were departing for Margate, Brighton and Bournemouth. We hunted among their serried ranks for one announcing its destination as Bombay. Having traversed the distance to Calcutta on the initial journey, Paddy Garrow-Fisher had decided to switch to Bombay for this second trip.

The coach we found, painted a khaki shade of yellow, was if anything smaller than the ones bound for various seaside resorts within four hours driving distance. And it was conspicuously older—considerably so—clearly designed to serve those same English spas in an earlier era. Other than removal of the last row of seats, to allow greater space for storage of baggage, tents and cooking utensils, it appeared to have undergone no special adaptation in preparation for a journey designed to last some eight thousand miles as opposed to eighty.

Day-trippers boarding their luxury clippers on all sides of us looked quizzically upon a vintage vehicle calling itself *The Indiaman,* and blatantly substantiating that appellation with a map of the route stretching the entire length of each side. One or two came over to inquire where we bought the tickets and how long the trip would last. We told them, quite truthfully, that we hadn't been provided with tickets or any specific dates, but we hoped the trip would not last longer than six weeks.

Paddy Garrow-Fisher arrived to take charge. In addition to running the company business at long-distance, with his secretary back in the London office to hold the fort, he was going to be our sole driver and guide for the entire route. With him was his diminutive Indian wife Moti, who took her place, cross-legged, on an enormous bed-roll at the front of the bus beside her husband. She was responsible for producing the right maps relating to every sector of the journey.

We found our seats, to which we laid territorial claims that would survive the entire distance. I sat in the last surviving row, immediately in front of the improvised baggage compartment. Alongside me was a sandy-haired young man my age, who diffidently introduced himself as Nigel Service. I was to find, as we progressed, that I had made a fortunate choice of travelling companion. Nigel and I established a friendship which long outlived the journey.

At Dover we boarded a ferry that headed into appalling seas. I survived the open decks longer than most, peering through my camera's viewfinder at a scene suddenly obscured by the descent of a giant wave that submerged me entirely. I had to dry out the camera, whose condition concerned me more than the state of my clothing. But since it was also necessary for me to get to my suitcase, I set out to accomplish both objectives at the back end of the bus, in the dark and deserted bowels of the ferry. This presented greater difficulties than I anticipated.

The pitching and yawing threw me around to the point where I couldn't keep my balance, leave alone change my trousers. In the midst of trying to perform this task, I was so overcome by nausea that I abandoned the bus, one foot caught in a trouser leg and the other out, hopping over to the bilges to throw up. The whole miserable ordeal was accompanied by further such interruptions until I feared I would pass out.

Crawling back upstairs, I found the entire compliment of passengers, and a large part of the crew, laid low by the ferocity of the seas we were taking on board. I made my way to the purser's desk, where I had been advised to get my passport stamped. A hand materialized over the counter, groping for the stamp with which to affix the necessary entry. I guided hand and stamp to the first empty page in my almost virginal passport. I learned later it was one of the worst crossings in living memory.

Getting from A to B

It was soon apparent that this would be no guided tour of interesting landmarks encountered en route. No explanations were forthcoming other than those obtainable from fellow passengers who had the foresight to arm themselves with guide books. Paddy's objective was to cover the distance from A to B as fast as possible. We had a long way to go and he knew conditions would deteriorate steadily the further we progressed. The good roads were where he planned to make the best time.

I wished I had prepared myself by reading more about the geography of Europe, but neither geography in general nor Europe in particular had figured high on my reading list. Nigel was a great deal more knowledgeable on both, and prepared to share that knowledge with me. He proved particularly useful in Paris, where I found the hotel and the food so prohibitively expensive that I envisaged my hard won savings running out before we reached Italy. It was Nigel who taught me the cheapest way to sustain myself was a loaf of delectable French bread and a hunk of cheese.

At Lyon he pointed out the "Canut" apartments, characterised by high ceilings to accommodate the machinery for silk-production and named after the weavers who had occupied them and made the city such a bastion of industry. The *bourgeoisie*, on the other hand, had constructed their impressive flats in the old neighbourhood around the city centre, notably along the Saône river, leading to the *Tête d'Or* park, where we watched old men playing *la boule*.

Somewhere past Grenoble, we took a wrong turn towards the Swiss rather than the Italian border. Once we'd sorted that out, we headed for Turin and Milan, where we paused for a visit to the cathedral and then pressed on to a camp site by the shores of Lake Como. There were many of us who had looked forward to Como, with its old town, basilica and *Piazza Cavour*, but no, time wasn't going to permit, so on we sailed, out of Lombardy and into Veneto. Here we demanded, and were granted, time to linger over Shakespeare's Italy.

The view has been expressed that Shakespeare must have been Italian because no less than fifteen of his plays have Italian settings. If so he would have been an Italian very poorly informed of his own country because in *The Tempest*, Prospero tells his daughter how they were put aboard a small boat at the gates of Milan and borne out to sea. In *The Taming of the Shrew* we hear of people "coming ashore" at Padua, while in *Two Gentlemen of Verona* Panthino warns Launce that he will lose the tide if he tarries any longer. Nevertheless, Italian or not, the plays were the thing, and to see those inland cities where they were set did not disappoint in any way.

For all aboard the good ship *Indiaman*, the crowning joy of Shakespeare country was the city where the Bard *did* get his tide tables right; glorious Venice. With or without its *Merchant* and its *Othello*, Venice swept us away. I strolled and strolled, bridge after bridge, canal after canal, lost in the wonder of shifting diaphanous auroras of light, dancing on bulging brick walls that had never been parted from the patterns and sounds of water.

I deliberately left to last the *Piazza San Marco*, described by the French poet Alfred de Musset as "the drawing room of the world". Certainly it was charging, for its time, drawing room prices. The cafeteria overlooking that hallowed, if pigeon-ridden expanse, billed me an outrageous five shillings for a cup of coffee. Since I had budgeted no more than a pound a day, that represented a quarter of my daily allowance.

Writing up an account of that day's giddy experiences, in the vineyard on the outskirts of Venice where we had erected out tents, I was so fiercely bitten by mosquitoes that my entire face swelled like a balloon and I was barely able to open my eyes the following morning. My first mosquitoes since India, and were they making up for it!

Accused of Espionage

It is the images held by the eye, rather than captured by the camera, that linger longest; our first view of Trieste, white in the sun, clinging to the coast of the Adriatic Sea, a cavernous restaurant below the castle in the old city of Ljubljana, the wide open squares of Zagreb, the wonderful parks and gardens along the Danube in Belgrade. And then, in a little mountain village near Nis, on the way to the Bulgarian border, something of an entirely different order, when we ran abruptly into a tragic-comic episode that brought us face to face with the realities of what it meant to be so far off the beaten track.

I had been recording picturesque village scenes with my early model Japanese camera, and Robin Whitelaw, one of the two Canadian architects in our party, had contributed to this souvenir gathering by using the camera on my behalf. He had just obtained a shot of me getting my dusty shoes pampered by a street Arab bootblack when a man in uniform approached, confiscated the camera and indicated that we were both to consider ourselves under arrest.

On what grounds? we demanded.

Espionage, he replied. We were to accompany him to the police station.

What was he? A soldier? A policeman? His uniform was so unkempt he might have been a minor official in the sanitary department, but his lack of English made it as impossible for us to ask him to explain. He conducted us to a grim looking building that looked more like a penitentiary than a police station.

"Abandon hope all ye who enter here," I murmured to Robin.

We were kept waiting an interminable length of time before we were conducted into a small, dark, sparsely furnished office where another man, speaking just a little more English, asked us what we had been photographing. I accepted responsibility for the camera and pointed out Robin was only involved because I had requested him to take a couple of snapshots of me. I assured our interrogator there was nothing in the camera except innocuous scenes of village life; women heading for market, a train of mules going past, that sort of thing. How much of this he understood was impossible to guess.

He regarded us in silence for a moment and then pointed out that if there was indeed nothing of importance on the photographic record—no military installations for example—we presumably wouldn't mid having the film developed. I asked a tactless question. Was a village so small, so remote, so primitive, capable of developing a film? I merely wanted to know because there were some attractive scenes I had recorded on that roll which I wouldn't wish to lose. This was not a good move, and his scowl made the point immediately obvious. With or without my permission, he had arranged to have the film processed by a local photographic studio. We were to accompany him to that studio to view the outcome.

We set off down the street, joined by our original captor and a small procession of children, to a shop that seemed anything *but* a photographic studio. The miscellany of articles on offer contained nothing vaguely suggestive of that possibility. There our wait continued, until an elderly man emerged from a curtain at the rear of the crowded premises, holding a dripping roll of processed film and a strip of contact prints.

The two "policemen" regarded the latter with keen intensity and then passed the prints, negatives and camera to me. They declared themselves satisfied that the photographic evidence bore out my explanation. We were free to leave.

"And by the way," said Robin over his shoulder, "do have yourselves a nice day now, you hear?"

"Come on, Robin," I murmured, "before we find ourselves charged with issuing unwarranted threats." Having a nice day appeared to be the last occupation they were prepared to permit, either on their own or on anyone else's behalf. I could only thank God it wasn't a roll of colour film in my camera. I didn't want to think what they might have done with *that*.

Byzantium Revisited

Some curiously Byzantine presence still lingered over Bulgaria. In 1014 the Byzantine emperor Basil II had won a battle over the Bulgarian army, after which he ordered fourteen thousand prisoners to be blinded. It seemed as if the current communist regime had condemned the entire Bulgarian populace to the same fate, more mercifully fulfilled by effectively putting blinkers on the lot of them.

In September 1944 the Soviet Union had declared war on, and rapidly occupied this miniscule country. In conjunction with the Soviet invasion, a communist-led coalition, called the Fatherland Front, seized power in Sofia. Under Todor Zhivkov, the communists consolidated their power and by the end of 1947 had completely eliminated their opponents. Bulgaria had since acquired the reputation of being the most loyal ally of the Soviet Union, slavishly imitating Soviet collectivization and industrialization policies. It had also acquired a reputation as the most inaccessible state in southern Europe.

Our visas stipulated we were granted twenty-four hours to traverse the country, and our cameras were sealed on entry. Thracians, Greeks, Romans, Byzantines, Turks and Slavs had swept across this landlocked territory through the centuries, leaving their traces in the physiognomy of its people, but we had a day in which to get in and out. Furthermore we were required to stay in the hotel officially approved for reception of foreign guests.

Moving slowly through the streets of Sofia, looking for this hotel, *The Indiaman* attracted the attention due an unidentifiable fleeting object. Men deserted their tables at outdoor cafés to come running after us, trying to comprehend the astonishing news of our origin and destination, as conveyed by the map spread across both sides of our vehicle. The looked up at our windows as if expecting to see green faces with pointed ears. Some clung to the partly open door behind Moti's bedroll, employing scant English in desperate appeals to be pulled aboard, to be hidden in our baggage, to be smuggled out of the country. They would be willing, on the spur of that incredible moment, to desert wife, children, home and country in order to be transported to another galaxy.

If we had no room for them, could we at least take postcards to convey to relatives outside the iron curtain that had descended across their frontiers? We sought Paddy's advice, and he pointed out that we risked compromising the strict conditions under which we had been granted our hard-earned visas, so we could only shake our heads and reluctantly decline those earnest, heartfelt pleas.

Stopped in front of our hotel, we were immediately surrounded by crowds, held back by a ring of security personnel, presumably policemen, who cleared a path for us through to the front door. The hotel, whose name I cannot now recall, looked old and grandly imperial, with enormous crystal chandeliers and vast expanses of carpet and marble. We checked into palatial rooms, enjoyed luxurious baths and sauntered down a sweeping staircase to the restaurant, where we were horrified to learn the cost of so much as a simple snack. Only visiting Soviet officials could afford prices beyond the reach of us mere capitalists. Nigel Service and I decided to retire to our rooms and consume the last of our stale loaves and cheese.

Paddy insisted on an early start in the morning, so that, stomachs grumbling, we boarded the bus to speed eastwards through deserted streets towards Plovdiv, Khaskovo and beyond. We had until sunset to reach the Turkish border. "Failing which," observed our hard-bitten and cynical Isabel, widowed in her sixties and travelling ever since, "we will all be lined up against the wall and given the option of blindfolds and last cigarettes."

If we made good speed on that journey, it was due less to the condition of the roads—in places barely meriting that description—than to the fact that there was nothing on them except the occasional ox-cart. The passing countryside was a rotating diorama chronicling agrarian antiquity, composed of frozen tableaux of men, women and children, looking intensely Slavic in appearance and costume, arrested in the act of tilling their fields or harvesting their crops. When they awoke from their daze as to what they were seeing, they would break into brave, cheerful smiles, waving scarves and doffed hats in our wake. Presumably the assumption was that if we weren't recognisable, we must be visiting Russian commissars who would expect to see happy workers contentedly cultivating their communes.

We swept through both Plovdiv and Khaskovo without pause, crossing the Turkish border well before expiry of our time limit, but the strain proved too much for Paddy. In the darkness, on the other side of Edirne, he pulled over on to the verge and fell asleep across the wheel. Moti made herself as comfortable as she could, curled up on the bedroll beside him like a cat on a beanbag. We looked at each other, wondering what to do. The scant food and drink we had brought with us had been shared out earlier in the day, in the best traditions of collectivist comradeship. It was too late, and too dark, to break out the tents and the leaky air mattresses from the back of the bus. Besides, we had nowhere to camp, for on both sides of the road stretched cornfields.

With barely a word of complaint, we snuggled down into the seats where we sat, determined to make the best of it. We were, after all, in Turkey, a third of the way towards our destination, and this was the first real inconvenience we had encountered. Paddy had accomplished a great deal on our behalf, and deserved to sleep undisturbed.

In the early hours of the morning, with the faintest suggestion of dawn lighting the east, I disembarked to find Isabel standing by the roadside, displaying the face and jaw-line of a disapproving Marlene Dietrich, left elbow supported on right arm to raise the inevitable cigarette to her lips. She breathed out a long plume of smoke that spread between us like the pale and insubstantial outline of a map of Asia. "Do you think we're going to make it?"

"To Bombay?"

"To Istanbul. I worry about him. He's pushing too hard, and we've hardly started. We've got all that desert before us, and we haven't crossed the Bosporus yet."

"Let's not burn our boats before we reach them."

On the Cusp of Asia

Our hotel in Istanbul was situated beside the railway station. My window overlooked its platforms and the street alongside, jammed with trucks delivering or collecting produce for haulage all over the city and its environs. The cacophony of horns prevented any possibility of sleep, but I enjoyed opening the shutters and looking down on a scene so evocatively reminiscent of Sealdah or Howrah or all those other railway stations of my youth. Even without crossing the straits, I felt I was back in Asia again.

The feeling was reinforced in the Kapalicarsi, the covered bazaar dating back to the 15th century, with its four thousand shops spreading through a labyrinth of arched alleyways into which suffused light descended as if through fathoms of water. The scents, the spices, the colours waylaid me like importuning beggars spreading carpets at my feet and whispering: "Ah friend, for you who have returned to us after all these years, we have very special bargains to offer."

Other hints of an unidentifiable familiarity, redolent of rajah's palaces and oriental ostentations carried over from my childhood, lay in wait at the Topkapi, less a single monumental structure than an organic growth, spreading across the tip of the peninsula overlooking the Golden Horn. Its various ante-chambers, seraglios, quarters for Nubian guards, kiosks, gardens and belvederes dated from 1466-1478, when the first Ottoman palace was founded in the newly conquered capital of their empire.

A Genoese merchant perfectly captured the mood of the palace in a letter dated about 1550, describing a visit to the wife of Suleiman the Magnificent:

> "When I entered the kiosk in which she lives, I was received by many eunuchs in splendid costume blazing with jewels, and carrying scimitars in their hands. They led me to an inner vestibule, where I was divested of my cloak and shoes and regaled with refreshments. Presently an elderly woman, very richly dressed, accompanied by a number of young girls, approached me, and after the usual salutation, informed me that the Sultana Asseki was ready to see me. All the walls of the kiosk in which she lives are covered with the most beautiful Persian tiles and the floors are of cedar and sandalwood, which give out the most delicious odor."

The Ottomans were contemporaries of the Moghuls of India. They reached their zenith in Suleiman, who conquered Belgrade and besieged Vienna in 1529, during the corresponding reign, in Delhi, of the first Moghul Emperor Babur, who considered himself Turk by nationality, Moslem by religion, Persian by culture and nomad at heart.

And then there were the mosques of Istanbul, the Blue Mosque with its six minarets and incredible azure tiles, the cascading domes of the Suleymaniye, where the Magnificent One himself lay entombed, and the Hagia Sophia, erected as a Christian church by Justinian I in the 6th century, converted to a mosque in

1453 and finally declared a museum of Byzantine antiquities in the year that I was born.

How could I not fall in love with the city that once was Constantinople, where Constantine in 330 AD had declared his "New Rome" by the sea of Marmara? The calls to prayer by muzzeins in their minarets summoned echoes from deep within my cloistered heart.

Disaster in Ankara

What I had not appreciated was how much of Turkey lay on the other side of the Sea of Marmara. It was a country with most of its foot in Asia and a mere toehold on Europe. There was no bridge across the Bosporus in those days. One went by ferry, which made you acutely aware of departing one continent and arriving at another.

Disembarking in Eastern Turkey, we wasted no time heading for Ankara, the capital founded by the amazing Mustafa Kemal Ataturk, twentieth century antithesis of Suleiman the Great, the reformer versus the conqueror. Both founder and first president of the Turkish Republic, Ataturk destroyed what Suleiman and his precursors had built, replacing fez and pantaloons with felt hat and three-piece suit, supplanting feudal despotism with the fabric and institutions of modern Turkey.

Ankara had been continuously inhabited since the Bronze Age. The very fine Museum of Anatolian Civilizations recorded the pulse of cultures that had flowed through Turkey's veins, from Hittites, Phrygians, Lydians and Persians to Galatians, Romans, Byzantines, Seljuk Turks and Ottomans. A small provincial town until Ataturk declared it the capital of the new Republic on October 13, 1923, Ankara had since developed rapidly, leaving the old settlement largely untouched, clinging to its hills like tide marks left behind by some historic flood.

It was the only city in Turkey with an urban development plan, dating back to the 1930s. Ataturk's Mausoleum, which I set out to visit the moment I parked my bags at our modest little hotel, dominated modern Ankara from its own hilltop. Completed in 1953, fifteen years after Ataturk's death and four years before I set eyes on it, the imposing limestone structure represented a fusion of ancient and modern architectural concepts. It suggested a sharp-edged Athenian Parthenon cut four-square. I arrived as the sun was setting, causing the rose-coloured stone to glow a warmer shade of red.

The following morning, I set out, with a group of my fellow travelers, to explore the old town, less impressive perhaps, but infinitely more atmospheric and full of life, than the severe grid structure of the new. We scaled one of the hills and looked down on a bone dry river bed, coiling through a ravine between our hill and the next. We saw parked cars, tractors and earth moving machinery apparently constructing a road, people wandering the river bank engaged in conversation. Then we turned away to photograph a noisy group of children vying for our attention.

Suddenly a hue and cry broke out, and people ran past us to crowd the parapet we had just vacated. Below us, an incredible raging brown torrent had erased all trace of the scene we had witnessed just moments before. Cars, machinery, people, all were gone. Further down the course of this instant ferment, other vehicles were tossed aside or carried bodily upon the flood, houses were crumbling from the impact and a wide swathe of destruction was spreading into downtown Ankara. Occupants of houses nearer to us, their lower floors already inundated by rising waters, were throwing out their possessions to friends and family still occupying dry land.

Under a cloudless blue sky, the spectacle was so incomprehensible that it defied explanation. Only later did we learn that a distant thunderstorm had breached an ancient dam and sent its contents hurtling towards the city, faster than the proverbial rumour of disaster that allegedly outstrips horse and telegraph. Hundreds of lives were almost instantly expunged.

The return to our hotel entailed a circuitous course and much trial and error, as we encountered flooded side streets too deep to forge. A conference that night with Paddy elicited the disconcerting news that the route we had planned to take out of the city was no longer passable. We would now have to make a wide detour far to the south, via Kayseri and Sivas, losing much time in the process.

But even on that route we ran into difficulty. An offshoot of the torrent had swept across the road and left a quagmire in its wake. For the first time since leaving London, we had to break out the shovels and put to the test both ourselves and our implements. We began to realise what a very low wheelbase *The Indiaman* possessed, and the implications of this once the inevitable desert sands replaced the mud.

Deep into Anatolia

The deeper we pressed into Anatolia, the more barren the landscape became. Villages huddled their haphazardly stacked, mud-walled shoeboxes into the groins of hills. By crowding those crevasses, they hoped to escape the worst of the unpredictable seismic tremors that had too often inflicted catastrophe upon similar flimsy structures of stone and clay. Increasingly the lack of vegetation created problems for our sanitary regime. We could no longer request a stop for "bushes" once the bushes were no longer there. And it was pointless walking out into the wilderness if you were still visible to fellow passengers even from a distance of several hundred yards.

Besides, there was the danger of running into terrifying Anatolian sheepdogs, with spiked collars like murderous bracelets, so ferociously loyal to their flocks, their owners and their tracts of territory that they set upon intruders like wolves. We had watched them racing towards our moving coach like avenging harpies, not just barking at, but endeavouring to sink their teeth into, our spinning tyres. Meet up with one of *those* in your most compromising posture and you might be left a great deal worse off than my lance corporal friend bereft of a slice of buttock on a Korean hillside. The only sensible alternative was to arrange for relief stops in relays, miles from any village or sheep flocks, with the women retreating first to the rear of the bus and the men following when the last of the first batch announced the coast was clear.

Magically, even here in the arid Anatolian landscape, water melons were in season. We were following the crest of a water melon wave that had carried us all the way from Venice and was to last us well into Iran. Stacks of these globular green fruit were sharing the rear of our bus with our luggage and our store of chianti wine bottles. The latter were acquired in Trieste, cushioned in their raffia baskets from the damaging concussions to which they were subjected.

Whenever we stopped to take our turns at the primus stoves, cooking up our evening meal, Nigel and I rationed ourselves to our customary omelette spiced with onion, green peppers and whatever other available garnish we might improvise. It became a standing joke; our culinary staple, bequeathed the title "Mosserve" as a compound of our two names. Finding a hillock on which to consume this dish, we would watch the sun sink over the continent left in our wake and bastardise verses from Fitzgerald's version of the *Rubaiyat of Omar Khayyam*:

> "Here, looking very much the worse for now, a loaf of bread, a flask of wine and thou beside me, seated in the wilderness, this wilderness can really seem a cow."

It seemed most *emphatically* a cow when the time came to pitch our tents. Aluminium tent pegs made little impression on a landscape compacted in fearful anticipation of the next subterranean upheaval. Mallets served only to contort these pathetic implements into misshapen metallic deformities. In despair, we would each end up winding our tent canvas around ourselves until we were entirely swaddled in its embrace. Then we would fall over, hopefully on to inflated air mattresses which, as often as not, would immediately breathe their last beneath this unexpected burden.

Morning would find us rolling free of our nocturnal encumbrance, like Cleopatra from her carpet, just in time to pack up and seek the safety of the coach before the next sheep farmer and his faithful hounds materialized on the horizon.

Kicked in the Teeth by a Camel

The road from Erzincan to Erzurum was one I would never wish to traverse again. Seldom wide enough for two vehicles to pass, it wound an infinitely convoluted course around the flanks of a spectacularly steep ravine, so perilously that we were informed it remained closed during spells of winter ice and snow. It is never a pleasant feeling to sit at the back end of a bus, directly over a wheel that leaves the road with a sickening lurch on practically every inside bend. It is even less so when you look down and see, far below you, the crushed remains of yet another truck or petrol tanker that took a bend too far and too wide.

But Paddy, as ever, proved his driving skills were more than adequate for even this challenge. Increasingly I learned to respect his quiet, confident manner, his unassertive but indisputable leadership, his phlegmatic acceptance of setbacks and his resourceful application of remedies to counter them. I learned little of his background other than the fact that he had for years conducted one business or other throughout west and central Asia, picking up languages, acquainting himself with national characteristics, learning the lore of the road in each and every territory. Always he had nursed, at the back of his mind, an ambition to launch the first overland bus service. Having already proved its possibilities once, he was planning to establish a regular, twice-a-year timetable.

"Each time I do it," he said, "is going to seem like the first. With this route, nothing is predictable. The potential for the unexpected is limitless. So each journey will remain a new adventure. That's why I don't want to hand the wheel over to anyone else. The time may come when it's necessary to do so, but I will let that eventuality take its course. Meanwhile, we have a new day ahead of us, and a fresh target to reach. So let's get going."

He had his perfect companion in diminutive Moti; unfailingly cheerful and responsive to his every need before he could even voice it. Seated in lotus posture on her bastion of bedroll, she would reach across and pass him cups of tea as he drove, or feed him spoonfuls of cold *dhal* and rice.

Beyond Erzurum lay Ağri, and beyond that Mount Ararat, on whose 16,853-foot summit Noah allegedly brought his Ark to rest, releasing its burden of animals to multiply and populate the land from which the Biblical flood was still receding. In the shadow of that mountain, a distant descendant of the patriarch's floating menagerie came a fraction of a centimeter from dislocating my jaw. It was my fault. Spotting a small herd of grazing camels, I crept up with my camera from behind, to avoid startling them, and so abysmally failed in my objective that one of the youngest took fright and lashed out with its back legs. Its toe grazed my lip and nearly broke my front teeth.

Beyond Ararat

Also in the shadow of Mount Ararat lay the Turkish-Iranian border, opening up to us a country that would be—next to India itself—the largest encountered on our journey, aside from being the most problematic and the longest to traverse. On the road to Tabriz we stopped by a village mosque, whose kindly imam invited us to spend the night. Lying side by side, our sleeping bags set in rows on a blaze of richly embroidered carpets, we slowly succumbed to sleep, too tired to continue staring in wonderment at our surroundings. But I resisted to the last, gazing up into that mini-firmament of a dome, inset with filigrees of pattern high above. I thought it the most beautiful setting in which I had ever laid my head, and for once I wanted to pray before I closed my eyes. In thanks for bringing me so far, for what the rest of the journey might bring and, beyond that, for the remainder of my life.

At the next stop, a village whose name is now beyond recall, we found a wayside inn advertising reasonably priced accommodations. While my fellow passengers settled for this, I had noted a similar sign but a mile or so back, quoting a cheaper rate that appealed to me more. Promising to return in the morning, well before scheduled departure time, I set off and discovered perfectly acceptable lodgings at a price better suited to my fast draining pocket.

The following morning, just after dawn, I headed back to rejoin my companions along an empty street suddenly filled with a clatter of horses' hooves. An entire detachment of mounted Iranian cavalry hove into sight, rifles slung across their shoulders, looking with amusement upon my sandaled legs loping along under admittedly brief but perfectly decent shorts. To a man, they whistled at the sight, and kept on doing so until I rounded a corner, lost to their gaze. It was not an experience I was prepared to relate to my fellow travellers.

The remainder of that considerable distance to Tehran was one long repetition of landscape and featureless, unrecordable monotony, devoid of incident. We drove through a continuous haze of dust so fine it penetrated the texture of clothing, lids and flaps of every suitcase and shoulder bag, hairs of ear and nostril, roots of scalp, rims of eyes and of clenched lips, no matter how firmly closed. We sat, we endured, we literally gritted our teeth and bore it.

When our eyes were open, we could see that all colour had deserted us. We were, each and every one, a uniform khaki grey from head to foot, with only our bloodshot, sand-grained eyeballs staring back in stunned adjustment to our altered circumstance. We were smothered in airborne motes raised by the marching heels of Alexander's conquering Macedonian army more than two centuries earlier. They may not have followed this precise route, but the winds of the desert carry a long way.

Refreshed and Refurbished

Arrived at last in Tehran, we filled and refilled our hotel bathtubs and wallowed again and again, scrubbing every clogged pore. Then we shook out our bags and laundered every item of clothing, used and unused, remarking how the cloth was already beginning to show signs of the disintegration we had been warned to expect.

Thus refreshed and refurbished, we set out on our separate voyages of exploration. First impressions were favourable. Here, in the midst of a vast, sparsely populated nowhere, was a city of prodigious size and consequence. Tehran, I learnt, meant *warm slope*. As a village in the suburb of the ancient capital of Ray, it bore the brunt of a massive population shift when inhabitants of that larger entity moved in after the sacking of Ray by the Mongols in 1220 AD.

Despite the fact that it had been declared a capital in the previous century, Tehran was still a city in the making, proliferating—though in a slightly more orderly manner—like a virus culture in a glass dish. Nine-tenths of the built-up area was set in square blocks with absolutely straight boulevards. From the walls of these blocks, from yardarms intersecting lampposts, from smaller portraits adorning coffee houses and restaurants, the visage of the last Shah of the Pahlavis (how were we to know this *then?*) beamed magnanimously down upon us in ubiquitous reminder of the source of all this rapid projection into the twentieth century.

Yet stray a few yards behind some of those boulevards and you stumbled into the equivalent of a cinema city back-lot, the behind-the-scenes revelation that much of the impressive façade was no more than that, propped up at the rear by structures still in the course of construction. The façade was everything, lining as it did the course of the royal limousine, progressing in convoy down wide boulevards with its paramount passenger, the Shah in person, nodding and perhaps half raising a hand to wave at passing subjects.

Much of the city's rapid growth had produced ontogenesis without style, regimented into square blocks, anonymous, lacking harmony in its shades of greyness, with never a flower box to relieve a window-sill. It was a monotony that the baroque and pretentious newer structures, particularly banks, did little to improve. Even Tehran's earlier monuments, erected by the Shah's predecessors, dated from the *fin de siecle* rag-ends of the nineteenth century. They bore the marks of a period when, everywhere in the world, taste had become degenerate and overblown, descending to endless replication of the same motifs.

In the open doorway of a still empty restaurant, for it was not yet noon, I paused at the unexpected sight of a wide tray of sheep's eyes, sizzling over a brazier. It seemed transported straight out of scrubland, from some bivouac encampment of itinerant nomads. Grinning at my bemusement, the robed, turbaned and bearded proprietor selected a sheep's eye and proffered it to me on the tips of his fingers. T.E. Lawrence would unhesitatingly have accepted, I felt sure, but for me the whole experience of being here at all was still too raw, too new. I smilingly declined and he shrugged, as if he had anticipated as much.

Past the Ayatollah's Stronghold

Paddy took us into his confidence. He had decided against heading due east, towards Masshad and Afghanistan. He didn't feel comfortable with the volatile Afghan temperament and neither, from what we had read and heard, would we. He favoured the southern route, via Isfahan, Yazd, Kerman and Zahedan, even though it meant crossing the Dasht-e Lut desert. There the *djinnis* were reputed to be so devilish that travellers were cautioned to sleep with the soles of their feet pressed against a companion's lying in the opposite direction, so that demons had no chance to steal their souls. Were we game for this longer route?

Offered that pearl of Islamic culture, how could we say no to Isfahan, even though it lay four hundred and thirty five kilometres from Tehran along some pretty indifferent roads? To get there we would have to pass Qom, where Ayatollah Khomeini had studied, was already preparing to undermine the Shah's regime and would later be arrested and condemned to exile, whence he would return in triumph in 1979, having engineered the Shah's downfall.

Back in 1957, Imam Khomeini hadn't quite perfected his talent for swaying Iranians with denunciations of every human vice, from drinking alcohol to reading Salman Rushdie's *Satanic Verses*, but the mood of things to come was already apparent. Paddy made it clear he would not be stopping at Qom, despite its importance to Shiite Muslims since early Islamic times, and the fact that, housing the lavish tomb of Fatima al-Masuma, it had been a goal of pilgrims since the 17th century. In case the bus was delayed there for any reason, all the women in our party were requested to have a head scarf ready for use, and to wear skirts instead of shorts and jeans. Qom's golden dome beckoned like a siren beacon as we passed, but we averted our gaze and spurned temptation.

Isfahan more than compensated. It lay at the heart of ancient Persia, both geographically and culturally, a veritable treasure house of all that was beautiful in Islamic architecture. Here flourished the golden age of Persian art, science and literature, during the centuries when Europe was still struggling to light the candles that would dispel the Dark Ages. Most of its landmarks had survived intact since its installation as capital of the Persian kingdom during the Safavid dynasty. Some, like the Shahrestan Bridge, dated from the 11th century.

Built by Shah Abbas I the Great, at the beginning of the 17th century, Isfahan's central complex was Maidan-e-Imam (Imam Square), twice as big as Moscow's Red Square and bordered on all sides by monumental buildings linked by a series of two-storeyed arcades. There we found the Royal Mosque, the Mosque of Sheyx Lotfollah, the magnificent Portico of Qeyssariyeh and the 15th century Timurid Palace, all bearing witness to Persian socio-cultural life during the Safavid era. So predominant were the pale blues of many of these paragons of Islamic design that it seemed the very air was tinged with aquamarine.

An early European visitor to Isfahan was Sir John Chardin, son of a Huguenot Paris jeweller, who arrived in 1666 at the death of Shah Abbas II, following which he observed the coronation of Shah Safi, who became Soleiman III. Chardin was fascinated by the pigeon towers he found in vast numbers around the city, and was amazed to learn these derived from the local obsession with melons. In a published account of his travels, he wrote that the people

> "live upon nothing else but melons and cucumbers . There are some that will eat five and thirty pounds of melon at a meal, without making themselves sick. During these four months, they come in such vast quantities to Isfahan, that I can't help believing they eat more here in a day, than they do in France in a month."

We were in luck. The melon wave had followed us to that true blue Islamic paradise, and we gorged to an extent that would have shocked even Sir John. From time immemorial, pigeon dung had been seen as the best manure for melon crops, accounting for one of the most remarkable eccentricities of Iranian architecture. The pigeon towers surrounding the city were built for the purpose of enticing the birds to nest in their tops, so their dung would fall to the bottom in conveniently harvestable heaps. Chardin noted:

> "I don't think there are any finer dove-cots in any part of the world. They are built with brick overlaid with plaster and lime, full within of holes for the pigeons to breed in. They reckon above three thousand pigeon-houses about Isfahan, all built for the sake of the dung. They call it "tehalgus". It is sold a "bisti" or four-pence, the twelve-pound weight on which the king lays a small tax."

On our way eastward, out of the city, Paddy stopped the bus alongside one of these towers, now deserted by its pigeon tenants but still so robust and durable that we could climb to the parapet and survey the countryside for miles around. "Oh for the wings, for the wings of a dove," we chorused.

Hedonist Pleasures

Heading for Yazd, we travelled mile after mile through a dehydrated, beige-coloured landscape, interrupted by groves of date palms to mark the possibility of human habitation. Where such settlements occurred, they were barely distinguishable from the terrain around them; clusters of mud-walled huts with domed roofs, incongruous as igloos fashioned of clay rather than ice to withstand a fiercer sun. Every dozen miles or so we would pass a small pile of boulders, beside which would be grouped perhaps two or at most three men, armed with shovels and standing at attention to watch us pass, as if instructed to convey the impression that some form of rudimentary road-works were in progress.

After such barrenness of vista, Yazd proved something of a surprise. Repeatedly, and almost desperately throughout history, Yazd had drawn attention to itself as the perfect candidate for elevation to the Persian capital. Like some exiled and hopelessly disqualified claimant to a distant throne, it had consistently failed in this endeavour. A township of modest proportions, it stood engulfed in disproportionately large and grandiloquent memorials of that abortive enterprise. Largely rebuilt between 1324 and 1365, the Jami Mosque was one of the outstanding 14th century buildings in all Persia. Crowned by a pair of minarets alleged to be the tallest in the country, the portal's facade was decorated from top to bottom in dazzling tilework, again predominantly blue in color. Within lay a long, arcaded court, behind which was a deep-set sanctuary chamber under a squat tiled dome, exquisitely decorated with faience mosaic. Its tall faience *mihrab*, dated 1365, was also one of the finest of its kind in existence.

But for me the principal delight of Yazd was the entrance to the 19th century bazaar. This magnificent display of ostentation, setting arch upon arch, aspiring to a crowning triumph of twin minarets rivalling those of the Jami Mosque, concealed a relatively modest marketplace that quickly extinguished my expectations.

There was much else in Yazd that, alas, I could spare no time to see; the Zoroastrian Fire Temple, the Towers of Silence, home of the last worshippers of the *Ahura Mazda* faith, the Dowlatabad Garden and its wind tower and the deep water-tanks, sunk six, eight or ten meters below street level to serve as reservoirs in the prolonged dry season. Finally there was the tomb of Sayyid Rukn ad-Din, all that remained of a complex erected on his orders to accommodate the Institute of Time and Hours, whose horological devices made it a wonder of its age.

I *could* have made the effort, but I was seduced by the hedonist pleasures of a steam bath in a genuinely ancient Persian bath house. Sunk into the ground, like the town's subterranean reservoirs, this was a maze of little domed cells with pools and water jars, where ferocious looking Iranian attendants waited with brushes, sponges and expressions of direst intensity to wreak vengeance on all infidels submitting themselves to their ministrations. I was pummelled, pulverised, scrubbed, rinsed, scraped almost skinless with loofahs and left for dead to sleep it off, which I did in such a blissfully disembodied state that I almost missed the bus.

Moon, Melon and Minaret

Somewhere between Yazd and Kerman, we were collectively lured into the home of a rug merchant. In a large courtyard, layered so deep in carpets our bare feet seemed to walk on spring mattresses, we were entertained with tiny cups of thick Turkish coffee while members of the household brought out roll upon roll of closely woven handloom for our contemplation. Seated, like us, on piles of cushions, the proprietor of this establishment held forth on the merits and qualities of these intricate and exquisite gems of the carpet trade while we wondered how we could (a) afford them and (b) get them home unsullied.

I don't think we purchased many. Even the smallest cost more than my greatly reduced allowance, now dwindling at a rate far slower than it had in Europe, but still evaporating like dew under a rising desert sun. I figured I would have to get by on about seven shillings a day if I was to make it as far as Calcutta. Our affable host didn't seem to mind that his coffers were not substantially supplemented by our presence under the billowing canopy above our heads. He pressed more coffee and conversation upon us, and invited us to make ourselves comfortable for the night. It was a tempting prospect, but I could see Paddy looking pointedly at his watch.

And so on we pressed on, made increasingly aware of a list to one side and a pronounced grinding sound each time we lurched over one of the many potholes Paddy could not avoid. Our fears were confirmed when we tracked down the one and only automobile repair shop in Kerman. We had a broken spring, and would have to send for a replacement. The delay would cost us at least two days. Ah well, we shrugged, better now than in the middle of the Dasht-e Lut desert, where the *djinnis* were waiting to suck us inside-out through the soles of our feet.

Kerman too had its curiosities; the Shazdeh garden, the Tomb of Shah Nema-tollah-e-Vali, the ancient Nurieh Hospital and Jabal-i Sang, or *Mountain of Stone*. The latter was one of the most enigmatic monuments of southern Iran. The purpose intended for its domed chamber, possibly dating from the late 12th century, could not be properly determined. For that matter, neither could its date with any certainty, for it was never finished. Most of these landmarks remained unvisited, for we were by now so culturally, spiritually and physically exhausted that few ventured to invest the effort required for their examination. Even the splendid public bath known as the *Hammam Gandjali Khan,* and named after a former governor of the province, proved a temptation I felt compelled to resist. Of vastly superior quality to the one I had patronized in Yazd, its principal doorway was adorned with murals depicting animal scenes. But the luxury of two public baths in the space of a week was one I could not contemplate on my diminishing reserves. Like the rest of us, I had learned to live with a paucity of ablutionary resources.

Instead we sat around in a coffee shop, killing time, discussing the rumour that, some three months earlier, a trio of tourists in a Land Rover had been ambushed, robbed and murdered by brigands on the edge of the desert, while waiting to cross at night, when the desert cools enough to make that venture possible.

I can't remember where it was. It may have been Kerman. But one night I sat under a full moon, gazing at a minaret silhouetted against the stars, a mouthful of watermelon spilling over my lips, and I thought

Whatever else, I won't forget
A moon, a melon and a minaret

The Dasht-e Lut Desert

With our spring finally fixed, we headed for the worst obstacle of the entire odyssey, the infamous Dasht-e Lut desert, spanning the first leg of a three hundred and forty mile journey to Zahedan. What we found more than fulfilled our expectations. We also encountered desultory and uninspiring evidence of an attempt to build a road across it. Teams of men—this time larger in numbers and actually busy being industrious instead of merely standing around looking decorative—worked with hand tools to deposit layers of stones, in the manner of Roman road builders two centuries earlier. But their labours seemed futile, for the surface kept sinking under the dunes as fast as it was slowly and painstakingly laid.

Again I wondered if the men were prisoners, employed on a predictably fruitless task to serve the dual purpose of keeping them busy while demonstrating that efforts were indeed being made to bridge that wasteland. The desert was far enough away from Tehran, and the Shah, for the latter's propaganda machine to keep this particular pot interminably boiling. I could picture a British adviser at the Shah's court, making the best of the scant evidence of progress by explaining to the press corps, in Oxford English tones, "It's a dashed elusive desert, dash it all."

Alfons Gabriel, one of the earliest explorers in this area, described the sand sea as a "confused mass of impassable tangled dunes". He noted dunes up to one hundred and fifty metres tall, of uniform size, almost perfectly round, and containing an admixture of volcanic material. A volcano with a small caldera lay on the western edge of the desolation, its topography creating changes in the orientation of prevailing wind patterns.

We took our place at the tail end of a convoy of trucks lined up in preparation to essay the worst of the void the moment the sun went down. Most of these were heavy-duty Mercedes diesels, with high wheelbases and six to eight wheels designed for maximum traction on minimum areas of purchase. Their drivers regarded our bus with initial amazement, quickly replaced by contempt. But they were sympathetic and hospitable towards those foolish enough to risk their lives in such an unsuitable and ill-equipped conveyance, inviting us to share with them their shade and their coffee.

Despite weeks on the road, I was still chronically unable to correctly gauge my required water intake, in this heat a deficiency that would prove especially troublesome. I was losing moisture through my pores faster than I could replace it. Having exhausted my vacuum flask, I had even tackled my shrinking supply of melons. The thick, glutinous coffee seemed only to exacerbate my thirst. Feeling myself dehydrating rapidly, I craved and shamelessly begged for water. One compassionate trucker squatted by the grille at the front of his Mercedes, turned on a tap and drained into a mug a warm liquid the colour of tea. In it floated flecks or rust. Radiator water, he explained. Perfectly safe to drink because thoroughly boiled. I drank greedily.

As the sun mounted vertically ahead of us, there was no shade left except directly under the vehicles, where we hollowed out sand pits to accept our supine forms, trying to avoid axle grease and oil drips. We made a few desultory stabs at conversation that petered out as, one by one, we drifted off to sleep.

At six o'clock, an angry red glow behind us in the west marked the demise of the sun, clinging to the lip of the land like the snarl of a ferociously large animal dragged to its death. We busied ourselves in preparation for departure. Paddy, sporting a coiled turban donated to him by a truck owner he had befriended, announced he had done a deal with the man in question, whom we promptly named Edward G Robinson for his startling resemblance to that pugnacious actor. The deal was that, for an undisclosed sum of money, his Mercedes would tow us across the sands, his crew working alongside us to keep both vehicles moving.

We had planks for the wheels, a plentitude of ropes and shovels, and shoulders to apply to the back end of the bus, the sides and everywhere that required such assistance. Just so did we work our way, foot by foot, yard by yard, through a darkness relieved only by frugal applications of torchlight to sort out where to dig and where to place the planks. At one point, scraping with my hands under one of the rear wheels, I saw in the pale torch beam a delicate, almost translucent scorpion poised in my palm. It brought back such a stab of memory that I was loath to release it, but the crew member alongside me struck my knuckles from below to dislodge the insect and then stamped it into oblivion.

In the pale glow of predawn, a hoarse cry from ahead conveyed the tidings that the Mercedes had regained the surface of a road beneath its wheels. The nightmare was over. Since sundown, we hadn't rested for more than three minutes at a stretch, for a mouthful of liquid or a quick cigarette. At least we had avoided the risk of falling asleep and allowing the *djinnis* to assault our bare feet, which I suddenly realised might explain why—aside from coolness—Iranians preferred to tackle this desert crossing at night. But the effort had taken its toll. We were too weary even to raise a cheer.

Marooned in a Cockroach Sea

It did not surprise us to learn that Zahedan was one of the most economically backward cities in Iran. Local industries included brick making, milled rice, live-stock feed, processed foods, mats and baskets, embroidered articles and ceramics. It had all the depressing forlornness of a frontier town verging upon one of the world's loneliest and least trafficked border crossings. Camping in the courtyard of the Iranian customs station, I groped my way through darkness to a latrine against the far wall and was mystified, while squatting over the open pit, to hear a slithering, rushing sound, as though water was flooding the narrow cubicle. Lighting a match, I saw myself islanded in a sea of cockroaches, pouring over my shoes, scaling my trousers, steadily engulfing me in a mounting tide of rippling chocolate. Nothing could be better calculated to expedite the process of evacuation.

On the other side of the border lay Baluchistan, largest province of Pakistan, with an area greater than the British Isles but a population of considerably less than a million, reined back by a dauntingly arid geography. Fiercely independent, the Baluchis never really took to the Moghul empire, but effectively retained their status as autonomous frontier tributary. In India they fought the Hindus and gained some influence in the Punjab and Sind. Survival demanded expedient changes of loyalty and allegiance, sometimes as swift as the shifting desert winds. They formed alliances, when necessary, with Moghuls, Persians, Afghans or whichever bordering state it might currently seem most politic to cultivate; even, when the time came, the British, who in 1841 were the last to arrive.

We headed for the Baluchi capital, Quetta, laid low by the devastating earth-quake of 1935, a month before my birth, but now almost entirely rebuilt. The name Quetta derived from the word *Kuwatta*, which meant a fort. Situated at 1692 metres above sea level, the city was surrounded by imposing hills and lay at the mouth of the Bolan Pass. Camping on the outskirts, we found the air cooler and sharper than we had felt on our skins for a long time, making for remarkable clarity of vision.

The following morning George, one of the eldest of our fellow travelers, remarked that he had been up brewing coffee before dawn and had seen what looked like a shooting star behaving very oddly, for it slowly traversed the sky from east to west, imprinting a brighter pinpoint of light against the dimming star canopy. Not until we reached Amritsar, days later, did we stumble across an explanation for this phenomenon, in a newspaper headline reporting that the Russians had sent the world's first spacecraft into orbit and had called it "Sputnik".

Nomadic tribesmen traverse the Bolan Pass each spring and autumn with their herds of sheep and camels. We came across an entire traffic jam of them, slowing our progress all the way down to the valley below. Snorting camels resisted efforts to direct them to the roadside, flocks of sheep suddenly erupted under our tyres. Owners with flailing sticks set upon their rebellious beasts, and seemed as likely to set upon us as well for provoking their mutiny. It didn't help that we camera enthusiasts demanded constant stops to capture the highlights of this irresistible colour and movement.

Shades of Bhowani Junction

Lahore made me feel I was already home. Seated in the garden of a palatial bungalow-style hotel in the Lahore cantonment, at the end of a busy day touring the city sights, I listened to the crows in the neem trees and felt my journey nearing its end. The film version of John Masters' *Bhowani Junction* had been released the previous year, and I recalled that a distant relative of mine—one of the kind Paul Scott would later label as *Staying On*—had lent her bungalow to the production crew seeking locations in this city, presumably for that part of the movie depicting the Anglo-Indian sector of the fictitious Bhowani community.

It had been a curiously unconvincing movie, based on a hardly more convincing book, but up to that point in time it was the only instance of either medium attempting to portray the Anglo-Indian experience, commendable for this reason despite its many inaccuracies and inconsistencies. Ava Gardner was cast as the Anglo-Indian heroine. Her most memorable line in the movie was "I thought I could overcome my guilt by becoming a Sikh!". A biography of George Cukor reveals that a scene where she used a toothbrush belonging to Stewart Granger, portraying a British officer, was cut from the film for being too risqué. Perhaps the world's first recorded instance of a prohibition on dental miscegenation.

There was much else to reflect upon in that crowded day. No other city had encompassed so many names familiar to me from the annals of Moghul rule. Islamic suzerainty began here when Qutub-ud-din Aibak was crowned in 1206, thus becoming the first Muslim Sultan on the sub-continent. Lahore was Akbar's capital from 1584 to 1598. He built the massive Lahore Fort on the foundations of a previous fort, and enclosed the city within a red brick wall boasting twelve gates. Jahangir and Shah Jehan (who was born in Lahore) extended the fort, built palaces and tombs, and laid out gardens. The last of the great Moghuls, Aurang-zeb (1658-1707), gave Lahore its most famous monuments, the great Badshahi Masjid and the Alamgiri gateway to the fort.

Robin Whitelaw and I visited both fort and mosque, the latter constructed entirely of red sandstone in a record time of two and a half years. The mosque courtyard was said to be the largest in the world, a claim we had no reason to dis-pute, for our bare feet were scorched, spanning every yard of it under a blazing sun, from the gateway to the sublime relief of the pool where we could bathe our blistered extremities. The marble domes covered seven prayer chambers. In niches above the gate were housed relics attributed to the Holy Prophet, his daughter and son-in-law, said to have been brought there by Amir Taimur.

During the eighteenth century, as Moghul power dwindled, Lahore suffered constant invasions. The 1740s were years of chaos, producing nine changes of governor. Lahore ended up being ruled by a triumvirate of Sikhs, of such loose moral character that the population invited Ranjit Singh to invade them. He took the city in 1799 and declared himself Emperor. The Sikh period saw much destruction of ancient Moghul monuments. Nur Jahan's Tomb was stripped down to its bricks. When the British arrived, in the early 19th century, they char-acteristically sighed with rapture over a "melancholy picture of fallen splendour."

Musing on those vanished glories myself, while ingesting cucumber sand-wiches delivered to me by a turbaned bearer on a silver-plated tray, I was brought to my senses by a shockingly large, dark brown object that descended with a crash on the tea service, scattering teapot, cup and saucer, and making off with the last of the sandwiches I had been meditatively contemplating in my fingers. I had been attacked by a kite hawk, its talons drawing blood from my thumb and fore-finger.

In the evening, a party of us hired a taxi to visit the famed Shalimar Gardens, the most complete Moghul gardens in the entire Indian sub-continent. Laid out by Shah Jehan in 1642 for the pleasure of a royal household which often stayed a day or a week at a time, its design conformed to the classic Moghul conception of three terraces of straight, shaded walks, set around a perfectly symmetrical arrangement of ponds, waterfalls and marble pavilions, all enclosed by flower beds and fruit trees within a wall. There were more than four hundred fountains, many of them still functioning.

Golden Pavilion on a Lake of Glass

Crossing the border from Pakistan into India, we found the latter's customs officials more zealous than those of Pakistan. The Indians were the first to insist on searching not just us but our vehicle. Since those were the days of rigidly enforced prohibition, we feared they would discover our last remaining cache of chianti bottles, concealed at the back of the bus under layers of carefully disposed luggage and tarpaulin. Viewing this mountainous region with distaste, an inspecting busybody lifted a flap of tarpaulin, which fell back to jet a cloud of dust over his immaculate uniform. "*Barparee barp!*" he muttered, beating a hasty retreat.

Pressing on to Amritsar, we were frisked for cigarettes at the gates of the Golden Temple, holiest sanctum at the heart of the Sikh faith. Tobacco and alcohol are forbidden in its precincts. We were also required—both men and women—to cover our heads. Once a quiet pool in the dense forest home of Guru Nanak, the temple was remarkable for its full golden dome and the gold-leaf which sheathes most of its upper structure. Its architecture drew on Hindu and Moslem artistic styles, blending both in a unique synthesis. Amritsar, meaning "pool of ambrosial nectar", was the original name of the ancient pool that inspired Guru Nanak to found his religion there. It later became the appellation of the temple complex, and still later was applied to the city that grew around it. Anxious to ensure we observed the correct etiquette, our guides steered us along a narrow marble causeway to a shimmering gilded island on a lake at still as glass.

We were granted an interview by an extremely dignified, white bearded elder, who sat cross-legged in a pavilion overlooking the pool. A rippling, dancing rhapsody of reflected light stabbed the room with tongues of flame, which I felt were penetrating my skull and imparting the wisdom of centuries. *Sikh and ye shall find,* I silently pondered. We were invited to pose questions, and they certainly met with frank and enlightening answers. We learned, for example, that the nearby border between India and Pakistan was of no consequence to the Sikhs, who barely deigned to recognise it and felt free to cross at any time they chose. After all, had they not conquered Lahore, and long held its people in subjugation?

What about Hindus and Muslims? Where did the Sikhs fit into the religious antipathies that still divided this sub-continent? Both Hindus and Muslims, we were informed, must learn to coexist in harmony with the Sikhs. The onus was on them, and not the other way around. The Sikhs were at the centre of all faiths.

Day of Tragic Mishap

Bound east from Amritsar, along the Grand Trunk Road to Delhi, we pulled in at a *dak* bungalow, anticipating that this regular stand-by of touring government officials, providing basic rest house accommodation, would serve us in good stead. Our expectations were dashed when we were informed that, although beds were available, we would not be served meals or allowed to use the kitchen utensils provided, because the establishment was under Brahmin management. Brahmins, of course, could not possibly permit their domestic implements to be employed by persons of lesser caste, including Europeans.

Why, we asked, were Brahmins allowed to run a *dak* bungalow when the sole purpose of such accommodation was to cater to all comers? From the looks we received, the question did not merit a reply. It was too late at night to seek alternative arrangements, so we reluctantly hauled in our battered saucepans and primus stoves to improvise a meal as best we could. Rattling our pots and pans to maximum audible effect, and grumbling our way through a discussion of India's iniquitous caste system, we reminded ourselves it should be left to he who is without caste to stone the first sin.

The following day was the worst of our entire journey, visiting upon us one major inconvenience followed by two outright disasters in quick succession. Traversing a narrow earth embankment, between recently flooded grain fields, we tried to negotiate our way around a bullock cart and slipped over the edge, grounding both wheels on the right hand side firmly in the mud.

The dreaded shovels, extricated from incarceration in the lowest strata of luggage mountain, where we had hoped never to set eyes on them again, were employed in relays as we tried to dig our way out of this mess. A team of labourers, engaged on road works nearby, graciously came to our assistance. In the midst of our combined efforts, one of the latter suddenly yelled that he had been bitten by a snake. Since he had been standing more or less in the middle of our group, we all started hopping around as if dancing on hot coals, but there was no evidence of the culprit to be seen. Yet sure enough, there were the puncture marks, clearly visible on his ankle. We had to rush him to the nearest hospital as fast as we could, and with no alternative means of transportation in sight, other than the still lingering bullock cart responsible for our predicament, this imperative lent renewed vigour to our toil.

Once the wheels were clear, we raced to a clinic some miles away, where we left the unfortunate victim of the mishap in the care of nurses already claiming that, without knowing what species of snake bit him, it was going to be difficult to administer the right antivenin.

Paddy was betraying the telltale signs of falling behind his timetable, so off we set, without resolving the mystery of whether or not the man survived, down a Grand Trunk Road becoming increasingly congested with traffic. The rules of the road in India dictate that two opposing vehicles bear directly down upon each other until, at some point in the final seconds prior to collision, the lesser concedes right of way. Paddy, mercifully having no inclination to participate in this contest of wills, would always pull over at first sight of the opposition hurtling towards him like a bullet from a duelling pistol.

We were especially grateful for Paddy's discretion when we came upon the consequences of an instance where neither driver had conceded defeat. The mangled wreck of a bus lay partly across our path, a great dent punched into its cab beside the driver's seat. Still extracting themselves from this mortally wounded vehicle were dazed passengers, holding their heads, carrying out the less fortunate, tending to screaming children. It was precisely the kind of tableau we had dreaded encountering, and had been spared until now.

"Is there anyone left inside?" asked Paddy.

Being nearest to the driver's cab, whose open door suggested the driver had not only survived but possibly even run away, I hauled myself up to take a look. In the front seat on the opposite side, which had taken the brunt of the impact, was a still living, still breathing, still conscious torso of a man, both limbs severed and gushing blood from his left side, pinned to his seat by imploded metalwork. He looked at me with a gaze beyond appeal, beyond hope, his eyes already glazing over. I dropped back to the road and leaned my head against the side of the bus, unable to speak. Paddy could see at once that he needn't ask again. He hoisted himself up to the scene I had witnessed, fell back beside me and gripped my shoulder. "Too late for him," he murmured. "We've got to summon help for the others."

Hastening on to the nearest police post, we reported the accident and left it to the duty officer to organise whatever succour was available. Nigel tried to console me. "Lightning can't strike *three* times in one day," But it did.

Barely an hour further west we came upon a horrific train crash, littering the rails alongside the road. In the early hours of the morning a passenger express had sped headlong into a goods train laden with fuel. The latter had caught fire, and the flames had engulfed survivors trapped in the wreckage. Although the collision had occurred several hours earlier, rescue teams were still hauling the living and the dead from crumpled carriages that had either compacted into each other in a concertina effect or had slewed in every direction, including upside down.

There was nothing we could do that wasn't already being done, and the day we had been through was so stunning as to leave us dazed with impotence.

Pillar of Lifelong Fecundity

For myself and Robin Whitelaw, the overland expedition was drawing to its close. Both of us had decided we must bid farewell to the others no later than Agra, at which point *The Indiaman* would turn southwest for Bombay and we would head east for Calcutta. After a day spent touring both old and new Delhi, we parked by the Kutab ruins, dominated by the slightly leaning red sandstone monolith of the Kutab Minar. In those days it was still possible to climb all four tiers of this majestic pillar, to gaze out over the distant city from which India had been governed for centuries. On the way up we counted three hundred and seventy nine stairs, engraved in characters whose import was beyond our speculation.

Scattered around the foot of the tower were rows of ruined columns and arches, also bearing their own inscrutable carvings. Commenced by Kutab Uddin Aibak in 1200 AD, the Kutab Minar was completed by his successor Shamsuddin Altamash in 1220. It tapered through its 238 feet from a diameter of 47 feet three inches at the base to nine feet at the pinnacle, where we crowded vertiginously together, laughingly holding on to each other. It seemed to me at that moment we gripped each other so tight not just through fear that we might slip.

Falling silent, we gazed at the point where the sun had already set, lost in our private thoughts and wistful reflections. Then we tore ourselves away, descending in a deliberately jocular mood, competing to see which of us could stand with our backs to the famed iron pillar in the grounds, guaranteeing lifelong fecundity by locking our fingers together on the far side. This pillar was estimated to have been cast in the Gupta period, some one thousand five hundred years earlier. It had stood there, in heat, dust and rain, for one and a half millennia without betraying the slightest trace of rust.

We looked around for some means of recording our own ephemeral companionship, within the considerably less durable existence of each contributing member, and could think of no way of doing this without defacing our surroundings by adding to their disfiguring graffiti. In the end we settled for a group photograph around the Kutab Minar, and another one around its metal column, and then each found something for the others to sign; a book, a scarf, in my case the cloth cap I had worn throughout the trip. Finally, in a ritual pact of undying friendship, we finished the last of the wine that had accompanied us all the way from Trieste.

We knew that, effectively, it was over. We had only one more stop where all of us would be together for the last time. And that was the Taj Mahal.

At the Tomb of Shah Jehan

It seems a travesty to attempt a description of the Taj Mahal. And more so to essay an account of how it looked to us that night in October 1957, on the eve of the fullest moon of the year. The following day the grounds would be awash with visitors, sharing the holiday mood of the full moon at the peak of Diwali, that glorious festival of light that had so captivated me as a child. But tonight we had that hauntingly beautiful mausoleum, that milky white magnificence all to ourselves. Entering from the main gate, which in any other setting would be monumental in its own right, we looked across the intervening expanse of moonlit gardens, pools and fountains to see a single orange glow at the entrance to the tomb, a tiny flame against a lake of ultramarine. Approaching in silence, awed by an experience already verging on ethereal, we discovered two guides and a lantern, hoping for just such nocturnal visitors as ourselves.

"Come," they said, beckoning. I could almost finish the sentence for them. "And you will see what you have not seen, know what you have not known."

Holding the lamp high to light our way, they led us down a flight of steps to where Shah Jehan and his Mumtaj Mahal lay side by side, two lovers permanently united in the most celebrated architecture ever devised to commemorate a romance. Rabindranath Tagore called it "a teardrop on the cheek of time". One tends to forget how long they had shared this mortal coil before she finally shuffled it off, dying in childbirth after delivering her husband's fourteenth heir.

It is claimed Shah Jehan built this colossal, entirely marble masterpiece because he was driven by guilt over the manner of his beloved's death. Despite her pregnancy, he took her with him on one of his many Deccan campaigns in the south. She had faithfully accompanied him on all his other energetic travels, just about everywhere else in India, but this proved one too many. The death so crushed the emperor that all his hair and beard were said to have grown snow white in the space of a few months.

The sorrowing widower's excessive indulgence, on this and other architectural wonders, provoked a power struggle among his sons, which led to the ruthless prince Aurangzeb deposing his father in a coup d'etat in 1658. A case of history repeating itself, since Shah Jehan had seized power from his own father, Jehangir. Aurangzeb had his Dad imprisoned in his own handiwork, the Octagonal Tower of the Agra Fort, from whose windows the old man could gaze out across the river at the wondrous tomb he would never again visit while still alive.

To further torment his father, Aurangzeb sent him a well-wrapped present with the message: "King Aurangzeb, your son, sends this to Your Majesty to let you see he does not forget you". Praising God that he was remembered, Shah Jehan opened an inlaid box to discover the severed head of his favourite son, Dara Shukoh, who had been his heir apparent until the coup. The old king went into convulsions and lost several teeth from a collision with a table.

But like King Lear, Shah Jehan had one faithful daughter, Jahanara, who nursed him back to health and remained with him until, after eight years of imprisonment, he finally died, at which point he was granted his last wish of returning to that longingly beheld mausoleum, two kilometres downriver from the fort, for interment beside his beloved Mumtaz Mahal.

Adieux to the Indiaman

The following day, Robin and I bid our adieux to *The Indiaman* and all who would sail on in her, bound for distant Bombay. Months later we would individually learn, through correspondence with those who remained in touch, of an explosive evening on the final lap, when around a campfire some minor disagreement mushroomed into a blazing row. All the pent up, unvoiced grievances, all the myriad and one suppressed recriminations, came flooding out. It was a bout of poison letting that left them reeling from the discovery of all those festering toxins running so close to the surface for so long.

Robin and I were spared that trauma, but at the same time denied the knowledge of whatever resentments they might have harboured against *us*. Best not to know, perhaps. Best to remember how we all were on that night at the Kutab Minar, when no matter what privations we had suffered together, we briefly, vainly and foolishly wished it would never end.

We headed for Agra Station to board the train for Calcutta. All we could afford were second class tickets, which condemned us to a compartment so crowded there was no berth or seat left, and barely enough space to squat on the floor. This was not how I remembered the experience of rail travel in India. I couldn't even see out of the windows unless I stood, and if I did so I risked encroachment upon my precious territorial claim from the sheer pressure of human flesh around me. I looked at Robin in wistful apology. When I assured him he was in for the experience of a lifetime, I had not meant this. But Canadians are nothing if not resourceful and phlegmatic. Robin shrugged and accepted it as the inevitable consequence of the fact that we were travelling in the busiest season of the year, when everyone in India was on the move, heading back to their families for the Diwali vacation.

Food and drink proved a problem, until by befriending those around us we established a system whereby the one nearest the door would make purchases on our behalf. Having refilled in this manner our sole surviving and now shared carafe, whose long consumed wine we had turned to water, Robin and I noticed a severe looking, elderly man a few feet away regarding us with disgust every time we passed the flask. Assuming we were guilty of neglecting to share this refreshment more widely, Robin offered him the bottle, whereupon this individual paled with horror and withdrew himself as far as his restricted circumstances permitted.

"I am thinking," he explained, "how shameful it is that your lips should be touching the same glass, for you see I am a Brahmin."

"Aah," replied Robin, releasing an exquisitely expressive sigh. "We know all about Brahmins. Please accept our commiserations on your condition."

The fulfillment of more immediately compelling bodily functions than hunger or thirst, which could not be as conveniently satisfied, required exquisite manoeuvring to place ourselves in position by the doorway, while the train was slowing for a station, in order to run like hell for the platform toilet so as to make it back in time for departure. And always we would remember to take our carefully hoarded shreds of newspaper with us.

At other stations where such urgencies were less pressing, I was forced back on my imagination. Every time the train ground to a halt I would listen for those evocative cries of *gurrum char* and *pan birri,* and picture the bustling scene outside the window, with its vendors, beggars, sweepers and sleepers, the living and the possibly dead. Beyond the familiar sounds, the calls of the tea and betel nut sellers, the dry coughs of asthmatic old men and women in their dhotis and saris, I strove to gauge the sonic dimensions of that vastness of plain that stretched around us in the night, faintly punctuated by the barking of dogs in far villages, the yelping of hunting jackals and the underlying depths of silence emanating from infinities of distance.

I was back in a landscape measured by a different scale of geography, stretching to horizons beyond horizons, in denial of accepted propositions that the world could be anything other than boundlessly flat. In my mind's eye I saw those vistas marching back in perspective, still echoing the rhythm of the rails churning in my head.

> Don't wake me up if you see me aboard,
> or pull the safety cord.

"Are you awake?" I heard Robin ask.
Opening my eyes, I saw that he was offering me a bread and butter sandwich.
I shook my head. "Only when I reach Calcutta."
"What?"
"Sorry. Something on my mind. Yes I will actually. Thanks. I'm starving."
He glanced at his watch. "We're due in Calcutta early in the morning."
"I know. That's what I was thinking about."

Back Where I Started

It was not yet dawn, but the tumult at Howrah station was indescribable, as if the entire city were in the process of evacuation. We had not encountered such crowds elsewhere on our journey. I could see Robin's eyes widen in disbelief at the carpet of people we had to step through and find our way over, just to reach the station entrance. Hands were thrust at us from every direction, fingers clawed back in age-old gestures at open and empty mouths. Somehow we forced our way though this, and through subsequent cordons of touts endeavouring to relieve us of our scant baggage, in order to reach the taxi ranks.

I gave our driver the address near Marquis Street where the parents of my old St. Xavier's classmate, Leslie Maidment, had agreed to put us up. Once again many-layered Calcutta overwhelmed my senses. On the surface it looked more dilapidated than ever; sinking deeper into putrescence and decay. But that only made the sheer miracle of its survival the more elusive and intriguing. How had it so defiantly outlasted conditions that had destroyed many lesser aggregates of human endeavour; those other derelict conurbations fading quietly, decently and decorously into history?

Here was a metropolis that should long have been abandoned to its crows and pariahs. Yet it persevered, its crowds more congested, its traffic more sluggish, all of the evidence more than ever palpable of a city that had outlived its infrastructure and was well into the age of frantic improvisation. There had to be something at the heart of this anti-dynamic that explained the enigma.

Barely inching its way through streams of horse-drawn, bus-heavy, rickshaw-crammed humanity converging on Howrah bridge, our taxi was stuck like a fly in a very old and unsavoury ointment. Even at this time of the morning, with the sun clearing the city's tatterdemalion skyline, the sidewalks were crowded with inert human forms, as if Calcutta had brought out its dead, the latest casualties of a plague growing ever more oppressive. We saw a policeman checking a comatose figure with his baton to establish if it were still alive.

It was a relief to regain the comfortingly familiar environs of Marquis Street, where the general state of urban decline seemed less marked. The Maidments had spent a holiday in Hastings some three or four years earlier, when our two families had been briefly reunited, reminiscing about the old days and discussing the changes that had taken place in India since independence.

Maidment senior was a sub-editor on the Calcutta *Statesman*, one of the continent's most respected newspapers, and I had entertained the foolish hope that he might somehow be able to find for me a vacancy in its editorial office. He quickly dispelled any such notion. My journalistic experience in England would be of no avail. India abounded in talented writers, fluent not only in English but their mother tongue, which I had quite noticeably lost.

He took me to his office and handed me a telegram from my Aunt Zena, who had known I was due to arrive at this address. It contained instructions that a berth had been booked in my name aboard the *S.S. Santhia*, sailing a few days hence from Calcutta's Kidderpore Docks, bound for Penang where she and Len would be picking me up. I was to be aboard that ship or risk the humiliation of repatriation to England as an impecunious vagrant.

It was the first time I had ever set foot in the offices of the *Statesman*. I wondered if its archives still held the winning crossword entries of my grandmother, who had proved so prolific she had been politely informed her further entries would be declined. From its windows one looked down on much of the obsolete apparatus of empire, left to clutter the Calcutta skyline a whole decade after independence. Below lay the intersection of Chowringhee Road and Dharamtolla, and beyond, to the south, the Victoria Memorial and Ochterlony Monument were visible on the *maidan*.

I had about two days in which to rediscover these and other old haunts, including the labyrinthian Hogg Market, the Fancy Lane quarters that Uncle Len and Aunt Zena had occupied when he was still in the Governor of Bengal's Band, the wide open vistas of the *maidan*, crowned by that astonishingly vast and empty tabernacle to Victoria, and my grandmother's grave at Tollygunge. The latter was a revelation; beautifully maintained—as was the entire cemetery—by a small army of gardeners and showing barely a trace of age.

I stood before the simple marble cross and tried to remember her. It wasn't difficult. She had been a stout little woman, who made up in magnetism what she lacked in size. I could recall her voice, her gestures, and most of all the bedside chat when she had wistfully wondered if I would ever be doing this, bringing flowers to her grave under a hot sun. Even now I could hear her asking "Where's your solar topi? You'll catch your death of sunstroke."

She had never failed to remind me that I came from a long rolling stock of railway people, who had cast their lot with India but looked over their shoulders at their supposed origins in Europe. She had never lived to see any of that faintly dubious provenance. I had, and it had not proved strong enough to hold me.

The Very Model of a Modern Indian Businessman

Roughly my age, Leslie Maidment offered to act as our guide. He was already heavy-set, bespectacled and looking the very model of a successful businessman in the making. To think that my brother Paul and I used to race his rickshaw home from St. Xavier's! To think we had ever been young enough to do that! He suggested a train excursion to see a jute mill belonging to one of the Maidment kin, situated on the banks of the Hooghly.

The platforms of Sealdah station were just as crowded as those of Howrah. Leslie explained this was all part of the huge overflow of Hindu refugees who had crossed the border with neighbouring East Pakistan in the bloody aftermath of partition ten years earlier. They had remained as they were, wherever they could end up, on the platforms, on the streets, in makeshift shanty towns, in whatever form of refuge they could find. One needed a torch to traverse the sidewalks at night, or risk constantly tripping over sleeping and sometimes dead bodies.

Again we had to run that gauntlet in order to reach our train, Our destination lay just a few miles north of Sealdah station on the Bengal Assam line. It was tempting to stay aboard that creeping caterpillar, encased in its sheath of freeloading stowaways, and cover the rest of the relatively short distance to Kanchrapara, but time wouldn't allow. We disembarked at Titigarth, south of Barakpur, and hired cycle-rickshaws to take us to the jute mill.

The latter, one of several lining the banks of the river, was enormous, filled with ancient, clanking machinery, looking like an archaic mezzotint of Dickensian working class conditions, except that the workers were clad in loin cloths and saris, sweating in the dank and fetid darkness of their cavernous worksheds. In all my years in India I had never visited a jute mill, and now did so only to eliminate that experience from the list of activities yet unventured.

What can one say in favour of jute? It's a versatile plant fibre used in the manufacture of sacks and rope. But then so is burlap and hemp, despite the latter's unsavoury reputation because of its source in the cannabis plant that produces marijuana. The jute plant is of a different species entirely, growing from six to ten feet in height and resembling, from a distance, fields of sugar cane run wild. The stem of the plant is covered with thick bark containing the harvested fibre.

India has long been the largest producer of raw jute in the world. The jute industry was established here late in the nineteenth century, with Scotsmen playing a key role in its foundation and owning most of the earliest mills. Nearly all of these were located in Bengal, many of them along the banks of the Hooghly, on whose waters the processed fibre was transported by sailing barges to Calcutta docks for shipment overseas. Leslie introduced us to the mill's manager, who conducted us on a tour of the factory sheds, where rows and rows of enormous and antiquated machines, working at decibels that must surely have reduced their operators to deafness in a matter of years, compelled us to communicate by gesture; a process which left me with a very confused impression of what was actually going on.

Emerging from that din, to breathe air uncontaminated by chaff and dust, we stood on the river bank, gazing out at sailing barges pressed down to the waterline under their huge cargoes of jute and hay. Propelled like Phoenician galleys, by rows of oarsmen working in unison on either side, they resembled lumbering and grossly overweight water beetles, helplessly vulnerable to predators on the open reaches of the Hooghly.

Severing the Strands

Many miles upstream lay Bandel, church of miraculous occurrences and scene of my confirmation to a faith already faltering. India was beginning to swell in my memory like a returning tide, carrying random debris from the past on currents grown stale and rancid from prolonged exposure to the sun. At first sight, nothing had changed; the topography was as I remembered. But time had raised invisible barriers between what was and what had been, and—having travelled so far to return—I had not brought with me the right keys to open the locks. Leslie and I bid farewell to Robin, homeward bound to his legal practice in Canada, and then it was my turn for leave-taking.

Boarding the British India Line's *Santhia* at Kidderpore Docks, I was reminded of my previous departure, alongside the Gateway to India at the other end of this sub-continent. These lower reaches of the Hooghly presented a different scene, cramped and confined, entirely devoid of pomp and circumstance. From our upper deck, we looked down on a crowded steerage class, swarming with humanity, livestock and little mountains of produce, reminiscent of scenes from *Lord Jim* or any of Conrad's other novels set in these waters.

Launched in 1856, the British India Line had just celebrated its centenary a year earlier. Its pivotal route from Calcutta to the Far East had appeared even more profitable in the immediate postwar years, owing to the removal of the Japanese shipping lines with which it had formerly been in close competition. The *Santhia* was one of three new vessels specially commissioned for that service. Launched in 1950, she weighed 8,908 gross tonnes, was just over sixty two feet long and equipped to carry twenty-five first class, 136 second class, and 1,619 deck passengers, most if not all of that complement seemingly aboard by the time we sailed.

We cast off into the stream, chugging our way south through twilit reaches of this offshoot of India's holiest river. From Kidderpore docks to the mouth of the Hooghly is roughly sixty miles as the fish swims; much of it unfurling an endlessly fascinating tapestry of riverside villages, half sunk beneath the plimsoll line of poverty, so close to the tide as to place them in immediate jeopardy when the next cyclone struck from the treacherous Bay of Bengal. Even the *Santhia's* wake came near to demolishing the fragile foundations of those cane and thatch structures, whose walls were coated with the same mud on which they stood. I wondered if it was a deliberate demonstration of faith in their Hindu deities that inspired the foolhardiness of electing to live under conditions of such extreme vulnerability.

The river banks on either side reproduced repetitive features like endlessly recycled appeals to arrest our progress. India seemed loath to forgo its claims on another shipload of evacuees, dreaming of riches beyond these coasts. But eventually the black and featureless fingers of delta and mangrove were forced wider apart around our curving course. To me they were separating filaments in a chain of memories, steadily becoming so thinly attenuated that eventually they would disappear below the horizon of recollection. Time would bear me away from all this jealously hoarded trove of experience as surely as the tide was bearing me away from these shores.

Dusk obliterated the unravelling spectacle before we passed the outermost reaches of the estuary and forged out into the open waters of the bay that has caused more loss of human life, from the severity of its hurricanes, than any other body of water in the world. At last we were surrendered to that empty nocturnal expanse, now almost docile in its placidity, leaving behind nothing but the self-erasing trace of a wake across an ink-black sea. A brilliant firmament of stars spread above me, transformed by tears to a shimmering *aurora borealis* in the luminous tropic night.

Postscript

And so here I am, back full-cycle to where I started. It's the spring of 1978, marking my first return to Bengal in more than twenty years. I'm on my way home to Hong Kong from London, with time on my hands, seduced by a whim to stop off at Calcutta's Dum Dum airport and revisit Kanchrapara. Of all the railway colonies I remember from my childhood, this one left the most lasting impression.

I look down the length of the starboard wing as our Boeing 747 loses height, circling over a slowly rotating chequer-board of paddy fields, reflecting the sky like a mosaic mirror, marred by small imperfections of greenery. My eye is drawn to a flight of tiny white darts, a flock of egrets skimming over that fractured, glassy sea.

Of all the thoughts that *could* spring to mind at such a time, I recall only the proverb I learnt from my years in Malaya, before the British, anxious to wash their hands of yet more colonial dependencies, and ideally represented for that purpose by their manipulative Secretary of State for Commonwealth Relations, Duncan Sandys, persuaded Prime Minister Tengku Abdul Rahman to merge his country into the incongruous makeshift mess of Malaysia. No matter how far and high the paddy bird flies, he always ends up in the shit. Irreverent perhaps, but somehow fitting and appropriate to this belated homecoming. No matter where I have roamed, in all those years since I last set eyes on it, I have returned more or less to where it all began.

With the dun-coloured earth rising to greet our wheels, I can already detect the spiralling, transparent veil of heat thrown across a landscape that seems perpetually on the point of coming to the boil. A couple of uniformed, rifle-toting Sikh security guards flash by on the airport perimeter as our engines go into reverse thrust.

When we file down the stairs, to walk towards a terminal building which, unsurprisingly, does not appear to have kept pace with the age of the jumbo jet, I hear a cacophony of crows receding into an immense, heat-deadened distance. Instantly I am made aware of the enlargement of spatial dimension this country has in common with other continental enormities like Africa, the Russian steppes and the Canadian prairies.

I brace myself for confrontation with India's least endearing feature, the bureaucracy it inherited from the Raj and has further convoluted to enmesh the country in its Laocoon coils. When I finally reach his counter, the immigration officer thumbs slowly through the pages of my passport, like a form master considering where next to apply his censorial remarks. He looks at me and I respond with a benignly patient smile. Applying his chop, he hands the document back to me.

In the arrivals hall I am beset by touts and taxi drivers, one of whom holds on to my arm and will not be shaken off. "Where you go? I have very cheap hotel. Excellent service, most conveniently located."

"I want the railway station."

"What for railway station? What is destination?"

"Kanchrapara."

"Railway station no use. Only goods trains go there."

"I don't believe you. I have always travelled to Kanchrapara by train."

"When was last time?"

I hesitate. "A few years ago."

He simultaneously shakes and nods his head in that uniquely Indian way that signifies both denial and acquiescence. "Today is no more passenger service. My taxi is more quick and very cheap."

"How cheap?"

"You will see. Very cheap." He seizes my suitcase, leaving me my carry-on bag. "Follow me please."

Before his Hindustan Motors taxi can go anywhere, he requires an advance so that he can deposit some petrol in the tank. Judging by the coughing and spluttering when he starts the engine, there is barely enough to get us to the nearby filling station, where I watch him through the dusty back window as he haggles with the attendant. I wind the window down to lean out for some air, and observe a pariah dog, thin as a clothes rack, sparing a benediction of urine for our hub cap as it gazes pityingly back at me.

We head north up an uncrowded road, clattering in the wake of trucks displaying a shameless, baboon-like exhibitionism in the colourful signs attached to their rear ends. *Keep Your Distance, No Kissing My Backside, Eat My Dust, Less Crowding Please.*

I sense that we must be quite near the frontier. "How close are we to Bangladesh?" I ask.

"Not far. Just over there." He points vaguely over to the right.

"Any problems?"

"No problems. Just too much refugees."

Large advertising hoardings flash by, extolling the merits of powdered milk and cosmetics or emblazoned with road safety messages and other public educational homilies like "Overtaking Leads to Undertaking".

"Look," says my driver triumphantly, "there is train."

He points to the left, where a long, segmented cylinder, encrusted with human bodies over its roof and sides, is hauled across the plains by an ancient and asthmatic locomotive, gasping spurts of black expectorant into the air.

I remember Enoch Powell, author of the controversial "Rivers of Blood" speech opposing immigration; the speech that the Bishop of Croydon described as giving "a certificate of respectability to white racist views which otherwise decent people were ashamed to acknowledge". An acquaintance of Powell has recorded the fact that much the same scene as I now witness, reviving countless childhood memories, prompted his resolve never to permit such sights in his beloved Britain.

In 1939, Powell enlisted in the army as a private, rising rapidly to the rank of brigadier and demanding more equal treatment for fellow Indian officers during his wartime Indian service. His ambition to become Viceroy had led him into Conservative politics. Yet it was he who decreed that someone carrying a British passport ought no longer to assume he had an inalienable right to emigrate to the British Isles.

I challenge my driver. "I thought you said there were no passenger trains."

"You wish to be passenger on such a train?"

"You sound like Enoch Powell."

"Who?"

"How many more miles to Kanchrapara?"

"We are almost there."

And so we are. Over to the left, just a few miles beyond where we saw the train, I make out a familiar building, the railway institute, rising as incongruous as a Greco-Roman temple from the agricultural flatlands. I try to keep the excitement from my voice. "I know that building. Take me there please."

We find the gate closed, and patrolled by a trio of youths brandishing *lathis*. Alongside is a sign announcing the annual district sports day of North 24-Parganas. I walk over to the gate and ask permission to enter.

The eldest and largest youth shakes his head. "Cannot. Institute closed."

"I have come a long way for this visit. I will not interfere with your sports day. I just wish to look around the institute."

He tightens his grip on the *lathi*. "Not permitted. Institute closed today."

Our exchanges continue in this unproductive manner, my conduct rapidly deteriorating into the worst domineering style of the bad old days of the Raj, while his becomes increasingly stubborn and truculent.

The stand-off is broken when a charming young woman in flowing dark brown sari appears on the scene. "Can I be of assistance please?"

As I explain the purpose of my visit, her eyes widen and her smile expands until she positively beams. "How very interesting," she murmurs. "Please come with me and permit me to introduce you to our chairman."

The gate is reluctantly opened by its trio of guardians and I am led to a group of people assembled on the lawn beside a marquee, where I am greeted by a dour-looking man dressed in a white linen suit. When I introduce myself, and repeat the summary of my reasons for being here, he nods and says he remembers my family. "I used to work under your father in the railway workshops," he explains. "He was not an easy man to get along with. Kept much to himself."

"That sounds very like my father," I agree.

He does not appear to find it particularly surprising that, not having seen Kanchrapara since the age of ten, I should now wish to return. "Will you join us? We are about to open the event."

He leads the way into the marquee, where I assume I will be shown to a seat in the audience. Instead I am conducted on stage, to join the dozen or so dignitaries seated there. I feel extremely awkward and out of place.

The chairman approaches the microphone and delivers his speech in Hindi, at the end of which he mentions my name and turns to indicate that I am to take his place. Overcome with embarrassment and stage fright, I see that it would be discourteous to ignore the summons. Quite possibly this is a test; his way of avenging himself for the sins of the father.

Composing myself as best I can, I replace him at the microphone, thank him for his introduction and embark on a rambling, disjointed explanation of how I come to be here this day. I spent much of my childhood in Kanchrapara, I explain, and it left such a mark upon me that I have long felt the urge to return. The honour I have been accorded, through this invitation to share in their sports day, will now contribute a further highlight to my store of memories.

I scan their blank faces. What a load of old bullock carts, they must be thinking. The close of my impromptu remarks is followed by a brief interval and then a scattering of polite applause that slowly swells in volume. Among those in the front row, applauding more enthusiastically than the rest and grinning from ear to ear, is my taxi driver.

I return to my folding chair and sit out the rest of the proceedings, following which we retire outdoors again for tea and sandwiches, very much in the style of English vicarage garden parties.

I apologise to the chairman for the clumsiness of my remarks, and for having left the audience in some state of confusion. They are surely bewildered as to why I have been permitted to gatecrash their sports day.

"Not at all," he replies. "They are most impressed that we have gone to the considerable expense of bringing you here as a VIP, to grace our opening ceremonies. In fact we'd be delighted if you can do this again next year."

I manage to avoid choking on this, not realizing that it is seriously intended and that, for years to come, I will continue to receive invitations to the annual North 24-Parganas sports day. Turning the discussion to the institute itself, I ask why they have chosen to erect their marquee in its grounds rather than stage the ceremony in that building's considerably larger auditorium.

The chairman explains that the institute has fallen into disuse. Except on very special occasions, it is generally kept locked. However he can arrange to have it opened for my inspection, should I wish.

I take him up on this offer and, as soon as I can decently withdraw from the gathering, I accompany the caretaker delegated to unlock the institute doors. When they swing open I am admitted into a high, vaulted gloom to which my eyes require some time to adjust. A musty smell of stale, trapped air pervades that cavernous darkness. I can make out the stage, to the right, and a long procession of chairs lined against the walls.

The stark reality is suddenly overlaid by images of past occasions—Christmas parties, costume balls, variety concerts and cinema matinees. The contrast is so great that I dispel them from my mind, thinking: not now, later, when I can afford to give way to the anguish. But I cannot shut out the voices, reaching me as if travelling great distances underwater; lapping on the shores of memory like foam on an unbidden tide.

I move on to the billiard room, where my father spent so many evenings with his friends, particularly those fleeting friends he made with servicemen passing through during the war. Dust sheets are laid across the tables, and cobwebs, suspended from overhanging lamps, swell in the unfamiliar current of air. I think for a moment I can see in that stagnant air the faint threads of cigarette smoke that once clouded this room and imparted its special atmosphere.

The realisation strikes me with painful clarity. The Bell Institute has become a mausoleum to a period of time that has no relevance, no bearing on the kind of occasion I have just witnessed in its grounds. So much has happened in the thirty years and more since I last saw it that I should not have expected otherwise. The wonder is that it should be here at all, preserved as an ungainly memorial to former folly; a temporary aberration in India's ongoing history that spans millennia rather than centuries.

The people who built it, to enshrine their own fleeting rituals, have disappeared like the lost tribes of Egypt, like so many other civilizations that have left behind their tantalising traces in fallen monoliths and jungle ruins. We Anglo-Indians have become an endangered species, our heritage steadily eroded until it must inevitably disappear into oblivion.

Fly away Peter, Fly away Paul,
Fly away Blackbird, Fly away All.

0-595-31373-6

Made in the USA
Coppell, TX
11 January 2024